SENTIMENTAL NARRATIVE AND THE SOCIAL ORDER IN FRANCE, 1760–1820

DAVID J. DENBY

School of Applied Languages,
Dublin City University

CAMBRIDGE
UNIVERSITY PRESS

Published by the Press Syndicate of the University of Cambridge
The Pitt Building, Trumpington Street, Cambridge CB2 1RP
40 West 20th Street, New York, NY 10011–4211, USA
10 Stamford Road, Oakleigh, Melbourne 3166, Australia

First published 1994

Printed in Great Britain at the University Press, Cambridge

A catalogue record for this book is available from the British Library

Library of Congress cataloguing in publication data

Denby, David.
Sentimental narrative and the social order in France, 1760–1820 /
David J. Denby.
p.   cm.   – (Cambridge studies in French 47)
Includes bibliographical references and index.
ISBN 0 521 43086 0
1. French literature – 18th century – History and criticism.
2. Sentimentalism in literature.   3. French literature – 19th century – History
and criticism.   4. Politics and literature – French – History.
5. Literature and society – France – History.   6. Social classes in literature.
7. Narration (Rhetoric).   8. Tears in literature.   I. Title.   II. Series.
PQ265.D46 1994
840.9'353 – dc20 93–15238 CIP

ISBN 0 521 43086 0 hardback

CE

CAMBRIDGE STUDIES IN FRENCH

General Editor: Malcolm Bowie (*All Souls College, Oxford*)
Editorial Board: R. Howard Bloch (*University of California, Berkeley*),
Ross Chambers (*University of Michigan*), Antoine Compagnon
(*Columbia University*), Peter France (*University of Edinburgh*),
Toril Moi (*Duke University*), Naomi Schor (*Duke University*)

Recent titles in this series include

A complete list of books in the series is given at the end of the volume

Cambridge Studies in French 47

SENTIMENTAL NARRATIVE AND THE SOCIAL ORDER IN FRANCE, 1760–1820

Much of Europe wept over narratives of misfortune in the eighteenth century. Why? This book places sentimentalism at the heart of the Enlightenment project. Working in the first instance on sub-literature of the late eighteenth century (Baculard d'Arnaud, Gorjy, Vernes) it moves on to consider texts by Rousseau, the *Idéologues* and Germaine de Staël, as well as a variety of social pamphlets, and texts and debates of the French Revolution. It proposes a formal definition of sentimentalism as a popular narrative structure dealing in happiness and misfortune, but at the same time representing the reaction of an observing subject. In this sense, sentimentalism figures Enlightenment theories of morality and language; it is the site for the working out of notions of equality and democracy, with all the ambiguities bound up with these notions in this period.

Spanning a crucial period of transition in the emergence of modernity, this book seeks to break down artificial divisions, between both periods and movements (the Enlightenment and Romanticism; reason and sentiment) *and* between disciplines. Denby reveals that sentimental writing is rooted in a set of social attitudes, and traces the evolution of a formal structure across types of discourse, changing historical circumstances and different social and political interests. This discerning study is interdisciplinary in approach, addressing problems in literary and social history, and in the history of ideas, mentalities and ideologies.

For John, Alex and Marian,
and in memory of Sydney

Les hommes ne sont naturellement ni Rois, ni Grands, ni Courtisans, ni riches. Tous sont nés nus et pauvres, tous sujets aux misères de la vie, aux chagrins, aux maux, aux besoins, aux douleurs de toute espèce; enfin tous sont condamnés à mort. Voilà ce qui est vraiment de l'homme; voilà de quoi nul mortel n'est exempt.

Rousseau, Emile, Book 4

Venez, nous pleurerons ensemble sur les personnages malheureux de ses fictions . . .

Diderot, Eloge de Richardson

Contents

Acknowledgements

Research for this book was made possible by a joint research grant from the Royal Irish Academy and the Centre National de la Recherche Scientifique, France; a research grant from the French Embassy, Dublin; and travel grants from Dublin City University.

I am grateful to the Musée de Louvre, Paris (Musées nationaux) for permission to reproduce Jean-Baptiste Greuze's *La malédiction paternelle* and *Le fils puni*.

Many people have helped over the years it took to complete this book, offering interest, encouragement, advice, help with preparing the manuscript, and free accommodation in Paris: Roger and Suzy Biehler, Jean-Claude Bonnet, Hugh Brazier, Marilyn Butler, Eileen Colgan, Zoë Devlin, Martine and Michel Dumas, Serge Fournier, Marie Frapin, Norman King, Jane Lamoine, Jean and Christiane Laudet, Ian Noble, Chris Prendergast, Tibby Sachet, Jacques Seebacher. Malcolm Bowie was generous in his encouragement, and in his attempts to persuade me to be less tentative. Most of all I must thank Claire Laudet, who believed that I could finish when I was less than sure.

Note on spelling

Some quoted material is taken directly from eighteenth-century editions, while in other cases a later edition or a secondary source has been used, where spelling had already been modernised. I have therefore modernised the spelling of all quoted materials, with one or two exceptions where the boundary between spelling and syntax suggested that the original should be kept.

Ellipses marked thus '...' are an important feature of sentimental writing. In contrast, to show where I myself have made cuts in quoted material, I enclose the ellipses in brackets thus '[...]'.

Introduction: the politics of tears

'Daddy, were the Indians goodies?' The question, delivered, like all the best unanswerable children's questions, over breakfast and without apparent warning, has a genealogy which takes us to the heart of the matter. A few weeks before, in response to questions about the story of the cowboys and the Indians, I had explained to my six-year-old son that there might be a way of telling the story other than the established one: the cowboys had landed in the Indians' country and, one way and another, had destroyed their society and all but wiped them out. Here was a liberal parent trying, gently and without melodramatic excess, to encourage critical thinking about a powerful collective myth of our society. My contribution – recounted here, needless to say, in adultspeak – had, essentially, been to attribute agency to the cowboys: *they* had landed, *they* had wiped out the Indians; implicit in my version was a state of harmony, a prehistory lying beyond the irruption of narrative; and, clearly, my intervention was a moral evaluation, in the sense that I was questioning the identification with the heroic cowboys and setting straight the historical record. John's delayed-action response, based as it was on a retranslation of my remarks into the logic of story-telling, demonstrated an impeccable understanding of what I had been trying to say. His question struck me then as a particularly vivid confirmation of the kind of links between narratives, value-systems and the construction of history which this book attempts to chart. Most importantly for the analysis of sentimentalism, this six-year-old had spontaneously reinterpreted the narrative function of *victim* as the moral function of

I

goody: the character who is devoid of agency, the one to whom things happen, is, in this system, the bearer of the positive moral charge.

Narratives of misfortune feature prominently in our society's discourse about itself. From the British miners' strike of 1984–5 to the Gulf War, from the Falklands to the demonisation of Gadaffi, the dominant media have shown that they know how to frame a hard-luck story in such a way that the right moral and ideological conclusions are drawn. Nor is this only a feature of the dominant media: despite the left's suspicion of 'sentimental' socialism – which, like Eugène Sue's, is superficial and unscientific – victims remain a crucial figure in the denunciations of injustice which figure in the left-wing press from *L'Humanité* to *Socialist Worker*. In fictional discourses, too, whether it be popular novels or the visual media, writers continue to portray the humanity of suffering heroes and heroines, and audiences continue to respond to these narratives' attempts to draw them into a charmed realm of identification with their protagonists.

In that sense, it seems to me that we are still operating within a nexus of relations which was constituted during the Enlightenment. The purpose of this book is to piece together these relations, and to demonstrate their structural coherence in late eighteenth-century France. Narratives of misfortune fill the pages of the sub-literature of the period. Of course, such narratives are not an invention of the eighteenth century, any more than the notions of pity and sympathy which they articulate, and which have a long religious and humanist tradition behind them. What is new is that fictional narrative becomes a privileged site for the self-conscious expression of such notions: this is part of a new relationship between text and society, mediated by the spread of reading and related, both as cause and effect, to the emergence of public opinion and to the whole process of secularisation. On the one hand, then, I want to show how sentimental narratives can be read as a figure of the social relationship which lies at the heart of the Enlightenment project: a project of social solidarity and sympathy, but also one in which notions of community and public opinion come to play an increasingly crucial role. Conversely, it will be necessary to look beyond narrative texts to areas such as historiography, political discourse, social pamphlets, in order to show their dependence on structures – narrative, linguistic, discursive – which belong to the tradition of the sentimental narrative. The ambition, clearly, is an interdisciplinary one: my aim is to trace a structure across boundaries, and to suggest the centrality of sentimentalism in the cultural patterns of the period.

Sentimentalism in the eighteenth century was, of course, not confined to France. Britain had the 'man of feeling', Sterne, Mackenzie; Germany had *Sturm und Drang*, Lessing, Goethe; Russia, the work of Karamzin.[1] This universality in itself suggests some fundamental social and cultural realignment to which sentimentalism is intimately connected: the emergence of new social forces, their increasing self-awareness as actors on the social and historical scene, and new definitions of the social subject. But if the fundamental question is that of the triangular relationship between sentimentalism, Enlightenment and these social transformations, it is perhaps the French case which is the most instructive. Various reasons may be advanced for this: the high degree of integration of literary and philosophical preoccupations in the French Enlightenment; its strongly developed self-awareness, related to social and ideological polarisation; and, the ultimate expression of this polarisation and self-awareness, the French Revolution itself which, as a discursive event, brings into perfect but short-lived focus the interdependence of narrative and history, of text and social project. At the same time, however, the Revolution represents a turning-point: the Terror represents a limit to the sentimental vision, and more than any one event signals a partial split between the sentimental vision and the historical optimism of Enlightenment. It is from this dissociation, and the concomitant realignment of elements of sentimentalism with an anti-revolutionary, anti-utopian, organicist vision, that some of what we call Romanticism will emerge.

In methodological terms, I believe that the key to understanding the social and historical insertion of sentimentalism is to define it in *formal* (as opposed to purely *thematic*) terms. That fundamental choice explains my preference for the term *sentimentalism* over the more familiar *sensibilité*. *Sentimental* and *sentimentalism* imply a formal structure: one can speak of a sentimental narrative, sentimental discourse, etc., whereas the French *sensible* qualifies the observing individual, and *sensibilité* refers to a phenomenon of a psychological or a socio-psychological order. Such dimensions are, of course, crucial: if *sentimentalism* can be defined in the first place as a narrative structure, in which the happiness and misfortune of the represented subject are the primary focus, it is equally important to see that onto this narrative structure is grafted a second level of meaning, which can be defined as a structure of *observation* or *perception*. As well as representing a reality, the sentimental text represents the reaction to that reality of an observing subject, and in that sense we are witnessing the codification of a kind of reception aesthetic. But the psychological and socio-psychological are to be seen operating *within texts*: *sensibilité*, for all its status as a documented form of social behaviour, has its roots in texts which represent, repeat and celebrate the act of being moved. Furthermore, the need for formal definitions is only strengthened if a corpus of minor literature is to be used: its power as a method of gaining access to past mentalities and ideologies lies in its absence of self-consciousness, its historical naivety, but a formal approach must be used to resolve the endlessly repetitive proliferation of narrative segments and features into a structure which makes historical sense and permits a movement outward to other levels of cultural patterning.

For a long time, attempts to understand the literary and social phenomenon of *sensibilité* in eighteenth-century France were framed by the now outmoded dichotomy between reason and sentiment. An analysis which attempts to demonstrate the fundamental solidarity of sentimentalism and Enlightenment obviously rejects that dichotomy; moreover, to the extent that the reason–sentiment opposition is replicated in a thematically based understanding of the relationship between Enlightenment and Romanticism, my approach adds weight to the view that the transition from one to the other, if transition there was, is to be understood differently – notably in terms of the nature of the relationship between text and society. The reason–sentiment dichotomy was perhaps most successfully challenged, from the early 1960s onwards, by Roland Mortier, who argued that its demolition would involve an interdisciplinary effort to break down 'les classifications thématiques coupées de toute référence et dépourvues d'une nécessaire insertion dans des ensembles cohérents'. For Mortier, the opposition was essentially a creation of polemicists of the Consulate and Empire, who sought to reject rationalism as having led directly to the Terror.[2] In his seminal 'Unité ou scission du siècle des Lumières?', Mortier argued that the effect of the Enlightenment–Romanticism opposition was to progressively empty Enlightenment of part of its historical meaning, and it was in this context that he called for a proper history of the term *sensibilité* in the eighteenth century.[3] Frank Baasner has recently filled this gap;[4] but others too have worked on the history of an interrelated set of terms having to do with sensibility, notably the late J. S. Spink in a series of very suggestive articles.[5] The work of the 'Centre d'étude de la sensibilité' at the University of Grenoble is also situated in a lexicological perspective, and Sgard and Gilot's contribution to *Le Préromantisme: hypothèque ou hypothèse?* is a highly intelligent discussion of the importance of 'la vie intérieure', that space which the sentimental novel seeks to claim as the heritage of the whole of humanity, but which, paradoxically, words can only partially externalise.[6]

Frank Baasner has shown how the reason–sentiment opposition informs much of the work on 'Preromanticism' done in France in the first half of this century, and before, by Lanson, Mornet, Trahard, Van Tieghem and Monglond.[7] A re-reading of these critics confirms Mortier's view that it is the contextualisation of the literary text which leads to a break-down of this false dichotomy: it is when they actually envisage the literature of *sensibilité* not just as a corpus of themes, but as a phenomenon possessing real social referents and historical meanings, that these authors come closest to breaking its stranglehold and suggesting the kind of links which are crucial to my analysis. A case in point is Mornet's highly critical review of the first edition of Monglond's *Le Préromantisme fran-çais*.[8] Monglond's fundamentally reactionary analysis is that sentimentalism fulfils its ultimate destiny when it becomes the preferred discourse of the Terror; the boundary between Pre-romanticism and Romanticism proper lies at the point where the corrupt excesses of Robespierre's vision give way to the cultivation of a more sober, religious introspection.[9] Mornet reacts violently to Monglond's analysis, and in doing so explicitly relates sentiment with Enlightenment preoccu-pations of justice and equality: the language of sensibility may appear degenerate to the modern mind, but this is no reason to conclude that 'il n'était pour ceux qui l'employaient, qui l'avaient découvert, qu'une vaine comédie'. Mornet goes on to defend the sensibility of the eighteenth century, and to suggest its continued relevance to the values of his day: the sensibility of these 'bourgeois pleurnicheurs'

a agi constamment, continûment et créé, sinon pour l'éternité, du moins pour un lointain avenir. Toute notre bienfaisance laïque, toute notre bonté sociale viennent d'elle; c'est elle que nous continuons dans nos sociétés protectrices des animaux, nos semaines de bonté, nos prix de vertu, nos récompenses aux sauveteurs, nos timbres anti-tuberculeux. On rencontre aujourd'hui dans Paris des cantines maternelles; il suffit qu'une femme se présente, que le lait sorte de son sein pour qu'elle trouve un bon repas; c'est une idée de Beau-marchais.[10]

Mornet, then, implicitly relates sentimentalism and the Enlightenment movement of social reform, and will develop these ideas in a few passages of his *Origines intellectuelles de la Révolution française*, published in 1933.[11] Van Tieghem, much of whose work is bound up in the Preromanticism debate, also shows an awareness of the continuities between sentimentalism and Enlightenment concerns: like Mornet, he emphasises that the stylistic infelicity of sensibility should not lead us to con-clude that its exponents are insincere:

c'est elle qui, en généralisant l'horreur de la souffrance, a réformé l'éducation, la justice, la société; c'est elle qui a, d'accord avec la 'philosophie' et peut-être plus efficacement, fait du XVIIIme siècle, suivant la belle expression de Lavisse, 'un siècle humain, succédant à un siècle dur'.[12]

My opening chapter examines three sentimental writers, one relatively well known and two quite obscure. Although the presentation of these writers is obviously meant to adumbrate the more abstract analyses which will follow, I have tried to allow the diversity of both texts and authors to speak for itself, rather than suggesting that all sentimental texts can be read according to one overarching ideological scheme. In the following two chapters, I adopt a more abstract and theoretical approach: in chapter 2, with a good deal of reference to Diderot, and using notions drawn from Propp, Michael Fried and Jay Caplan[13], I develop a double model of the sentimental text as *narrative* and as the site of an exchange between observed and observing subject; chapter 3, which makes extended reference to Rousseau, examines at some length the relationship between the process of sentimentalisation and the problematic of the place of the subject in the social hierarchy. Although I have chosen not to formalise the structure in this way, these three chapters in a sense form a unit: together, they move towards a general interpretation of sentimentalism as a social and ideological project. The following three chapters take this semi-abstract model as the basis for a return to texts: I examine the place of sentimental narrative and language in some key texts of the Revolution (chapter 4), the milieu of the *Idéologues* (chapter 5), and the work of Germaine de Staël (chapter 6). In these last two chapters the analysis is extended into the post-Revolutionary period; here, I have chosen to restrict myself to writing which remains fundamentally faithful to the Enlightenment tradition, no doubt out of personal prejudice, but also because my objective is to see which part, if any, of the sentimental heritage remains available to 'progressive' thinkers in the post-Revolutionary situation.

CHAPTER I

Three sentimental writers

BACULARD D'ARNAUD

Baculard d'Arnaud (1718–1805) is the most well-known of the three sentimentalists presented in these case-studies. This reputation does not rest on literary merit, but rather on his enormous popularity during the eighteenth century, amply documented in Robert L. Dawson's 1976 study. Baculard's works were constantly reprinted during his lifetime, and *Les Époux malheureux* ranks as one of the most popular works of the century. Periodicals which serialised his works included the *Almanach des muses*, the *Discoureur*, the *Journal des dames*, the *Mercure* – from which he held a pension – and the *Année littéraire*. Grimm, despite his disdain, was obliged to acknowledge that the popularity which Baculard enjoyed must testify to talent of some kind. Baculard's reputation extended throughout Europe, and, as Dawson points out, in the restricted society formed by the republic of letters in the eighteenth century, Baculard d'Arnaud was acquainted with nearly everyone of import, ranging from Voltaire, his protector in the 1730s who eventually fell out with him in the Berlin affair, to Marie-Antoinette who possessed his works in a personally emblazoned copy.[1] Henri Coulet concludes:

> Si à nos yeux, avec deux siècles de recul, il paraît ne jamais sortir des poncifs moraux et sociaux, il faut reconnaître qu'il a été l'un des premiers à les créer et à les répandre.[2]

Baculard's fiction is indeed representative of the preoccupations and structures of sentimental fiction in the late eighteenth century: obsessively, and loquaciously, he returns to the same standard themes, apparently safe in the knowledge that his unoriginal exploitation of tried and tested formulae will continue to be popular. This repetitiveness is in itself representative, in that one of the striking features of sentimental literature in the period is the faith in a particular set of categories and structures which is implied by the literature's endless repetition and proliferation: the more monotonous the rehearsal of sentimental themes, the stronger is our impression that they point to the unquestioned assumptions, the moral culture of a whole epoch.

But if Baculard stands as a representative of eighteenth-century sentimentalism, he is by no means an unproblematic figure. He raises, in particular, the question of the compatibility of sentimentalism with the Enlightenment project. Ridiculed by Diderot and Grimm, published by the *Mercure* and by Fréron's *Année littéraire*, Baculard is generally considered to be an enemy of *philosophie*, an analysis which rests on the twin foundations of his anti-rationalism and his religiosity. His anti-rationalism is in my view a minor contradiction: to see Baculard as an anti-Enlightenment writer on such a basis is implicitly to validate an equation between Enlightenment and rationalism which is false. The preoccupations which his fiction dramatises are consistent with the mainstream views of Enlightened opinion: the primacy of the heart in conjugal relations and of the voice of nature over the claims of established authority, the essential humanity of all men and women transcending – but, as in enlightened opinion, only up to a certain specified limit – social and hierarchical differences.

Baculard's religiosity represents a stronger challenge to the view that his sentimentalism is fundamentally consistent with Enlightenment attitudes. Jean-Louis Lecercle[3] insists on the rewriting which *Les Epoux malheureux* underwent between 1745 and 1783, representing a toning-down of critical attitudes towards the church: the vicious priest Audoin who stands for the anti-humanist intolerance of the church is replaced by a tolerant disciple of Fénelon who instigates reconciliation in the divided La Bédoyère family. Dawson, for his part, confirms that religious preoccupations become more marked in Baculard's work as his career progresses. Indeed, a group of works bespeaks a fascination with the cloister which it is difficult to reconcile with Enlightenment positions. These works include the aptly titled *Euphémie, ou le triomphe de la religion* (1768), the *Mémoires d'Euphémie* of the same year, and *Ermance*, published in the *Epreuves du sentiment* in 1775. Euphémie, for instance, is faced with a choice between her former love for Sinval and her vows to the monastic institution, and the title of the play tells us the direction which she finally chooses. Texts such as this dramatise the conflict between the experiential truth of the heart and religious duty, with the latter winning out in terms of the binary choices which the text presents. Moreover, in the 'Précis de l'histoire de la Trappe' published in conjunction with *Les Amants malheureux*, Baculard offers an apology for the monastic way of life, considered as a necessary recourse for those whose lives have led them into dissolution and disorder which require remedy. All this seems very far removed from the militant anti-monasticism of Voltaire and Diderot, and the analysis of François Vernes's *Mathilde au Mont-Carmel* will demonstrate later how a more radical reading of the political meaning of such narratives can be made within the sentimental tradition of the period. Yet I would still wish to press the continuities rather than the dichotomies. In Baculard's narratives, the imperative of renunciation operates, almost by definition, as one pole in an opposition, the other pole being the 'natural' promptings of the human heart which the sentimental text typically places at the centre of its preoccupations. If Euphémie sacrifices her love, then one function of that sacrifice is to throw into sharper relief the magnitude of the happiness which is being renounced: in a discursive movement which may be described either as circularity or as a repeated oscillation between two poles, the projected (and remembered) happiness only seems to remind the heroine of the sacrifice she has made. Despite the apparently programmatic nature of the plot as it opts for renunciation over fulfilment, sentimental plenitude remains the discursive centre of the text: but it seems that this plenitude remains at one remove from the moment of enunciation, the text seeking to circumscribe and hold it, but succeeding only in grasping its trace, the mark of its passage from one site to the next.

In this sense, the meaning of texts like *Euphémie* is perhaps not as far removed from Enlightement as it might appear. Baculard's approach to religion is above all a *sentimentalised* one: whether one chooses to call it deism, or natural religion, it involves a typical Enlightenment shift from the transcendent to the immanent dimension, Protestant in the sense that the voice of justice, reason, nature, is envisaged as speaking directly to the individual subject – the distinction between heart and mind is not made by narrative – rather than finding expression in the form of institutionalised authority. Religious experience in such a vision is part of the same order of experience as human love, beneficence towards the poor, tolerance of difference: the opposites apparently dramatised by *Euphémie* belong to the same continuum, in a shift which anticipates nineteenth-century definitions of *laïcité*.

I am arguing, then, that Baculard's opposition to *philosophie* and his preoccupation with religion, while they pose problems in an analysis which sees sentimentalism as a progressive discourse linked to the political and social project of the bourgeoisie, should not be seen as the centre of gravity of his writing. If, as appears to be at least partially the case, Baculard's narrative is popular or semi-popular, addressing social groups who were likely to remain untouched by the great philosophical and religious controversies emanating from the commanding heights of culture, then there are good reasons to maintain that the more immediate social preoccupations of the text should be our concern here. Part of the readership of such fiction represents the people who will remain unaffected by superstructural change, by the representations which history produces as it makes itself – the people who, through the last years of the century, and even through the trauma of Revolution, will continue to live lives dominated by the local, in which new modes of thought and aspirations must negotiate a place alongside inherited beliefs and attitudes. The anti-clericalism of Voltaire, or of the Revolution, need not, in short, find reflection in semi-popular narrative. The following pages will

accordingly concentrate on the social interpretation of Baculard's sentimental narrative, analysing how the process of
sentimentalisation is linked to the constitution of certain bourgeois social attitudes. I shall look first of all at the role of love in
narrative, and its relationship to social hierarchy; I shall then
go on to analyse Baculard's attitude to social hierarchy as
articulated by his treatment of questions of poverty, inequality
and wealth.

Les Epoux malheureux (1745), one of the most reprinted novels of
the century, and Baculard's first major success, is a fitting
introduction to the role of romantic love in the sentimental
narrative. It is based on the true story of the chevalier de la
Bédoyère, whose marriage to an actress, Agathe Sticotti, was
challenged before the Paris *parlement* by his father, a leading
Breton noble, in 1745. The chevalier lost the case, although a
subsequent reunification did take place, and some sort of
family reconciliation was arrived at before the death of the
father in 1759. Rousseau, who was in Paris at the time of the
trial, alluded to it in a note to letter 2 of part 2 of *La Nouvelle
Héloïse*. The context of this letter emphasises the crucial thematic and structural similarity between the two novels: in this
letter, milord Edouard is pleading in favour of the free choice
of the heart against the desires of the parents for their children's marital future. The note, with its indirect reference to
the case, was suppressed by the censor, and Rousseau's view of
the case is contained in subsequent correspondence with
Malesherbes. Rousseau's view, it must be said, is ambiguous:
acknowledging the father's right to 's'opposer de toutes ses
forces au mariage de son fils', he insists that to break up the
marriage and disinherit the son after the event was an act of
cruelty.[4]

Whatever Baculard's considered view of arranged as against
romantic marriage – we shall see later that his opinion is
divided – he identifies unequivocally with the cause of the son
in the novel which was in the bookshops by the end of 1745, the
judgement of the *parlement* having been delivered on 18 July
of that year. In taking the side of the ill-fated lovers, and

making their misfortunes the sentimental focus of the work, Baculard clearly opts for one of the central imaginary clichés of the sentimental novel throughout the eighteenth century. Sentimental love, the spontaneous experience of the heart, dictated by nature, is pitted against the social prejudice which sets obstacles of birth and fortune in its way, and the sentimental identification of the text is all on the side of the victims. Sentimental love, in these narratives, is firmly embedded in discourse about society, and functions as a bearer of democratic values.

The notion of misfortune is crucial to the novel, as it is crucial to the sentimental novel in general. Without misfortune, the whole process of sentimentalisation, dependent as it is upon the existence of a victim, would be compromised, as would the sense of protest or outrage which sentimentalism generates. But the role of misfortune in *Les Epoux malheureux* is an ambiguous one: at a primary level, it is treated with all the hyperbole of melodrama, generating, as J.-L. Lecercle has shown, sentence upon sentence of inflated evocation of their *états d'âme*.[5] Misfortune, then, is the prime moving force of the narrative, the obstacle to happiness, and as such it is to be deplored. But at this point, other discourses intervene: one of these insists that the misfortune which has just been evoked so hyperbolically is nothing, an existential bagatelle when compared with the love which the unhappy couple feel for each other, and which is the only firm reality. Perhaps more revealing is the way in which, in a novel based on the quest for happiness, unhappiness is celebrated. Misfortune is seen as setting the victims apart from the rest of society and conferring upon them a superior status:

Sans amis, sans secours, étrangers sur la terre, n'attendant qu'une mort inévitable, et quelle mort! la donnant à un troisième infortuné [the child about to be born], victime de nos désastres: voilà quel était notre état. Dieu! que dans ces moments cruels on connaît toute la bassesse, toute la dureté, toute l'inflexibilité des hommes! qu'on a droit alors de les mépriser, de les détester! qu'on est trop assuré qu'ils sont sans vertus, sans sentiments, au-dessus [sic] de la Bête la plus grossière et la plus féroce! qu'on saisit alors le dur airain dont le coeur est armé! il faut être malheureux pour les surprendre dans leur vrai point de vue; le masque tombe enfin; plus d'illusion, et c'est-là le fruit de l'infortune; c'est de-là que naît cette philosophie qui ne trompe jamais: oui, la raison est le partage des malheureux.[6]

Only the unhappy know the truth: anything short of the most desperate misfortune seems to be dismissed as superficiality, illusion, as a mask to be stripped away to lay bare the reality of human existence.

In 1783, as was noted above, the novel was expanded to accommodate a happy ending. A series of peripetiae brings about reconciliation between the generations, after which the father can die happily, and our hero and heroine live happily ever after. Part of Baculard's intention was to bring the novel more into line with the reality of the case as it evolved between 1745 and 1759, the year in which La Bédoyère senior died. Such rewriting and expansion of previous work was nothing new to Baculard, but Lercercle believes that the change is part of an ideological shift on the part of Baculard, towards a more conservative, anti-philosophical position in which the happy ending can defuse the element of social criticism inherent in the sentimental figure of misfortune.[7] It is certainly true that the mechanics of the rewriting involve a toning-down of the polarisation between the victims and those who persecute them: the wicked Audoin is replaced by a priest of more moderate persuasion who convinces the hero's mother to accept her son and daughter-in-law back into the family. One can of course see how the Manicheism of the first version can be read as more in line with a 'philosophical' intention, the extremism of the forces persecuting the hero and heroine being an uncompromising reflection of reactionary social forces; but, on the other hand, the rewriting does involve the explicit affirmation of a tolerant and reformist religious programme. Reading ideological meaning into variations in dénouement is a risky business.

The La Bédoyère case was experienced in Paris in 1745 as what has come to be called a 'courtroom drama'. Baculard certainly gives the profession of barrister its sentimental credentials when he describes it in these terms:

un emploi qui est peut-être celui où soit attaché plus de dignité et de noblesse; prendre en main la cause des malheureux, porter les larmes de l'innocence, ou du pauvre opprimé, aux pieds de la justice, combattre, punir le coupable puissant, être, en un mot, l'organe du sentiment et de la vérité.[8]

It is as though the advocate were the agency whereby the innocence of persecuted virtue seeks to declare itself to the hostile world. The advocate's aim is to establish transparency where obfuscation reigns. A few pages later, Baculard has his hero reflecting in a particularly self-conscious way on his role as his own advocate before a sympathetic public.

Je défendais les droits de l'amour, ceux de la probité, de la religion. Je l'avouerai: il y a des moments où je m'applaudis, pour ainsi dire, de mes malheurs: sans eux, aurais-je goûté ce plaisir si pur, si doux, qui enivra tous mes sens dans cette occasion? Quelle consolation, quelle jouissance délicieuse pour un infortuné de voir tous les coeurs s'ouvrir à sa sensibilité, se pénétrer de ses peines, toutes les bouches prêtes à parler pour lui, et à prononcer un jugement en sa faveur! Voilà sur quel spectacle enchanteur se fixèrent mes regards; je vis même couler des larmes: quels éloges valent ces pleurs! [...] ce même jour m'a appris que les hommes ne sont pas aussi dénaturés qu'ils paraissent l'être: le sentiment est assoupi dans leur âme: il ne faut seulement que [sic] l'y agiter pour le réveiller: il est vrai que cette secousse affaiblie et dissipée, ces êtres si difficiles à émouvoir retombent ordinairement dans leur léthargie, et la sensibilité est la vie véritable: c'est la sensibilité seule qui nous fait goûter le prix de l'existence, et les mouvements qu'elle procure à l'âme, produisent nécessairement les vertus et les bonnes actions. (pp. 195–6)

The passage exhibits the faith, essential to the sentimental text, that all humans possess to some degree the basic quality of *sensibilité*, which can be stirred by the spectacle of virtue in distress, to produce virtuous and good actions: as such, this invocation of sensibility could be set beside hundreds of comparable passages from the period. However, this extract hints at other important features of sentimental narrative. The audience to which La Bédoyère appeals in this scene is a specific one; but the crowds who flock to the scene of the trial figure a broader community of sensitive and enlightened souls whose posited existence is a crucial condition for the text (both

La Bédoyère's fictional speech and the text which we read) to have meaning. As Jay Caplan has suggested,[9] the sentimental text is dialogic in its very essence, in the sense that its aim is to draw into itself, and thus to consecrate and consolidate, a receiving community. It is when the sufferings and joys of a human subject are *recognised* by other members of the human community that the values of sensibility are most effectively proclaimed, and that the possibilities of a broader community based on such recognition are foreshadowed. The process of communication between the different subjects in this dialogue is explicitly described and commented upon in this passage, predominantly in terms of *looking* and *showing*: the narrator's presentation of his case is the spectacle to which the crowds flock, but these onlookers in turn become a spectacle for the narrator, and in their tears he sees the reflection of his own suffering, but also of his power.

In *Les Epoux malheureux*, then, love is defined as a force which transgresses the rules of social hierarchy: indeed, the steadfastness with which it sets itself against social expectations, and, conversely, with which society excludes it, is the measure of its authenticity as romantic love. *Fanny, histoire anglaise*, provides some insight into this dialectical relationship between displacement within the social hierarchy and the representation of sentimental truth. Milord Thaley meets and loves Fanny, the daughter of James, a farmer on his estate. The dynamic of the story, then, is once again the romantic love which knows no class boundaries, recognises only the language of the heart and of virtue, and resists all attempts to thwart it in the name of social acceptability. A poor farmer's daughter, all that Fanny has to recommend her is her virtue, matched only by that of her father. And yet, the presentation of James introduces a further element of mobility: 'Destiné dès le berceau à l'emploi de ministre, il avait fait d'excellents études à Oxford: des disgrâces inattendues l'avaient forcé d'embrasser un autre état; mais son caractère eût anobli les conditions les plus obscures'.[10] It is as though, in order to enhance James's status as the representative of virtuous obscurity within the opposition hierarchy/virtue, a second degree of social displacement were necessary: throughout the story, James functions as the honest poor man, but the initial sentimentalisation of the character relies on this displacement down the social scale, which throws into relief the hierarchy-transcending category of virtue.

Thaley finally succumbs to the persuasions of his evil and class-obsessed uncle, the aptly named Dirton, and contracts a bogus marriage with Fanny, entering into real vows with the aristocratic bride of his uncle's choice. This is not before Fanny has become pregnant. The villainy of which his family has been the target enables James to confront Dirton with this reproach, perfectly expressive of the dynamics of the story: 'Je suis un pauvre fermier; mais, milord, je suis père, et un père outragé. . . J'ai pour moi la nature et la vérité' (p. 44). The story, of course, vindicates this view: Thaley's wife dies, and he returns to find Fanny in her 'chaumière', tilling the land to support her child and her father, now an invalid. The lovers marry, and Fanny goes to London, where 'elle servit de modèle aux ladys, et prouva par sa beauté et par ses moeurs, que les grâces et les vertus naissent souvent au village plutôt qu'à la ville' (p. 76).

It seems possible to offer two mutually exclusive and contradictory readings of a story such as this. The first reading – and, in view of the biographical evidence concerning Baculard, perhaps the most plausible – would attribute a fundamentally conservative message to the text, in the sense that it questions not the existence of social hierarchy, only its abuse, and the final promotion of Fanny can be read as the reintegration into polite society of the family which had fallen from grace due to James's 'disgrâces inattendues'. It is a happy ending because Fanny is one of the lucky ones: and the existence of the lucky ones proves that a hierarchical system is not necessarily a closed one, but admits into its ranks those whose nobility is of the soul. Similarly, it can be claimed that James is not really a poor farmer at all, and that the meaning of the sentimentalisation of the poor man who is really a gentleman is, precisely, to marginalise the question of the virtue, merits and rights of the truly excluded. And yet for many eighteenth-century readers, it seems inconceivable that tales such as *Fanny* were not in some sense the bearers of democratic aspirations, in that they demonstrated that the life of the soul was the prerogative of the humble as well as the exalted. Such notions are of course relative, and it is certain that the downtrodden of sentimental fiction frequently serve as proxy for the aspirations of the rising bourgeoisie, couched in terms of natural justice and equality. Nevertheless, this type of identification is one of the explanations of the great success of Baculard, and of sentimental writing generally in the period.

Baculard serves here to illustrate a fundamental feature of the economy of sentimentalism: some kind of social displacement or difference, an explicit denial of the validity of social hierarchy, is necessarily involved in the sentimental text's central task of representing the ideals of natural virtue and justice. Viewed from the point of view of the enunciating subject, this is an important and revealing feature. That subject, whether bourgeois or aristocrat, is at all events a member of a class which possesses a material stake in society, and is, moreover, not inclined to give up that stake. In that sense, the emphatic and repeated enunciation of a form of discourse which makes the devaluation of material wealth the condition for articulating the notion of virtue must be significant. In social terms, this may be described as bourgeois morality constituting itself by denying its bourgeois status; but it is the textual dimension which interests me at this point: textually, it is as though, once again, the fundamental moral notion towards which the text is directed can only be fully grasped through a discursive move which shifts the reader's attention from one site to another. It is that shift from one site to the next, the moment of *différance*, which constitutes the sentimental apogee, the nearest the text will come to seizing the elusive plenitude of sentimental meaning.

Les Délassements de l'homme sensible is a series of anecdotes published between 1783 and 1787. It describes itself as 'une espèce de registre où doit se consigner tout ce qui peut servir l'humanité', and it draws much of its material from the realm of everyday anecdote, while continuing to use some of the discursive procedures of sentimental narrative. As a result, the text points the way towards a differential analysis of sentimental representation, highlighting the differences between fictional and non-fictional discourses. A fictionalised commentary on the question of marriage, and the respective merits of the 'mariage par intérêt', the 'mariage par inclination' and the 'mariage raisonnable' counsels a middle road between the twin reefs of parental authoritarianism and youthful romance. Baculard starts from the assumption that his readers will identify immediately with the anti-authoritarian message of the first anecdote, concluding, in line with the general run of sentimental fiction: 'voilà ce qui résulte des mariages d'intérêt. Nos parents, en contraignant nos coeurs, en voulant soumettre notre inclination à leurs caprices, à la convenance, la fortune, l'éclat, font de leurs enfants de malheureuses victimes.' Baculard invites his young readers to peruse the second anecdote, in which a marriage based solely on the promptings of the young heart founders. The moral? 'Encore une fois, ce n'est pas l'amour qui fait les mariages heureux: c'est une convenance d'humeur, d'état...'[11] Passion, we conclude, is fine on the page, but real life is another matter: a gap is revealed between the fictional discourse of *Les Epoux malheureux* or *Fanny* and the harder-headed attitudes of the moralistic–realistic text.

Similar ambiguities can be found in Baculard's representation of wealth and social hierarchy. The most constant element in the twelve volumes of this work is the celebration of sensibility and *bienfaisance*, defined either through acts of charity performed by those who have towards those who have not, or by the gesture of the poor who refuse wealth and status in favour of virtue. Here then, as in the love stories previously analysed, sentimental categories are defined by opposition to the worldly criteria of success and status. Two episodes characterise this tendency in its most radical form. In 'La vraie noblesse ou la noblesse d'âme' – the title is itself a recurring sentimental cliché, with its substitution of a moral for a temporal quality – the hero, Frémont, the son of a grocer in the rue des Lombards in Paris, foregoes his 50,000 francs of lottery winnings, giving them to his friend Verneuil so that he can set up in business and thus be enabled to ask for the hand of

Frémont's sister. In the happy ending, Verneuil, now a success-
ful businessman, reimburses his friend handsomely (charity
pays). The disdain for worldly status is articulated strongly in
reference to Frémont's lack of an 'état': 'un état est pour la
plupart des individus ordinaires de la société ce que sont des
lettres d'annoblissement pour un parvenu sans mérite. Le
troupeau de graves insensés excite réellement le rire de l'indignation, ou plutôt de la pitié: ils vous parlent d'un état comme
on parlerait de la vie...' Frémont, in short is 'un de ces êtres
rares, qui ne dépendent point des accessoires, ni de ces *sup-
pléments* presque toujours étrangers à l'homme' (Arnaud's italics).[12] Derrida reminds us, that for Rousseau, the *supplément* is
that which is added to nature, and which stands in danger of
taking over the natural functions of humanity: and Frémont is
humanity in its pure expression, by virtue of his refusal of the
supplément.[13]

A similar point is made in 'La Pauvreté vengée'. Pierre is a
farm labourer who has come to Paris for a cataract operation
which is carried out free of charge by a charitable surgeon;
when the comte de ... refuses to put up Pierre during his
convalescence, a virtuous coalman intervenes, and his good
deed of course confers on him the right to moralise for a few
lines:

J'aime mieux être ce que je suis; je n'ai pas le sol, je me donne de la
peine comme un pauvre chien; mais, voyez-vous, j'ai une âme! et je le
disputerais pour cela à tous vos seigneurs de la cour: eh bien s'ils sont
plus riches que moi, je suis plus heureux qu'eux avec tout leur étalage
et leurs filles d'opéra [...] Je me plais à sentir mon coeur, Monsieur.[14]

It is as though the absence of all externality is conceived as the
condition of experiencing to the full the joys of the internal life:
the more the trappings of wealth are pared away, the more
obvious are the heart and soul which constitute the essential
humanity of the hero. The similarly entitled 'Le Peuple
vengé'[15] dwells in much the same way on the contrast between
the hard-hearted (urban) rich and the kind (rural) poor;
although not made explicit, a Physiocratic indignation at the
inversion of values between those who produce the country's
food and those who do no more than consume it, while giving

themselves an air of superiority, is present in both these episodes.

So far, the *Délassements* provide confirmation of the place of social hierarchy within the textual process of sentimentalisation: sentimental truth is constituted, as in the typical love narrative, in the movement which sacrifices position and wealth to an overriding moral imperative. This discourse would seem to find explicit expression, verging on class hatred, in the following statement: 'On est porté à médire les riches, et il faut avouer que la plupart font leur possible pour justifier l'espèce de haine qu'ils excitent, et qu'ils méritent.' Wealth is the dividing line between the virtuous and the non-virtuous. And yet these are the opening lines of an anecdote entitled 'Le Riche digne de l'être'[16] in which, predictably enough, the rich man's sensibility and charity in the face of the misfortunes of others are read as the sign that he at least deserves his wealth because, precisely, of the humanitarian use to which he puts it. A very important restriction is immediately placed on the sentimental discourse of contempt for wealth and status: the sensibility of the owning classes, if it finds expression in charitable behaviour, renders their privilege legitimate and socially useful. Such attitudes are of course perfectly in tune with mainstream enlightened attitudes towards charity in the eighteenth century. Baculard is as impressed as many of his contemporaries by the characteristic charitable institutions of his century. The opening of a workhouse in Norway in November 1785, for instance, draws gushing praise. 'De quelque côté que l'homme vertueux et sensible tourne les yeux, il voit la bienfaisance se répandre sur la terre comme un beau jour qui se lève et s'étend sur l'horizon. Les rêves du bon abbé de Saint-Pierre seraient-ils prêts à se réaliser?' Baculard praises the solemn opening ceremony, 'si respectable, si touchante', which concluded with the distribution of clothes to the girls who were to spin cotton in the factory 'd'après la manière anglaise'.[17] Elsewhere, in a chapter entitled 'L'Esprit du vrai négociant',[18] which spells out the rules of good management and economy which will lead the merchant to a prosperous and virtuous life, Baculard insists, in a manner almost liberal for his century, that we must help the poor, and that even those who are poor through some fault of their own, are no less worthy of our commiseration. Yet another chapter sets out some of the elements of what Baculard calls 'la science d'obliger', which consists essentially in giving alms in such a manner that the recipient's delicacy is not offended. 'L'homme est porté à haïr tout ce qui paraît s'élever au-dessus de lui, et un bienfaiteur est le premier des supérieurs; tout maître doit chercher à se faire aimer: il en sera bien plus puissant [...] cet art de faire le bien est rempli de difficultés innombrables.'[19]

The fragmentary, episodic text of the *Délassements* serves, then, to elucidate the real social insertion of sentimental attitudes. The processes by which sentimental meaning in its strongest, most rhapsodic form is produced are in no sense the direct reflection of social praxis. Contempt for wealth in texts which are framed as 'fictional' becomes transposed, in texts of direct social comment or moralistic prescription, into the legitimation of wealth through certain social practices based on sentiment. The social or moralistic text is more immediately readable, essentially because the social coordinates of enunciation are more explicit.

Baculard is not a coherent social thinker, and my purpose is not to present him as such. The poem of 1789 entitled *La Vraie grandeur, ou Hommage à la bienfaisance de son altesse sérénissime Monseigneur le duc d'Orléans* displays a particular collocation of attitudes towards poverty, which I do not take to be representative of Baculard or, *a fortiori*, of his century, although neither is it crucially at odds with its time. As the title suggests, the purpose of the work is to praise the efforts of the future Philippe-Egalité in favour of the victims of the cold winter of 1788–9. The poem demonstrates one particular way in which indignation at the injustice of deprivation may be combined with a respect for hierarchy. Indeed, this double attitude might be said to be definitive of this eulogy of the beneficence and sensitivity of the great man: it is precisely the duke's superior social status which makes his charity the more remarkable and praiseworthy. His is the greatness of the prince who, from the door of his palace, is not blinded to the sufferings of the inhabitants of the *chaumières* which cover his estate. No hint here of social protest: the function of *bienfaisance* is to knit together the fabric of society in a kind of unity which simultaneously minimises and draws its effect from the existence of hierarchy. The 'esprit de bienfaisance'

> Rapproche tous les rangs, remplit tous les espaces,
> Des citoyens divers unit toutes les classes.[20]

The charitable gesture, it seems, does not aim to abolish social difference; rather, its proper effect is to make social difference appear unimportant.

The *Discours préliminaire* to the poem justifies the fact that the work will dwell upon the depiction of misfortune. In the sense that this is what the vast majority of sentimental works of the period do, it is worth observing Baculard's argument. He writes from 'un vif désir de peindre le malheur, parce que l'homme aux prises avec l'infortune, en devient plus sensible, et que la sensibilité conduit nécessairement à la vertu' (p. v). The desire to depict and celebrate the charitable actions of virtuous souls who, it goes without saying, are reluctant that their works should be trumpeted far and wide, is also explicitly connected in Baculard's mind with a theory of education: it is exposure to examples of such virtuous behaviour which will lead others to adopt it as a model, and the mechanism through which this influence takes place is one of *signs*. Baculard quotes in a footnote the example of the administrators of the Collège des Grassins: in order to inculcate in their pupils a sensitivity to the plight of others, these wise teachers encouraged their charges to become involved in the charitable works which the college undertook. In this way, the pupils were exposed to the

spectacle des divers infortunés qu'ils sont allés secourir: ils ont éprouvé un attendrissement qui a été jusqu'aux larmes: ce tableau douloureux s'est gravé dans leurs âmes, et il n'y a point à douter qu'ils ne demeurent humains, sensibles, compatissants, le reste de leur vie. (p. 46n)

The crucial pedagogical relation is between a scene witnessed visually – *spectacle*, *tableau* – and the mind, imagined as parch-

ment or wax in which, according to another dominant metaphor of the period, an experience 'se grave'.

This preoccupation with signs – the term is Baculard's – is
another feature which will emerge as a common concern of the
sentimental text. I wish only to allude briefly to it here. One
development of the theme is in the pedagogical direction
already alluded to: the use of signs is conceived as an effective
means of communicating messages, given that men are 'plus
faits pour sentir que pour raisonner'. The pre-linguistic, pre-
intellectual is seen as dominant in the human constitution. The
theme emerges in the description of a 'fête de la nature' held at
Prades, Roussillon, to celebrate the Saint-Jean in 1784. The
culminating point of the ceremony was a distribution of alms.

Ce moment a intéressé tous ceux qui étaient présents [...] Il y a
longtemps que nous répétons que c'est par les signes qu'on parle aux
hommes, qu'on les persuade, qu'on les entraîne. Une semblable fête
en dit plus au peuple que tous ces ouvrages peinés de métaphysique
[...] voilà l'origine des hiéroglyphes et des allégories mythologiques;
il serait donc à souhaiter pour le bonheur général qu'on s'occupât
davantage du soin de multiplier l'usage des signes: c'est la langue
universelle [...] Ce sont-là, sans contredit, les armes des despotes
adroits.[21]

Baculard's primitivism paradoxically leads to a position where
he prefigures the use to which the Revolution put the *fête*; but
at the same time, it verges on an anti-intellectualism which
raises questions about his place in the philosophical camp.
Elsewhere, Baculard uses the same argument in favour of the
pedagogical usefulness of the theatre, accepting and turning to
pedagogical profit that which forms Rousseau's rejection of the
theatre as a debased form of social communication.

   The other important insertion of the sign in the sentimental
text is an expressive, mimetic one. 'Et, en prononçant ces mots,
le duc de Montagu laissait éclater cette touchante sensibilité,
cet attendrissement si honorable pour son âme, qui, bien plus
que tous ses titres, le distinguait de ses concitoyens; *on voyait
aisément qu'il était plein de ce qu'il exprimait avec tant de chaleur*'.[22]
The awkwardness of the expression is what makes it interest-

ing, for it dramatises the dichotomy between the linguistic and the non- (or pre-) linguistic expression of the life of the emotions. Baculard is celebrating here the possibility of sentimental transparency: words may betray, but other signs permit others to know the inner life of the subject, and the signs of sensibility figure high among the elements of this universal language. That which finds expression through linguistic signs has an independent and prior existence within: 'il était plein de ce qu'il exprimait...' In the scientific epistemology of the period, experience is the bedrock upon which the intellectual superstructure of language and conceptualisation is founded; and one of the tasks of the sentimental text is to make visible the inner experience of subjects, as a first step in the construction and celebration of a social morality.

JEAN-CLAUDE GORJY (1753-95)

Practically nothing is known, it seems, about the life of Jean-Claude Gorjy (sometimes spelt Gorgy). All that we can say about Gorjy, then, is based on his writings, which are in some ways surprisingly inventive and stimulating for a writer who has sunk into almost total oblivion in the eyes of history. His production is concentrated in the period 1784–1792, and the works which will concern us here are, chronologically:

Le nouveau voyage sentimental, 1784
Mémoire sur les dépôts de mendicité, 1789
Blançay (3rd edition 1792, first edition in or before 1789)
Victorine, 1789
Tablettes sentimentales du bon Pamphile, 1791
Ann'Quin Bredouille, 1791–92

Gorjy's sentimentalism confirms the importance of charity and *bienfaisance*, and introduces or extends two further important aspects of the sentimental vision: a preoccupation with the representation of the internal life of the subject and the relation of signs to meaning, and, secondly, the political uses of sentimental narrative in the specific context of the French Revolution.

Le Nouveau voyage sentimental – the reference to Sterne is deliber-
ate and self-conscious – confirms and extends alms-giving as a
sentimental topos. Here, it is articulated around a double
opposition: rich-poor and town-country. The narrator, witnessing scenes of poverty in the streets of Paris, is first of all
shocked at the insensitivity of the rich, which contrasts with the
charity of those who are themselves poor. This leads into the
second opposition: while the country is idealised as the seat of
peace, harmony and sufficiency, the city is the site of shocking
contrasts: 'Je rentrais chez moi pensant à ces deux infortunés,
de classes si différentes, que j'avais vus, en si peu d'heures, prêts
à périr de besoin au milieu d'une ville dans laquelle chaque
instant voit des sommes immenses consacrées à des super-
fluités.'[23] These 'malheureux' are described in little vignettes:
the group of paupers who come to sing and play in the rest-
aurant where the narrator is eating; the unemployed porter
collapsing from hunger in the street; the Bohemian poet and
actor, faint from hunger, met at 'une Académie bourgeoise',
who lives in a fifth-floor room with his 'grisette' – she living
from her work as a seamstress and praised for her resolute
refusal of the brilliant offers of rich men. These scenes are
marked by a refusal to enter into discussions about the merits
and demerits of the victims' case:

– Vous êtes bien bon, Monsieur, mais ne voyez-vous pas que c'est un
homme saoul?
–Qu'importe? En souffre-t-il moins? (p. 102)

Such expressions of undiscriminating liberality appear at
variance with the message of Gorjy's *Mémoire sur les dépôts de
mendicité*. This text is largely representative of the enlightened
debate about begging and poverty which took place during the
latter third of the century, in that its fundamental concern is
the definition and management of the distinction between the
deserving and the undeserving poor, the *pauvre méritant* and the
pauvre valide.[24] The *dépôts de mendicité* (set up by royal decree in
1767) 'affligent l'homme sensible, et découragent l'administration humaine par la difficulté apparente d'y réunir les prin-

cipes de sévérité, d'après lesquels doit être traitée une partie des individus qui y sont détenus, et la charité que l'on doit aux autres'.[25] The institutions were set up to fulfil a function of 'bienfaisance et humanité', but have in many cases been reduced to catering for a semi-criminal clientele of vagabonds and vagrants who in fact deserve punishment, but who cannot receive it as long as they remain in these institutions. The task of an enlightened administrator, Gorjy continues, is therefore to ensure that no individual in any particular district falls into the category of the 'mendiant forcé', and the means which Gorjy proposes in order to achieve this end is the provision, essentially through the private sector, of work. Employers should be encouraged, through various premiums payable by the authorities, to take on beggars able to work. Such a system, once it is in operation, will permit the authorities to categorise those who are still not working as 'mendiants volontaires' who should be sent to the *maison de correction* and not released until, by their work, they have amassed a certain sum of money which would be the tangible proof of their rehabilitation. The *dépôt de mendicité* would, by extension, revert to its original vocation as a place of shelter for those who are unable to work.

The notion of work is crucial in Gorjy's taxonomy, as in the general enlightened view. Those who can work but refuse to, deserve no pity, and become the just object of punishment; those who are unable to work become the object of sentimentalisation, inasmuch as they are powerless victims; only those who can work and are given a job to do seem to remain invisible in this system, disappearing into the normality of everyday economic activity which conveys no status, no category. The language of sensibility and the language of political economy manage to coexist in a text such as the *Mémoire*, precisely because the task of the analysis is to delimit their respective areas of competence. But a comparison with the discourse on charity of the *Nouveau voyage sentimental* suggests that the fictional work and the political essay inhabit different spaces: the function of the former is to celebrate sensibility, ignoring or obscuring distinctions and limitations which the political text seeks to bring out. This appears to offer some reinforcement of the point made earlier (p. 22 above) in connection with Baculard's *Délassements de l'homme sensible*.

Blançay and *Victorine* may be treated together. Both novels are very definitely of their period, in that they testify to the emergence of melodrama from sentimentalism which takes place in the closing years of the century:[26] the intrigue of the novel gains in complexity and imbrication, and depends more on a model of disguise and revelation in which characters already present turn out to be long-lost sons, daughters, mothers or fathers. Both novels are based on intrigues of this type, moving frenetically towards happy endings in which reconciliation and happiness triumph. In *Victorine* Azakia says to M de Belgis, whose daughter has been lost in one of the numerous shipwrecks which punctuate the text: 'Tu la retrouveras [...] bientôt les feuillets du malheur seront déchirés'.[27] And at the very end of the novel, in a piece of literary mannerism which demonstrates clearly the influence of Sterne, is a print purporting to show us the 'livre du destin': this tells us that page 195 was, according to the great plan, 'le dernier feuillet noir'. The text, then, functions in an extremely self-conscious manner as a gradual excision of 'le malheur', that category which is woven into the fabric of every sentimental (and melodramatic) text. A curious feature of the novel's dénouement demonstrates how the narrative overcoming of misfortune is perceived by the author as equivalent to the relief of misfortune through alms-giving: an anonymous 'princesse' – perhaps the comtesse d'Artois, to whom the novel is dedicated – and who has a real existence outside the novel, intervenes in the plot to bring about the happy ending. She is eulogised in these terms:

Heureuse du bien qu'elle fait, aimant à se dérober à l'éclat de son rang, uniquement occupée d'oeuvres charitables, Elle se dévoue à des travaux qui ont le pauvre pour objet. La vue de l'infortune, dont ses bienfaits ont tari les larmes, est le spectacle le plus doux pour Elle [...] Sans cesse on peut avec assurance implorer sa bonté pour l'être vertueux qui gémit sous le poids du malheur. (vol. 2, p. 200)

The beneficence which seeks to assist the poor and unfortunate, and the intrigue of a novel, share a common purpose: both are placed under the sign of misfortune, which it is their task to transform into happiness.

Blançay and *Victorine*, together with Gorjy's subsequent works, develop much further the question of the problematic expression of the internal life which, as I suggested in my analysis of Baculard, is a characteristic preoccupation of sentimentalism. Gorjy in fact returns on various occasions to a pantomimic theory of the expression of emotion, in which the dichotomy between linguistic and non-linguistic expression, as well as the power of the imagination, are investigated. In certain cases, the theme can be seen to be perfectly consonant with the ordinary run of sentimental description: in *Victorine*, for instance, when Verval confesses his love for the heroine in the presence of his kind step-mother, 'tous trois, ivres de ce bonheur que donnent les sentiments honnêtes, nous gardions un silence religieux. Des larmes, des baisers, des serrements de main étaient nos seules expressions' (vol. 1, p. 70). Similarly, in *Blançay*, the good Mme Péters is moved by the hero's account of his sufferings: 'sa respiration gênée, des soupirs retenus, ses yeux humides se tournant vers le ciel [...] Quel langage articulé aurait pu être plus énergique?'[28] At the end of the *Tablettes sentimentales du bon Pamphile*, the comte de Guérinval is so overcome by emotion at his reconciliation with the peasants of his estate that words fail him: 'le comte était tellement suffoqué qu'il ne pouvait articuler un seul mot. Il y suppléait par les signes les plus expressifs; et ses yeux étaient pleins de larmes.'[29] But two cases in particular develop the theme significantly further, introducing the imagination as a complicating factor. The first episode, from the *Tablettes sentimentales*, concerns a mother who is given hope that her sick child will survive. Gorjy describes

le cri de joie que fit cette pauvre mère, ou plutôt [...] une suite de cris coupés et se succédant si rapidement, qu'ils paraissaient n'en faire qu'un. En même temps ses yeux deviennent étincelants, sa tête est renversée, ses bras sont tendus vers le ciel: elle ne peut rien articuler;

mais elle n'en exprime pas moins, elle n'en exprime que mieux la foule de sensations que lui fit éprouver ce rayon d'espérance. (pp. 94–5)

Later, the narrator and the lady undertake a journey, and he witnesses a strange reaction on her part. Every time their carriage crosses a river, she manifests signs of terror, and once, when they pass close to a furnace glowing in the night, she cries 'encore un château'. The internal life, and its problematic relation with the outside observer, is thus made into a kind of enigma which the narrator and reader seek to elucidate (pp. 119–22). The lady is of course reliving imaginatively the catastrophe which deprived her of her father (the comte de Guérinval). Moreover, this catastrophe is said to have 'fait refluer le lait vers sa tête' thus affecting her reason; but her madness is considered an extension of normal human psychology, and simply serves, as it will in the work of Vernes to be analysed later, to heighten the processes whereby emotion seeks a form of expression other, and more intense, than language.

In the second episode, taken from *Victorine*, an even more extended description of the pantomime is offered. Azakia is describing the shipwreck in which she lost (or rather thought she lost) her daughter:

Elle s'arrête. Elle croit voir les flots écumer devant elle. Une de ses jambes est repliée sous elle-même, pour éviter leur atteinte [...] l'autre étendue, se cramponne sur le terrain, pour résister à leur effort. Son corps est porté en arrière autant que l'équilibre le permet. Les mains en avant repoussent le spectacle que son imagination lui présente. Sa bouche est en même temps béante et contractée. Son oeil, ouvert de toute l'extension des paupières, a le regard fixe de l'effroi. L'arc de ses sourcils est déformé. Le mouvement brusque qu'elle a fait en prenant cette attitude, l'élévation forcée des muscles de son front, la violente crispation de ses nerfs, ont comme hérissé ses cheveux [...] Sa respiration est suspendue [...] Après quelques instants d'une effrayante immobilité, 'Mon époux, ma fille' s'écrie-t-elle, avec un accent déchirant, et faisant le mouvement de vouloir les arracher aux flots. Puis, se relevant, et versant un torrent de larmes: 'Azakia n'a plus d'époux'.[30]

As in the first case, this episode illustrates the power of the imagination to replay previous sensations in the mind of the victim of misfortune. In both cases, moreover, if the mind is the theatre of the imagination, such is the interconnection of the physical and the moral that the impressions being experienced by the subject translate themselves into physical signs which are witnessed by the external observer. And here, as in the previous case, the scene is presented as an enigma, and as an interruption of normal social intercourse: while the pantomime is taking place, the narrator and the other spectators are reduced to an uneasy impotence as they observe the playing out of something which is beyond their grasp because, precisely, it belongs in the inner world of another human being. Paradoxically, within an aesthetic explicitly committed to the celebration of communicability, of sentiment as the basis of human interaction and sociability, the *distance* separating different subjects is emphasised.[31] That the sentimentalist should be attracted to such manifestations, given that they are situated within a continuum which includes the common or garden 'torrent de larmes', is scarcely surprising; what is more interesting is the fact that, with this extreme case of sensation, we begin to leave the realm of celebration, and move towards explorations whose attraction has more to do with the anxiety which they provoke than with an easy, consoling message about the joys and rewards of the life of feeling.

The fifth volume of *Ann'Quin Bredouille* contains a section of seventy or eighty pages which puts this concern for pantomimic expression and sign-language into a political context. This is a curious anecdotal work, loosely based on the journey formula and combining sentiment and satire in a moderately fierce attack on the Revolution besetting France, thinly disguised as the land of Néomanie. One of the crackpot schemes which the thirst for novelty has engendered is a project 'de l'intérêt le plus majeur' which aims to standardise language in Néomanie by eliminating regional languages. This is to be done in accordance with the principle that 'en parlant tous une même langue, tous auront bientôt un même sentiment'. In order to achieve this aim, it would be necessary to pass through a phase of total silence, enabling the people to become used to the absence of the familiar support provided by their habitual language; and the proposed method for doing this is the impo-

sition of a period during which the entire country will communicate entirely by sign-language. Monsieur Gobemouche, the
happy originator of this project, agrees to put his 'système
pantomimique' to public test by attempting to communicate a
message to a provincial peasant who speaks no French. A
pantomimic dialogue between Gobemouche and Gliondo
follows, in which, as in the scenes analysed above, the reader is
called upon to reconstruct the meaning of an enigmatic non-
verbal message. The dumbshow begins with Gobemouche
holding his stick horizontal, running his hand the length of it;
Gliondo comes down from the dais on which he is standing,
and places himself beside Gobemouche. Gobemouche then
places a liberty cap on the stick, which he holds aloft: 'Gliondo,
avec l'expression de la joie la plus vive, jette en l'air son
chapeau'. Gobemouche then hides the cap and stick in a
corner; Gliondo follows him, and shows some displeasure.
Gobemouche offers Gliondo a slice of bread and jam: 'Gliondo
le repousse d'un air très-piqué, et persiste à en vouloir au
bonnet et à la canne.' Gobemouche then hides the cap and
stick behind a bundle of bramble branches: 'Gliondo, en
colère, arrache le fagot, sans s'inquiéter s'il se déchire les
mains, et emporte avec un air de triomphe la canne et le
bonnet.' Gobemouche proceeds proudly to translate his pantomime into discursive form: when presented with the notion of
equality, Gliondo came down from his dais 'pour se conformer
à cette égalité universelle'; his behaviour towards the cap was
proof of his attachment to the principle of freedom, in the face
of attempts to seduce him (by the use of offers of jam today) or
terrorise him (by the use of brambles) into support for the
aristocratic principle. In short, the validity of his system is
confirmed: not only has the peasant understood what is being
referred to, but his enthusiasm to grasp the red bonnet is proof
of the fervour with which he supports the revolutionary cause.
This of course is subsequently deflated when an interpreter
translates from the peasant's patois the true message, which is
at complete variance with Gobemouche's enthusiastic revolutionary interpretation: Gliondo simply wanted a new cap
and stick. The 'système pantomimique', then, is conceived as

yet another scatty revolutionary idea. The only merit which the narrator can find in the whole scheme is the notion of linguistic standardisation: the Revolution has led to a proliferation of new words, as the 'plumaliers' seek to mask the vacuousness of their ideas beneath a veneer of linguistic sophistication: 'Convenez que les mots nouveaux, les mots intervertis, les mots rapprochés, les mots empruntés aux voisins, les mots affublés d'une signification nouvelle, les mots livrés à 24 000 000 d'interprétations différentes [...] ont cruellement bouleversé cette pauvre Néomanie.'[32] Louis-Sébastien Mercier's *Néologie ou Vocabulaire des mots nouveaux* will not appear until 1801.

The fundamental interest of *Tablettes sentimentales* and *Ann'Quin Bredouille* is that they show us a sentimental writer reacting in a relatively explicit fashion to the Revolutionary situation in France. Both works, as we shall see, use the basic stock-in-trade of sentimental fiction, but this material is put to the service of a political point of view. I propose to deal with the *Tablettes* first: this is a novel with a single, unified plot, and as such offers a clearer illustration of the political use of sentimental intrigue.

Published in 1791, the *Tablettes* are set in August–November 1789, in other words the period of popular ferment following the *Grande Peur*. Pamphile narrates the story: fleeing Paris, the seat of the 'esprit de parti', he decides to visit Mathieu, a humble and virtuous peasant and basket-maker whose acquaintance he had made during a trip to the country in happier times. Approaching the village where Mathieu lives, he comes upon a recently burned castle inhabited now only by an old woman who explains how the master, 'hautain mais charitable' – he gave bread to his peasants and built a church for them – fled and was accidentally drowned when the castle was pillaged by the politicised and misled peasantry. She is patiently awaiting the return of the master's daughter, who disappeared at the same time.

The narrator finds Mathieu much changed, worn by care and the troubles of the day. His particular grief is reserved for Antoine, the grandson who already, when Pamphile first met the family, was estranged from his rural background by virtue of time spent in the town, learning to read Latin and behave like a 'Monsieur'. Antoine returned from the town one day wishing to 'prouver que nous allons tous être égaux': now, he has joined the 'brigands', a decision which will surely lead to his eternal damnation. We then meet the lady whose panto-mimic displays have already been discussed. Pamphile is sensi-tive to the charms of this unfortunate but loving mother, and, as her health is restored under Pamphile's guidance and super-vision, he falls in love with her: she, however, speaks enig-matically of her Charles – husband? brother? – whom it is her absolute priority to find.

The narrator's peregrinations now lead him to a meeting with a hermit – frère Eusèbe – who is ashamed of the begging which he is forced to do, and whom Pamphile, naturally, treats with all the sensitivity and delicacy of the true man of feeling. 'Les peines sont à mon gré une sorte d'aimant, qui attire vers ceux qui en éprouvent', Pamphile confesses. The great revela-tion now occurs: the hermit is none other than the comte de Guérinval, who had been of assistance to Pamphile in his youth in Paris. 'J'essaierais en vain de décrire ce que j'éprouvai, en retrouvant ainsi inopinément l'homme à qui j'avais de si grandes obligations, et en le retrouvant malheureux.' It also transpires, of course, that he is none other than the master of the sacked château, that he had not in fact drowned but had been rescued by poor fisherfolk, and that he is now searching for his daughter and grandson. The count expatiates upon the injustice of his fate, the ingratitude of his peasants: 'En échange d'un vain tribut de respects, il n'était rien qu'ils ne pussent obtenir de moi.'[33] Indeed, his charity is such that he and his companion frère Gervais have come to the assistance of Antoine, injured in some dastardly revolutionary escapade: such charity is the direct opposite of the ingratitude of which Antoine is guilty, for it is given to one who defines the count as an enemy. Antoine repents: 'j'étais fou, j'étais forcené. Le dégoût de mon état, l'envie contre ceux qui étaient mieux que moi, avaient commencé le mal ... Monstre que j'étais! Ils [his family] pleuraient, et je n'ai pas été attendri!' (p. 185)

Pamphile is now given the task of returning to find the parish priest, who is to serve as an intermediary between the count and his estranged people. The priest addresses his parishioners, repeating the message which the reader has surely already digested:

Il était bienfaisant votre Seigneur, il était charitable. Le pauvre, vous le savez, ne l'a jamais imploré en vain. Dans les années de disette, ses greniers nous étaient ouverts. (pp. 195–6)

As Pamphile takes over, and recounts the story of his encounter with the count and his charity towards Antoine, 'les larmes ruisselaient de tous les yeux'. The count returns, the object of Pamphile's affections turns out to be the long-lost daughter, whose husband – Charles – also materialises, saved from the shipwreck which was supposed to have been his end. The only one excluded from this happy ending, then, is Pamphile, whose love cannot be requited: 'Il est partout, le bonheur, excepté dans le coeur du trop sensible Pamphile' (p. 229).

Two features are established here which will be developed, repeated and exploited in *Ann'Quin Bredouille*. The sentimental narrative, with its characteristic movement towards a happy ending which resolves misfortune into unity, now operates in the service of conservatism: it is the pre-Revolutionary society, with its organic links uniting disparate classes in one hier-archical structure, which the narrative seeks to recreate. No question here of the ideological indetermination alluded to in the discussion of Baculard. The message is a conservative one rather than simply one of national reconciliation, in the sense that the noble's role is considered pivotal in the functioning of the society. This is the meaning of the repeated insistence on the charitable nature of the count, who is seen as amply justifying his elevated position through the good works which are his hallmark. But this in turn is part of a wider trend in the novel, which will be systematically repeated in *Ann'Quin Bre-douille*: charitable action, the relief of misfortune, sensitivity to the woes of others – all of which are, as we have seen, central figures of sentimental discourse – are the very knot which holds together the narrative representation of society. Pamphile's

assistance to the count is the reciprocation of the kindness
which the latter had, conveniently, shown to the narrator years
before; the count's merit is finally demonstrated by the succour
offered to Antoine; and, indeed, the count owes his life to the
assistance of the 'pauvres pêcheurs' who saved him from the
river. It is this chain of obligation which ties the microsociety of
the novel together; these moments of *attendrissement* become
tokens of moral worth which circulate within the text. At
strategic points in the narrative, they perform a dynamic or
diachronic function, facilitating progress forward to reconciliation and happy ending; at the same time, they perform a
function within the moral structure of the novel, operating as
the external, visible signs of the internal qualities which separate the *sensible* from the ordinary mortal.

Ann'Quin Bredouille (whose subtitle *Le petit cousin de Tristram
Shandy* acknowledges the Sternian tradition) is an anecdotal
work, which, as the Prospectus announces, was to appear in
monthly volumes from February 1791 onwards. Six volumes in
all were published, the later ones dated 1792, which suggests
that the originally planned rhythm of publication was not
adhered to. The final volume, moreover, contains a highly
self-conscious, Sternian passage suggesting that the work was
interrupted by some political misfortune befalling the narrator:
the latter's uncle, Jean-Claude Ann'Quin Bredouille, has
decided to burn the remaining memoirs and to return to his
village.

Adieu donc cher Lecteur. Veuille le ciel vous envoyer un avenir qui
vous dédommage de tous les maux dont j'ai été témoin ... Mais ...
car ... O mon Dieu! entends, exauce les voeux de la véritable
philanthropie![34]

Whether this is an artfully constructed fiction suggesting that
Gorjy was the object of some type of political persecution we
cannot tell. It is however certainly the case, that this is his last
known work, and that the obscurity which generally surrounds
his life becomes complete from this moment on.

In a 'note trouvée dans le porte-feuille de mon illustre
parent, M. Tristram Shandy', Gorjy offers this description of

the formula of the sentimental journey, which will apply equally well to Vernes's *Voyageur sentimental* as it does to Gorjy's own work:

La charité et la bienveillance y sont toujours inspirées et recommandées. Quelquefois, il est vrai, je cours les champs et les grands chemins, sans autre projet que celui de jouir du bienfait de l'air et de la liberté. Mais un objet de pitié se présente-t-il à moi, je l'offre aussitôt à la pitié publique.

C'est ainsi que je vaguais dans l'insouciance, aussi innocemment qu'un enfant qui joue en cheminant, et que je ne revenais à moi que lorsque l'humanité, posant sa main sur mon sein, m'arrêtait tout-à-coup, et me tirait à part: j'étais alors dans mon fort. (vol. 6, pp. 40–1)

This accounts perfectly for the anecdotal structure of the work: the journey provides the principle of free movement within time and space, while this sentimental attraction to misfortune represents the recurrent preoccupation uniting the disparate episodes which are hung onto the journey structure.

Political conflict in 'Néomanie' is between two classes: the Altidors, who habitually use stilts to place themselves above the common mortals, the Surtalons. The destruction of the aristocratic principle is referred to, within this satirical system, as the casting aside or the breaking of the Altidors' stilts. In an extension of the techniques used in the *Tablettes*, sentimental narrative is employed to reveal the stupidity and cruelty of the revolutionary creed, and to recommend reconciliation between Altidors and Surtalons. Volume 1 offers an extended anecdote, telling the story of the narrator's meeting with 'la fausse villageoise'. She is first seen milking a cow to feed her daughter; the narrator and his companions are given milk. The brother of the 'villageoise' then appears on the scene, astonishing the travellers by virtue of the fact that he bears all the signs of being an Altidor. In answer to his reproaches, she defends her decision to cast aside her stilts and join the people: walking on stilts had become a delicate operation, and she feared hurting her daughter in a fall.

–En descendant doucement de moi-même, je l'ai ménagée, et je me suis assurée du bonheur de ma vie.
–Le bonheur, en se réduisant à marcher terre-à-terre?

–Mon bon ami, cela te paraît difficile. Je le croyais aussi. Eh bien, je t'assure que c'est le fantôme qui disparaît quand on le touche. (vol. 1, p. 132)

The brother remains unconvinced. Some chapters later, the 'villageoise' is seen giving assistance to a man with a broken leg: he turns out to be a Republican, who proudly boasts of the number of Altidor stilts and skulls he has smashed. Her charity in tending his wounds in spite of his politics is of course described as 'sublime', and the young Republican's father (the equivalent of Mathieu in the *Tablettes*) develops the theme:

Elle a toujours été l'appui du faible, la consolation du malheureux, la ressource du pauvre. La plus chétive chaumière, le plus triste grabat, rien ne la rebutait. Elle laissait à la porte ses grandes échasses, et descendait tellement au niveau de ceux qu'elle assistait, que ceux-ci auraient pu croire qu'elle avait tout le temps marché comme eux terre-à-terre. (vol. 1, p. 174)

The brother then arrives – on foot. The episode which has brought about his conversion again shows the central role of the charitable act as a hinge, a turning point in the narrative. He had tried to cross a flooded stream, and found himself in difficulty. Who should come to his aid but 'un vieillard de la classe des Surtalons' whose garden the thoughtless Altidor had only minutes before trampled underfoot 'sans aucun égard pour ses avis'. 'Dès qu'il voit mon danger, il oublie mes torts, quitte sa bêche, se prosterne à genoux pour demander l'assistance de l'Etre Suprême, s'élance dans le torrent.' Afterwards, of course, the good peasant refuses payment, and the aristocrat, in gratitude, smashes his stilts there and then: 'c'est avec elles que j'avais dévasté le jardin de mon libérateur'. Finally, in a typical movement of synthesis, it is revealed that the virtuous old man was none other than the father of the young Republican succoured by the 'villageoise'. The chain of charity has come full circle, enabling the moral to be articulated: 'Ainsi la véritable humanité ne connaît ni les classes, ni les distinctions, et rapproche par un échange de bienfaits, les êtres les plus opposés' (vol. 1, pp. 179–82). The charitable action overcomes revolutionary *and* aristocratic ideology: the message is clearly less onesided than that of the *Tablettes*.

The particularity of this use of sentimental categories in the articulation of a message of reconciliation is that the actions of an individual are put forward as a factor transcending any attempt to categorise people by their class. When it has been said that Dormeuil's father provided Alexis with an education, that the virtuous peasant assisted the very man who had trampled on his cabbages, all has been said. The narratives which bear this message are indeed terribly commonplace in character, and the good action which will swing the story in the right direction always comes, predictably, at the right time, as an afterthought which requires no preparation or naturalisation in the text. But this only emphasises the total faith which is placed in narrative as a means of resolving conflict and contradiction: as Baczko has shown, the story is an adequate representation of history, and the individual destinies which are charted by the *récit* are a sufficient basis for statements about the nature of society. If the *esprit de parti* is a theoretical construct which is poisoning the minds of Frenchmen, stories such as these demonstrate the belief that this can be transcended by a good *péripétie*.

Ann'Quin Bredouille concludes with an episode entitled 'L'aristocrate converti, ou le retour de Coblentz' (vol. 6, pp. 126–54). This follows the interruption of the narrative already described, and is presented in a 'printer's note' as an addition to the manuscript. The episode may therefore not be by Gorjy, but its analysis of the relationship between individual virtue and political theory ('esprit de parti') is consistent with the rest of the work. The narrator of the episode went into exile with the comte de . . ., and is recounting his story from the point of view of one who has seen the futility of such fidelity, and has returned to France in order to support the Revolution. The count had 'pris soin de mon enfance, et je devais à ses bienfaits l'existence assez honnête dont je jouissais dans le monde'. The starting point is a familiar one. At the time, the narrator failed to see through this charity: 'Ici la bienfaisance se montrait; je ne soupçonnai même pas qu'il fût possible qu'elle couvrît cette jouissance aussi orgueilleuse que féodale, qui résulte du bien répandu sur un inférieur.' It was the reading of the works of 'nos patriotes les plus zélés' which opened his eyes, and convinced him that behind this individual kindness lay yet another manifestation of the aristocratic plot. From this point on, we are treated to a very witty rewriting of a conventional sentimental analysis. Despite his hardship, the count continues to be the unsparing benefactor of the narrator: in the new discourse, this is translated as follows:

Mais ce que je lui reprocherais le plus, depuis que mes lectures m'ont éclairé, et parce qu'en effet j'y vois le comble de l'astuce, c'est qu'au milieu des déplaisirs qu'il éprouvait, il n'a pas diminué d'un sou ses charités d'usage. Il a même porté la ruse, l'hypocrisie jusqu'à partager avec les habitants, dans le moment de la disette, sa provision de blé, jusqu'à leur donner à crédit au prix des années moyennes. (p. 133)

Once the system is in place, no evidence can shake the conviction which it has instilled: he speaks of the 'audace imperturbable avec laquelle le Comte soutint jusqu'au bout son rôle d'attachement et de bienfaisance', and admits that, upon his return to France, the Count spoke to him 'avec le ton d'une sensibilité si vraie, que pour n'en être pas la dupe, j'eus besoin de me cramponner de toutes mes forces à mes nouveaux principes'. What this story dramatises, then, is the way in which a mental and ideological system, a theoretical explanation of the world, obscures and corrupts the transparence of virtue and good actions on the part of an individual. In that sense, it is the exact reverse of the narratives of reconciliation which have already been analysed.

If the individual transcendence of class and party divisions through virtuous action is the explicit message of *Ann'Quin Bredouille*, a certain class analysis does emerge in a nascent form. If the privileged site for narratives of reconciliation is the country, the seat of purity as opposed to the decadence of the city, then the corollary of this is that the parties reconciled are predominantly the peasantry and the aristocracy: the Surtalons represent a very restrictive interpretation of the Tiers Etat. One episode (vol. 6, pp. 12ff) does however include an explicit representative of the bourgeoisie, presented in an entirely negative light. On the one hand, the avaricious Serre-l'Aulne exploits his apprentice: 'au lieu d'être payé pour les services que l'on en exige avec tant de dureté, c'est lui qui paie pour un apprentissage prolongé pendant plusieurs années [...] logé dans un grenier dont l'été fait une étuve et l'hiver une glacière'. On the other, Serre-l'Aulne is the Revolutionary ideologue, responsible not only for the death of innocent victims of the Terror, but also for massacring the French language by his use of a tortuous, theoretical mode of expression which serves, precisely, to mask humanity and individuality beneath a veil of abstraction. Gorjy, in short, is tempted by a sentimental alliance of people and aristocracy against the self-interest of the bourgeoisie – a theme which will be pursued in the nineteenth century, both in melodrama and in the work of Eugène Sue and the young Hugo.

FRANÇOIS VERNES

François Vernes (1765–1834) is an approximate contemporary of Gorjy, but his literary career stretches forward into the nineteenth century, including work published after 1830. His work is therefore doubly interesting, in the sense that its roots lie in the sentimentalism of the late eighteenth century, but that it goes through the crucible of history; one particular consequence of this, which is exhibited especially by Vernes's later work, is a compensatory function, whereby the deceptions of recent history (Histoire) are subjected to a reworking through the medium of imaginative narrative (histoire). The earlier work, however, reinforces many of the features of the sentimental aesthetic which have been noted in Baculard and Gorjy.

The milieu from which Vernes comes is the rising Protestant bourgeoisie of Geneva. His great-grandfather, Pierre, left the Vivarais after the Revocation of the Edict of Nantes, and was naturalised a citizen of Lausanne in 1702. Pierre's son, Jean-Georges, born in Lausanne, obtained the status of *bourgeois* of Geneva in 1722. Vernes's father, Jacob (1728–91) is the author of the *Lettres sur le christianisme de J.-J. Rousseau* (1763), a defence of Protestant orthodoxy against Rousseau's vision in

the *Lettres de la Montagne*. It is, however, the future development of the family which most clearly illustrates their social
ascendancy: through a cousin of Vernes's, Jacques-Louis, who
is already established in business in Lyon in 1784, the family
will in due course return to France. Jacques-Louis's son
Auguste-Charles-Théodore, born in Lyon in 1786, is set up in
business in Paris in 1811; by 1820 he is a member of the
hierarchy of the Protestant church in France (Consistory of
Paris, then Conseil général des églises réformées de France),
while his business career takes him, in 1832, to the rank of
sous-gouverneur at the Banque de France. His younger brother,
Félix (b. 1801), is the founder of Félix Vernes et Cie, destined
to become the Banque Vernes of today, and which in the 1840s
operated as père Enfantin's agent for his investments in the
railway boom. As for François's direct descendants from his
three marriages, some will remain in Geneva, but Guillaume-
Théodore (b. 1820) follows in his second cousin's footsteps
when he enters the Consistory of Paris in 1853.[35]

As for the biography of Vernes himself, certain details can be
gleaned from correspondence conserved in various archives in
Geneva.[36] In 1784 and 1785, at the age of nineteen and twenty,
we find him in Brussels, reluctantly attempting to make a
debut in a business career which has been wished on him by his
father. By 1786, the year in which his first work is published,
Vernes is in Paris. Christmas 1787 sees our hero back in
Geneva. From this point on, the available evidence suggests
that Switzerland will remain Vernes's base throughout his life:
he figures, as we shall see, in the political hierarchy of Geneva
in the 1790s; at least some of the children from his three
marriages are born in the area; and the notices in the Genevan
press which announce his death in 1834 speak of him as a local
celebrity who has remained associated with the town
throughout his career.

In political and ideological terms, Vernes is clearly associated with the 'patriotic' movement for political reform and
extension of political rights in Geneva. His father was exiled to
Constance in 1782, after the collapse of the attempt by the
Représentants to challenge the political supremacy of the oli-

garchic *Petit Conseil*. Vernes himself appears as a member of various political and administrative bodies of the city after the Revolution of 1792 had finally achieved the aims of ten years before: 1793–7, member of the *comité d'administration*; 1794, *comité législatif*; 1796, *sénat académique*. Furthermore, his participation in the symbolically important restoration of the *fête de l'Escalade* in December 1793 actually included the composition of a 'hymne en l'honneur de ceux qui étaient morts pour la patrie';[37] this festival had been suppressed in the wake of 1782, and was now restored at the request of the Club fraternel des révolutionnaires genevois to mark 'le premier anniversaire de la votation populaire qui consacrait les vrais principes de l'égalité'. There is, in other words, clear involvement in public political activities of the egalitarian side of the political divide. His correspondence also contains letters to and from J.-B. Say, the editor of the *Décade philosophique* and liberal economist, who appears to be operating as a kind of literary agent for Vernes in Paris in ventôse Year 5.

An episode from *Le Voyageur sentimental* represents a direct echo of the Genevan revolution. It recounts the narrator's meeting with a group of exiled Genevan patriots at Constance. The key to the sentimentalisation of these figures is that they have preferred separation from their loved ones to the betrayal of patriotic political principle: they are heroic victims. The central figure of the group is an old man for whom the *patrie* is explicitly presented as the equivalent of the lovers, wives, children and families which the younger members of the party are leaving behind. The episode demonstrates the structural equivalence which exists between certain recognisable features of the process of sentimentalisation – a father's love for his family, affection for friends or lovers – and devotion to a political cause. There is no mistaking the clear conjunction of the sentimental and the political. 'Le ton, ces mots que seul un Républicain peut prononcer, et qu'un Républicain seul peut entendre, me bouleversèrent', 'un ruisseau de larmes échappa de mes yeux'. The episode is immediately followed by the return to the narrator's family in Morges, which is described thus:

Le commerce de la vie y est agréable; le luxe n'y offre pas son insultant étalage; on ne s'y pique pas de cacher la misère domestique, et celle de l'esprit, sous d'éblouissants dehors; on n'y rit pas de l'union conjugale et des douceurs qu'elle procure; une fausse philosophie n'y écrase pas les vertus par ses désolants systèmes; l'heureux esprit d'égalité y règne plus qu'ailleurs; le risible préjugé de *noblesse* n'y fait pas de tristes et ridicules séparations.[38]

Le Voyageur sentimental, ou ma promenade à Yverdon was published in the second half of 1786, a first edition appearing in London (printed by Cazin) and a second in Neuchâtel, published by Mourer. This, then, is during Vernes's period in Paris. The work clearly enjoyed a certain reputation at the time, since a reprint appeared in 1792 and a slightly modified edition again in 1825; the title pages of certain of Vernes's later works identify the author as responsible for the *Voyageur sentimental*, suggesting that this might be read as a recommendation by contemporaries.

Most of the features which have been illustrated from the work of Baculard and Gorjy find a place in Vernes's *Voyageur sentimental*, but two themes in particular will enable me to extend and deepen the analysis offered in the previous sections: the sentimental journey as a form which permits the enactment of a certain notion of social solidarity; and, once again, the importance of signs, both as an explicitly evoked category and as an implicit feature of the sentimental aesthetic.

The dominant meaning of the adjective *sentimental* is suggested in the following apostrophe to the reader in the opening pages:

Pardon, Lecteur! à l'exemple des Voyageurs, j'aurais dû vous donner des descriptions topographiques du Lieu de notre départ; vous marquer, exactement, sa latitude, sa longitude, sa distance de la Capitale; vous parler de son Eglise, de son Château, de sa Bibliothè-que, etc. J'avoue, à ma honte, que ce superbe genre d'érudition n'est pas le mien; vous ne le verrez que trop au cours de mon *Voyage*. Hélas! une nuance de sentiment me frappe et m'attache plus que tous les *Panthéons* et toutes les *Colonnes Trajanes*. (pp. 8–9)

The sentimental is opposed to the topographical; if the journey is designed to make us see something, then what is being shown is less immediately visible than the stuff of tourist guides, and, crucially, the showing requires the presence of a narrator, for it is through his sensibility that sentiment can be made subject to evocation. Vernes's novel provides confirmation of what was apparent in the case of Gorjy's *Nouveau voyage sentimental*: the narrator is central to the narrative, in the sense that he is the only common thread running through the book. He is the link between the various discrete elements which make up this most episodic of works. These episodes are as it were the sentimental punctuation which is hung around the unifying thread of the narrator's presence. But the narrator is more than simply a device for linking together disparate elements, and making these available to the reader: he does more than simply deliver a version of external reality to the reader, in the sense that what the text repeatedly dramatises is the moment at which an observing subject *reacts to* that reality. The repeated scenes of recognition which punctuate the narrative should be read as the textual enactment of a possible social practice, the prefiguration of a sentimental community.

In a journey narrative, it seems almost tautological to say that the episode takes the forms of the meeting: it is the person or persons *met* on the journey who supply the sentimental punctuation in question. Typically, their role is passive, in the sense that their meaning lies in the charitable reactions which they provoke on the part of the narrator: Vernes speaks of *bienfaisance* in essentially the same way as Baculard or Gorjy. The characters met by the narrator possess certain almost visible characteristics which guarantee them a place in the narrative. The first such character to be introduced in the narrative is 'l'homme au mouton':

Chemin faisant, je m'accostai d'un homme, dont les habits, autant que le jour naissant me permettait de le voir, portaient l'enseigne de la misère, enseigne dont tant d'hommes détournent les yeux, parce qu'elle leur donnerait la tentation d'une bonne oeuvre; et que tant d'hommes méprisent, parce qu'ils ne savent pas voir le mérite, que souvent elle cache. (p. 17)

The man is travelling with a sheep, and deep affective bonds obviously unite man and animal. When the man tells his story, we learn that the sheep was his favourite among a whole flock which his master ordered him to slaughter, and that he preferred to lose his job and take to the highway rather than sacrifice his only friend. Thus his poverty, which he interprets when he says, his eye lingering on his fleecy friend, 'je suis bien pauvre, mais je ne te le reproche pas'. The narrator, is, of course, moved, and gives money, taking the precaution of actually presenting it (one would love to have further details) to the sheep, 'de peur de blesser la délicatesse du maître', reproducing Baculard's concern for the ethics and aesthetics of alms-giving. The episode ends with an exhortation to the reader to imitate the example of the narrator if ever he meets the man with the sheep (pp. 16–22).

Another episode raises the giving of alms to the status of a moral precept, adding a commentary on the nature of the relation between religion and secular ethics. The narrator is in an inn with two ecclesiastical gentlemen, one of whom is a believer in the dogma of orthodox Christianity and the other a partisan of 'une religion plus humaine'. The innkeeper enters, asking for contributions for a traveller who has been robbed on the highway near the inn. It is, of course, the latter of the two clerics who digs into his purse for the unfortunate victim; and it is the narrator who arraigns the traditionalist, pointing to the 'petit écu' given by the enlightened cleric and saying 'Monsieur, voilà la bonne Orthodoxie' (p. 80). The quotation highlights a metaphorical structure common to many sentimental texts, in which sensibility is substituted for some socially marked value. The commonest form of this is the one which occurs in the case of Maître Cukin, a former aristocrat who has fallen upon bad times and is reduced to driving a carriage. The narrator consoles him with the reflection: 'Maître Cukin, la sensibilité de l'âme, voilà la vraie noblesse' (p. 141). Sensibility, as evidenced by the act of charity, is an alternative, democratic basis of social meaning.

Two final cases will perhaps serve to show to what extent the *dramatis personae* of Vernes's text are the stock sentimental figures easily recognisable to readers not just of eighteenth-century literature. One cameo has two such characters, an

orphan and a crippled soldier, confronting together life's vicissitudes, the little orphan bravely giving up half of his *étrennes* to
help the former hero; in another, the pair is constituted by a
blind man and his daughter, the father having, again, fallen
upon hard times after working for forty years 'à la sueur de son
front, pour amasser quelques centaines d'écus'. The cause of
his downfall is coyly referred to as 'des banqueroutes', and 'il
n'avait pas su se relever de ses échecs' (p. 159).

The feature common to all the foregoing episodes is that the
text, in particular through the journey form, dramatises the
meeting between a man of feeling, the narrator, and various
victims of misfortune. That point of meeting is to be read as the
infinitely repeatable gesture founding some notion of social
solidarity: each is a case of virtue in distress, as each gesture of
humanity on the part of the narrator is a manifestation of
humanity, *bienfaisance*, universal categories on which any
society should be founded. Behind these brief cameos, some
sort of ideological project is to be found: the text is, in some
minimal sense at least, about equality, democracy, the religion
of humanity as a basis for social coexistence.

This formulation represents one of the underlying hypotheses of the present study, and it will be extended, analysed
and criticised at various other points in the following pages.
But one episode in particular from the *Voyageur sentimental*
stands as a very serious question-mark over this attempt to
enrol sentimental texts as bearers of Enlightenment values of
democratisation and equality. The chapter is entitled 'le
Clavecin'. The harpsichord is the brilliant invention of a
scientist, who has imagined and realised a method for con-
fining a number of cats within a frame. The keyboard operates
a set of pins which prick the cats 'sous la queue', and, since the
cats are drawn from the whole range of cat ages, the resultant
complaints cover the entire musical scale. Such is this ingeni-
ous instrument, redolent of medieval mythologies but strangely
transposed into an Enlightenment vision, not least in the
scientific precision with which it is described, which is such
as to make one feel that a *planche* would not be out of place.
Like the *clavecin oculaire*, the device draws on the century's

fascination for phenomena which transcend the boundaries between fields of experience or between the different senses: the pain of the cats produces (notionally at least) aesthetic pleasure, just as the variations in the physiology of the cat over its life-span translate into a precisely spaced range of notes. This is not the only sense in which sensibility is the key to this strange episode. For while the inventor is demonstrating his brainchild, one of the cats escapes and comes towards the narrator, 'paraissant implorer ma protection et me dire, plaintivement, qu'il n'aimait pas la musique. Son maître, fort en colère, le saisissait pour lui faire reprendre sa note tonique: j'intercédai pour lui, et j'obtins sa grâce.' The fortunate creature's first gesture as a free cat is to come rubbing itself against the narrator's back, 'me remerciant à sa manière de ce que j'avais écouté la loi naturelle' (pp. 70–1).

The challenge which the episode represents to a reading of sentimentalism as an ideology of equality and democracy is clear. The process of sentimentalisation is so intimately bound up with a reduction of the sentimentalised object to the status of victim that the two processes are seen as interdependent: the powerlessness of the victim is not a fortuitous, given fact, rather it is the condition willed by the observer, since without it the subsequent act of mercy would have no reason to exist. The episode, in short, seems to blow the cover, to display to public gaze the trick which the sentimental text performs all the time, but in less blatant form: sentimentalisation, far from being a liberation, would in this view be an act of enthralment, an expression of the power of the dominant to *choose* to behave with humanity towards those placed under them.

The text, then, enacts scenes of solidarity, even though the nature of that solidarity is hedged about with political ambiguity. Vernes is explicit in identifying the *sign* as crucial in the process whereby the sufferings of humanity are recognised and relieved by the sensitive subject. An episode occurring immediately after the encounter with the 'homme au mouton' explicitly dramatises the notion of sign. The narrator is settling down before the fire in his room at the inn at Orbes, when he hears sounds coming from beyond the wall.

Il n'en fallut pas davantage pour exiter ma curiosité; les signes de la douleur m'attirent plus fortement encore que ceux du plaisir. Trait d'une profonde sagesse dans l'Auteur de mon être. (p. 57)

The terminology used points to the extent to which theories of language and sensibility elaborated within the discourse of scientific investigation have penetrated enlightened culture: the initial recognition of suffering is attributed not to language, but to the workings of a system of *signs*, which trigger the sentimental reaction on the part of the observer. These signs are perceived as operating involuntarily upon the man of feeling: the nature of sensibility, as a faculty uniting the physical and the moral, is such that an individual possessed of it cannot but react when (s)he recognises those signs. The man of feeling is a finely tuned *sensorium* constantly awaiting the opportunity to register and react to external stimuli.

In this episode, investigation by the narrator reveals a truly touching scene, perceived, in the first instance, precisely in the static, visual way which the term suggests. A father and five children are grouped round the bed of their dead wife and mother, their gestures concentrating all the reader's attention on the passive corpse, as in a Greuze painting or a sentimental print. Then comes the moment when the body must be removed, and the gesture with which the children mark this most highly charged emotional point in the narrative is to offer sweets from their pockets to the mouth of the dead woman. The sweets were the gift of the narrator, we learn at this point. And then the narrative breaks off: what might be called an aesthetic of the ineffable intervenes. 'Nature, prends tes pinceaux; je pose ici les miens; quand je pourrais broyer tes couleurs, mes larmes les effaceraient!' Language cannot carry the full emotional meaning of the experience (pp. 57–60).

The sweets in the episode just quoted bring me to the second aspect of the sign in Vernes's text. I am tempted here to use the term *emblem*, although there is clearly overlap between the phenomena I am seeking to distinguish. The distinction is this: the *sign* is an explicitly hypostatised feature of the process of communication by which the narrator is alerted to the presence of suffering humanity; the *emblem*, on the other hand, is a feature of the aesthetic of the sentimental text. Sentimental texts of the late eighteenth century possess an extraordinary capacity for investing very heavy affective or moral charges in what appear to be the tiniest of details. If the sweets offered by the children to their dead mother represent one case of this – and a particularly baroque one – then the sequence which best illustrates this tendency is somewhat different from the brief episodes already quoted, by virtue of its greater complexity and extension. My analysis therefore involves a brief narrative parenthesis.

The sequence begins with the narrator observing a funeral which is taking place in the cemetery close to his room at the inn. A bystander informs him that Marianne is being buried, and proceeds to tell her story which appears to fit perfectly within the conventional framework of eighteenth-century narrative. The starting-point is thus a static, pictorial one, but in this case a relatively extended narrative lies behind the initial *tableau*. Marianne was poor but virtuous, and all who knew her loved her, not least for her *sensibilité*. She was in love with Adémar, who also had the misfortune to be poor, and her father was opposed to the marriage. The father accepts a marriage request from a rich suitor who presents himself, and is insensitive to all his daughter's arguments, expressed in the following terms: 'Il est riche, dites-vous; mais qu'est-ce que l'or? Peut-il nous rendre heureux quand nous l'arrosons de larmes?' (p. 89). Marianne runs away and imprisons herself rather than give in to parental violence; the father and the suitor then have recourse to deception, forging letters which purport to come from Adémar, telling how he has married a richer woman. Marianne believes them and goes to the altar with the husband of her father's choice, only to discover that the story is an elaborate lie and that her husband is a violent and insensitive man. Her death is the proof of her virtue and the cruelty of her persecutors; the father's eventual death, on the other hand, is the price of sinning against the eternal laws of humanity for the sake of pride, money and social status.

Our traveller is leaving the cemetery, already sensitised by this heart-rending story, when he comes upon a man on crutches at the gateway, holding out a knitted woollen bonnet in which he hopes to collect alms. The narrator gives, but the coin passes through a hole in the headgear and ultimately, after a certain amount of exaggerated dumbshow from the beggar, he penetrates the meaning of the message which he is being given: the hole is not exactly large, and yet the coin passes through, *ergo* a larger coin is required. This detail is conceived as picturesque. Then comes the detail which provides the crucial link with the story of Marianne: the bonnet which has been the central locus for the act of asking and giving was knitted for the poor man by the even more unfortunate Marianne. It is as though the sentimental meaning which attaches to the episode were able to circulate through the text, attaching to an object such as the knitted woolly hat and thus being transmitted to the different context of the beggar's quest for alms. One could multiply instances of comparable textual procedures: the investment in a detail such as the bonnet is parallel, for instance, to the process of immobilisation which is at work in the constitution of the *tableau*. The effect, which appears to be coterminous with the notion of sentimentalisation, is to hold up for contemplation a particular feature which, by a sort of synecdoche, expresses the full emotional charge of a long sequence of events. It is as though the best way to express the sublimity of the emotions and values involved – for behind emotion, there always lurks a moral universal – is to exert increasing pressure on the description, reducing the narrative sequence to some ultimate expressive unit in order to maximise the effect of the emotional burden which it is forced to bear.[39]

Vernes's *Voyageur sentimental en France sous Robespierre*, published by Paschoud in Geneva and Maradan in Paris in Year 7, i.e. between September 1798 and August 1799, takes the character with whom the reader is familiar from the previous work and transfers him to a new context, which is identified in specific-ally political terms as Robespierre's France.[40] The book appears four years after the historical experience on which it claims to be a reflection, but this in no sense invalidates its interest. It is part of the proliferation of post-Revolutionary writing which seeks to analyse the meaning of the unprecedented events which have just (but only in one sense) come to an end. This new *Voyageur sentimental* is a particularly useful prism through which to view the relation between a sentimental vision and the experience of the Revolution and of the Terror: it performs this task more explicitly than the works of Gorjy, although both belong to the same genre.

Les opinions, en général, tenant nécessairement de la faiblesse et de l'imperfection de l'esprit humain, je cherche à prouver que les sentiments bons et généreux du coeur, doivent prédominer sur elles, être écoutés sans cesse comme la seule voix qui ne trompe point. Ah! C'est après les jours de sang et d'infortune par lesquels nous avons passé qu'il est plus important que jamais de rappeler de tels principes.[41]

The heart is an antidote to the 'esprit de parti': reaction to the excesses of the Revolution is one of the origins of the dichotomy between head and heart, reason and sentiment which has marked historical interpretations of Enlightenment since the Revolution. Vernes goes on to justify the evocation of the sad events of recent years with the familiar argument that 'l'expérience des maux les plus cruels devient bientôt nulle pour l'homme, si l'on ne la grave pas dans son âme, en lui en retraçant sans cesse le tableau'.

The difference between the experience of the sentimental traveller in the first book and now is that in the Revolutionary situation, the narrator cannot go about his business of charitable activity in the same open way as before: he would lay himself open to the charge of assisting the enemies of the Revolution, 'la pitié allait me criminaliser aux yeux de ceux que le courage de la férocité rendait tout-puissants'. Such accusations of counter-revolutionary motivation were of course directed at the language of pity in the years 1793–4, and chapter 4 will attempt to analyse that particular discursive formation in more detail. Vernes of course disclaims any such reading of his intentions, stating, in my view sincerely, his political credo:

Partout l'auteur y professe les sentiments et les principes d'un républicanisme épuré; partout il y prêche le respect dû aux lois et au gouvernement; partout enfin il plaide la cause de l'humanité.

A *ci-devant* aristocrat whose family are murdered in an orgy of egalitarian violence by a group of villagers; an unfortunate young bourgeois whose father and brother were executed in Montagnard reprisals against the federalist uprising of Lyon; a *prêtre déporté* who is the object of injustice from his uneducated and highly politicised guards: these three characters are met during the narrator's peregrinations, and their story, according to the well-established sentimental procedure, is recounted in response to the curiosity aroused by their present condition and in an attempt to explain narratively how it came about. At first sight it would appear that these victims, so essential to the functioning of the text, are all drawn from the ranks of the enemies of the Revolution, and that Vernes's sentimentalism has indeed turned counter-revolutionary. It is certainly the case that these episodes draw a political moral, but in each case it is possible to show that the position from which they are written is a moderate republican one. Le capitaine de Volny, the *ci-devant* in question, whom the narrator meets on the roadside in the company of his daughter, is carefully represented as having renounced the splendours of court life before the Revolution, in favour of withdrawal to his family estate. This unpretentious and humble country existence is presented in a typically Rousseauist fashion, with the captain operating as the benefactor of the local population and a servant of the 'patrie'. As a result, the outbreak of Revolution had caused the good captain no concern, and he had indeed been one of the first 'à adopter le systeme républicain, et à renoncer à de vains titres; de grands abus demandaient de grandes réformes'. These conclusions are, moreover, the result of philosophical study on the captain's part theorised in the following terms:

Le riche contracte envers le pauvre la dette de son superflu, et l'acquit de cette dette, en satisfaisant l'âme sensible, est plus encore un bienfait de la Providence pour celui qui le place que pour celui qui le reçoit. (vol. 1, pp 28–9)

The financial metaphor is typical. Volny appears as a middle of the road constitutional Girondin, and it is this enlightened and reasonable man who falls victim to the violence of peasants who previously had considered him their benefactor and 'père'. The familial metaphor, again typical, allows the violence of the villagers to be presented as bordering on parricide. Indeed, a whole range of characteristically sentimental techniques is employed to wring from the confrontation its full emotional meaning: the attack takes place on the wedding-day of the captain's daughter, and the groom falls victim to the violence; a concomitant feature is the insistence with which the violence of the villagers is described, and which ties in with a colourful fascination with violence pervading the whole book, worthy at times of the adjective 'Gothic' (vol. 1, pp. 26–38).

Similar ideological precautions are taken by Vernes in the presentation of the two other episodes which have been referred to. The narrator meets a young woman weeping by the roadside, and an old man accompanying her tells her story. Felix, her lover, shot by terrorists in Lyon for having sought to save his father and brother from their extremism, has impeccable credentials as a man of sensibility and reason, but nevertheless he is led away:

Oh! Qui peindra cette scène d'attendrissement et d'effroi! Partout on entend les noms de père et de frère: les coeurs les plus barbares sont émus, et sentent qu'ils tiennent encore par quelque fil à la nature humaine.

and it is left to the narrator to draw the moral in terms totally consistent with Protestant Enlightenment:

Ici le vieillard fit une pause pour donner un profond soupir aux malheurs de Lyon, à ceux de la France, et je crus voir dans le moment le fanatisme politique agiter le poignard dont s'arma le catholicisme au jour de la Saint Barthélémi. (vol.1, pp. 96–7)

The third episode mentioned develops the religious theme, and is, incidentally, an echo of the chapter entitled 'Le petit écu' from *Le voyageur sentimental*. The *prêtre déporté* is being escorted from France by two gendarmes, and the meeting with the narrator takes place at an inn. Observing that the gendarmes are drinking wine while the priest is confined to water, and judging that 'le père avait une figure de martyr', the narrator intervenes and offers the priest wine. The gesture is interpreted similarly by the two parties present: the gendarmes immediately conclude that the narrator is nothing more than 'un prêtre, un aristocrate' (the judgement, of course, being negative), while the priest sees in his benefactor a fellow Catholic. It is precisely at this point that the narrator intervenes to introduce a complication into the ideological simplification: he was born a Protestant, and his gesture conveys upon him the necessary credit to justify the lesson in humane religion which follows, together with an injunction to the priest to swear allegiance to the civil constitution of the clergy, the rejection of which is surely the reason for his imposed exile. Such a course would, according to the narrator, enable the priest to continue the non-partisan humanitarian work which is, in his view, the proper vocation of the clergyman. The priest, 'qui avait cru me dire une insulte en m'appelant philosophe', is finally persuaded, and gives the narrator his purse in recognition of his help and advice. The episode ends with several lines of apostrophe of this 'petite bourse de cuir' as a symbol of human *bienfaisance* (vol. 1, p. 136).

Several other episodes could be analysed in detail to support the claim which is being made here: that the procedures of sentimental writing developed by Vernes in his first work are used in this new version of the *Voyageur sentimental* to present a vision of the Revolution and the Terror which addresses a number of key topical issues and which can be identified as moderate republican in political conviction. Sentimental categories are never far from the surface in the presentation of the fourteen 'vierges de Verdun' led to the scaffold dressed in virgin white; of the reconciliation of the émigré aristocrat and his son of revolutionary sympathies; of the man who is prepared to take his friend's place on the scaffold so that he may live; of François, the patriotic hero who returns to his village from the armies of the Revolution ('J'ai perdu ma jambe en faisant mon devoir, tout ce qui me fâche, c'est de n'en avoir plus qu'une au service de l'Etat'); and, finally, of the blind old man condemned to rot in the prisons of the Terror. A common structure is present here: if disruption and misfortune are produced by the excesses of revolutionary ideology, then resolution is found in a creed of moderate republicanism, patriotism and a vaguely Protestant humanitarian deism.

What seems to be emerging, then, is that the Terror represents a limit for the sentimental vision. The presentation of Robespierre, and more specifically of his notion of virtue and of the possibility of representing it through the *fête*, gives a particularly clear insight into the nature of this limitation. The narrator is present at the Convention, and hears Robespierre proposing a series of 'jours de fête pour les vertus'.[42] The narrator's reaction is one of indignation: the man responsible for plunging a whole society into an orgy of death and suffering cannot be sincere when he speaks in this way of virtue, and this evident truth leads to a rigid separation between the reality of virtue and its theatrical representation. Robespierre's *fête* in fact reproduces in microcosm the central failure of city life: those revolutionaries – Danton, Hérault, Simond – whom we see going to their deaths, are reaping the rewards of seeking to live through the opinion of others, of being prepared to enter into the economy of political representation (vol. 1, pp. 250–6). This interpretation is clearly an application to the revolutionary experience of Rousseau's denunciation of city life and, more generally, of civilisation. And it takes on its full meaning when it is seen as part of a structure which is systematically developed in Vernes's book: the opposition between country and city. A *fête villageoise* which the narrator witnesses in the later stages of his journey as he returns to the calm of his native Switzerland, is described in the following terms:

Qu'on ne confonde point cette fête avec les imitations théâtrales qui dans les grandes villes nous laissent froids et indifférents; ici les acteurs sont les agriculteurs eux-mêmes; les actions de grâce qu'ils rendent aux Dieux des campagnes, leurs chants, leurs actes, les signes représentatifs de leurs travaux, de leurs jeux; les expressions naïves de leur félicité, rien n'est fardé, tout est réel, et le tableau de cette journée se compose de ceux de toute leur vie. (vol. 2, pp. 379–80)

The *sign* has been diverted from its proper task. The relation of immediacy between the external and the internal has been broken; the relation of transparency has been blurred. And it is precisely that transparency which represents the basic premiss of the sentimental text; sentimentalism is the celebration of that transparency, of the immanence of moral and emotional meaning in the everyday.

Le Voyageur sentimental en France sous Robespierre is a long, jumbled book, packed with episodic narratives displaying a series of fundamentally contradictory tendencies. In the face of historical confusion, one option which tempts Vernes is a retreat into nostalgia for the stability of a feudal society, the historical equivalent of the idealisation of the country over the city. But, on the other hand, the city also exercises its own particular fascination. It is as though the city is the force which pushes Vernes's writing from the sentimental mode into one much closer to melodrama and Gothic. The Paris of Balzac, but also of Hugo in *Notre Dame de Paris*, is already present in Vernes. That the boundaries between these modes should be so thin is one of the most interesting lessons of *Le Voyageur sentimental en France sous Robespierre* when compared to its rather juvenile predecessor. The city is more than a backdrop in the book; it fulfils an important function as the force drawing men and women to their downfall in several of the anecdotal narratives which fill the pages of the work: in this sense, it functions as a villain. But it also takes on what might be described as an explicative function in certain cases. In the previous work, the episode followed a basic structure whereby an initial meeting with a victim of misfortune was followed by a narrative phase in which the *devenir* behind the tableau was laid open to view. It was this, moreover, which constituted the victim as a deserving one: the story he or she told demonstrated that no fault lay with the victim, that it was a case, in other words, of *malheur*. Narrative here is performing a function of deculpabilisation, the origins of which in the eighteenth century can certainly be traced to Defoe (*Moll Flanders*) and to *Manon Lescaut*. This is still frequently the case in *Le Voyageur sentimental en France sous Robespierre*, but a number of episodes can be seen as exceptional: in them, it is as though the very fact of being the victim of misfortune in the city is a sufficient statement of merit. The physical complexity and extension of urban life somehow doubles for the narrative extension of the previous model.

Perhaps the most interesting feature of this text's response to the experience of Revolution, and the clearest indication of the author's desire to vindicate progressive political values, is the proliferation of imbricated narrative sequences which function as a repeated projection into various fictional and historical spaces of the problematic of a Revolution based on virtue and justice which somehow led to the Terror. The aim of this projection is somehow to neutralise the threat represented by the descent of the Revolution into Terror, and to reactivate a vision of history in which enlightened definitions of virtue still apply, the virtuous are rewarded, and transparency is finally restored.

The most striking common feature of these narratives when compared to the sentimentalism of Vernes's first work is their increased narrative complexity, achieved essentially by the introduction into the narrative of the appearance–reality dichotomy which has already been identified as crucial in the presentation of the city experience and in the analysis of the role of the Terror. In narrative terms, this of course implies a movement in the direction of melodrama. The process whereby the innocent are vindicated is interrupted and complicated by a whole series of *péripéties* in which things are not what they seem, in which appearances must be scanned before being accepted as realities: the saviour thrown up by the narrative may be a persecutor in disguise. It is, then, above all this obsessive working out of the fear of disguise which suggests that the narrative can be read as a commentary upon the political situation in France.

Some of the narratives in question specifically reflect Revolutionary events. Such is the case with the story of Montuson, with whom the narrator shares a cell in the Conciergerie. Montuson had been a monk in the latter years of the *Ancien Régime*; he had fallen in love with Almaïse, and the price he had to pay for obeying the voice of humanity was to be thrown into prison at the instigation of his order. Released in 1789 – the equivalent at the individual level of the storming of the Bastille – he is now once more imprisoned thanks to the injustice of his 'persécuteurs déguisés en révolutionnaires' (vol. 2, pp.

125–37). Equally explicit historically is the story of Lépervier, who is first introduced as one of the narrator's guards in the Conciergerie. His tobacco tin is a Chouan's skull, and his values are the ruthlessly pragmatic ones of an ignorant man who has made the Terror his own: he is profoundly unsentimental in that nothing can surprise him. Lépervier finally tells the story of his part in the Vendée wars, and his love for Orélina, the daughter of a royalist leader who is in fact first glimpsed in the midst of battle, cradling her dying father in her arms. The ruthless Lépervier is moved to pity by the sight of innocence persecuted. But the lessons which should be drawn from the story gradually shift; the Republicans become the victims of Vendean atrocities, and General Hoche himself appears as a figure of moderation and enlightenment. It is indeed he who marries Lépervier and Orélina; the civil ceremony has a place in the sentimental narrative. And if Orélina finally dies, morally exhausted by the ideological conflict taking place in her soul, the fault is placed firmly with her brother, who writes cruelly accusatory letters insisting on her betrayal of family and religion. The story of Lépervier and Orélina, then, projects a possible resolution of Revolutionary violence: between the extremes of Royalism and Terror there lies a middle way of moderate, enlightened Republicanism (vol. 2, pp. 49–75).

Some of the narratives which form part of the paradigm are unexplicit in their historical reference. Vernes even manages, for instance, to introduce the story of Héloïse and Abelard, where the conflict between natural love and denatured monastic institutions echoes the story of Montuson; but the point, again, is that even in a distant historical setting, rather than indulging in reactionary nostalgia, Vernes introduces *conflict* into his evocation of the past. Time and again – and it is the repetition which points to the underlying structure – the narrative attempts to enact scenarios of reconciliation. The irony, of course, is that the primary narrative line around which these secondary *récits* cluster is in total conflict with the message of reconciliation, in that they are all flights of fantasy or memory away from the grim reality of 1793–4. *Le Voyageur sentimental en*

France sous Robespierre is a crystalline example of the narrative imagination functioning as escape, compensation and alternative historical model.

Le Voyageur sentimental en France sous Robespierre represents the irruption of history into the sentimental text, in three important senses. Firstly, and most obviously, in that a commanding historical event, the Revolution, is the problem around which the book is organised. Secondly, because historical projection, the use of narrative to enact historical scenarios other than the real one, is an important function within the work. Thirdly, in the sense that some of these historical projections are actually set in a remote past. *Mathilde au Mont-Carmel* (1822)[43] raises the last two features to an organising principle, in that this is fundamentally a historical novel the sub-text of which is concerned with contemporary political issues. The work has its roots in controversy, and its meaning may therefore be said to be explicitly ideological: it is a continuation and rewriting of a novel published by Mme Cottin in 1805, entitled *Mathilde*, the philosophical and political implications of which Vernes deplores and seeks to correct. A further element in the circumstances of the book's composition is relevant, although less centrally: during the composition of *Mathilde*, Mme Cottin was in contact with Joseph-François Michaud (1766–1839), who was to become a leading Ultra intellectual during the Restoration, well-known as the author of the anti-Bonapartist *Histoire des quinze semaines* (1815) and as editor of the Royalist *La Quotidienne*. The correspondence clearly shows that Michaud encourages Mme Cottin in the writing of a novel set at the time of the Crusades:[44] indeed, a 'Tableau historique des Croisades' was published as the introduction to *Mathilde*, and this may well have been the starting-point of Michaud's own mammoth involvement with Crusade history, resulting in the publication, between 1811 and 1822, of his *Histoire des Croisades*, reprinted many times, not least in 1867 in abridged form, in the revealingly entitled 'Bibliothèque de la jeunesse chrétienne'.

Mme Cottin's *Mathilde* is a sentimental novel, in the sense that its primary object is the presentation of love.[45] In its dramatisation of conflict, it belongs to the literary movement of which its near contemporaries *Atala* and *René* are the most illustrious representatives. It is also, by its setting, an historical novel. The narrative takes place during the second Crusade, after the recapture of Jerusalem by Saladin in 1187. The heroine is the sister of Richard I (Coeur de Lion); destined for life in a convent, she leaves, at the beginning of the novel, for a pilgrimage to the Holy Land. The journey, of course, introduces unexpected reality and adventure into a life meant to be free of all wordly taint: her boat is captured by Saracens, at which point Saladin's brother Malek-Adhel enters the story. The young princess's terror at such ordeals gradually gives way to a realisation of the humanity of her captor, and the love which Malek feels for the defenceless Christian is soon requited.

The extended narrative proceeds from this point to tell of the tribulations of love in the face of a series of obstacles. Two principal oppositions can be identified. In the first instance, romantic love is set against reason of state: Mathilde refuses the hand of Guy de Lusignan, and in doing so she affirms the primacy of feeling over the demands of the social order. This represents a continuity with narrative themes of Enlightenment fiction, where the heart knows better than cruel parents seeking to impose a socially desirable choice on their innocent offspring. There is also an echo of eighteenth-century preoccupations, perhaps more specifically of the *conte philosophique*, in the fact that this love knows nothing of the boundaries between religions: Mathilde's love for Malek is the discovery of his essential humanity, which a philosophical author would have developed into a lesson in religious relativism and the primacy of a lay morality. The path followed by Mme Cottin is, however, different: if social demands on love are swept aside, it is to highlight the inevitability of the conflict between love and religion. Mathilde can only marry an infidel if she is prepared to renounce eternal happiness, and Malek feels no more inclination than she to renounce his religion. The latter solution is, however, imposed when the treacherous Lusignan murders Malek, who is converted to Christianity as he is dying. The obstacle of religion is only removed, then, to make way for a tragic form of love: Mathilde marries her loved one on the edge of the grave, and it seems that the love which provides the whole dynamic of the plot is only fulfilled to be dashed again. Death, it seems, is the only possible resolution of the conflict between love and religion. Saladin allows Mathilde to bury Malek at the convent of Mount Carmel. The Saracens who are present at the burial are converted to Christianity, and the last image of the novel is of Mathilde, about to enter a convent in a far-off land, watching the sails of the English ships disappear towards the horizon and home.

There can be little doubt that a reversal has taken place here with respect to the dynamics of much eighteenth-century fiction and to the ideology of happiness which underlies it. To proceed from that observation to a claim that *Mathilde* is an example of an anti-Enlightenment novel seems excessive: above all, such a reading begs the question of the admissibility of a straight political reading of the nascent Romantic aesthetic. Moreover, *Mathilde* is the expression of the impossibility of choice rather than of a definitive validation of the ideology of sacrifice. This is apparent particularly in the rhythm of the prose:

Jamais peut-être le devoir et la vertu ne remportèrent un plus beau triomphe; Mathilde, pieuse et soumise à la voix de l'Eternel, immole son bonheur et son amour; Malek-Adhel, généreux et magnanime, à la voix de celle qu'il aime, abandonne ses espérances et ses désirs: tous deux sont libres cependant; ils s'adorent, ils pourraient vivre toujours ensemble, et ils vont se séparer, se séparer peut-être pour jamais.[46]

The sublime lies in the tension between happiness and sacrifice, and this prose dramatises the circularity of the operation.

Michaud's *Histoire des Croisades* does not in itself provide any elucidation of Mme Cottin's text and its possible ideological significance: that a reinstatement of religion is part of the ideological programme of Ultra royalism no longer needs stating. Michaud's *Histoire* does however shed some light on the context in which Vernes's text was written, to the extent that it demonstrates how a concern with history becomes part of the reactionary creed. This is a complex issue; Norman King has shown, for instance, how the *groupe de Coppet* integrate an analysis of the Middle Ages into their historical quest for a liberal value-system, so that a rehabilitation of that period, or even of the Crusades, should not be seen as sufficient proof of Ultra leanings.[47] In Michaud's case, however, this does appear to be a legitimate conclusion. The desire to speak of and to contemplate the past is predicated upon a supposed hostility on the part of Enlightenment towards the past (and in the case of Voltaire's vision of the Crusades, one would not have to look very far to see Michaud's interpretation vindicated). Thus the Revolution is, for Michaud, 'une époque fatale, où la mémoire des ancêtres n'est plus révérée, où les peuples dédaignent les institutions religieuses':[48] the past and religion are indissoluble. In the *Histoire*, history itself is presented as fundamentally conservative in its effects:

C'est en vain qu'un esprit dédaigneux repousse les souvenirs des âges passés et que nous protestons en quelque sorte contre notre propre origine: nous y sommes sans cesse rappelés par nos goûts, par nos sentiments, et en quelque sorte par nos plaisirs. En effet, si, d'un côté, notre raison formée à l'école des idées nouvelles ne trouve rien que de révoltant dans le moyen âge, pourquoi, de l'autre, notre imagination émue par le spectacle des passions généreuses aime-t-elle à se représenter les vieux temps, et se plaît-elle avec les preux et les paladins? Tandis qu'une philosophie sévère blâme sans mesure les coutumes barbares de la féodalité et les moeurs gothiques de nos aïeux, pourquoi les souvenirs que ces coutumes et ces moeurs nous ont laissés inspirent-ils encore à nos poètes des tableaux qui nous paraissent pleins de charmes? Pourquoi ces souvenirs sont-ils reproduits tous les jours, avec le même succès, dans nos poèmes, dans nos romans et sur nos théâtres? Serait-il vrai de dire qu'il y a plus de patriotisme dans notre imagination que dans notre raison, puisque cette dernière voudrait nous faire oublier l'histoire de notre patrie, et que l'autre nous la rappelle sans cesse?[49]

This is a programme for a historiography based on spectacle and evocation rather than on any intellectual analysis of processes of causation, continuity and discontinuity.

The latter approach to the writing of history presupposes the acceptance of the temporal distance separating the historian from the object of study; it is diametrically opposed to the process of identification which Michaud appears to be advocating. Parts of his history, nonetheless, do adopt this more analytical approach; in that sense he can be seen as a contributor to the growth of nineteenth-century historiography in its main current, even if his analyses of the legacy of the Middle Ages tend to be conservative in their conclusions. The coexistence of these two approaches to the work of the historian does however lead to a certain tension. In the middle of an enthusiastic and spectacular description of the Council of Clermont, Michaud breaks off to make the following observation:

Au milieu de l'entraînement universel, aucun sage ne fit entendre la voix de la raison. Ces scènes si étranges, dans lesquelles tout le monde était acteur, ne devaient être un spectacle que pour la postérité. (Book I, chapter 1)

This tension between identification and the recognition of historical distance seems characteristic of the period; generalising outwards, one could observe that such contradictions between conscious ideological commitment and the intellectual tools forged by the Enlightenment are the mark of the impossible intellectual dilemma of reaction in this period.

The preface to *Mathilde au Mont-Carmel*, in which Vernes indicates his objections to Mme Cottin's novel, places religion firmly at the centre of discussion. He disapproves of the 'sacrifice' with which the novel culminates, but, more generally, the object of his criticism is 'la lutte des préjugés dont cette catastrophe avait été la conséquence'. He then proceeds to anticipate an objection which may be made to his argument, and provides a reply:

En vain me dira-t-on que Madame Cottin fait agir et parler ses personnages suivant l'esprit de leur siècle; comment me feront-ils espérer un résultat utile, si cet esprit est faux; s'ils parlent et agissent à rebours du sens commun, qui est tous les temps?[50]

He fears that this 'esprit du siècle' may become 'celui de ses lecteurs', and concludes by expressing his desire for 'l'abolition de ces tristes restes des siècles d'ignorance et de barbarie'.

This Preface is a systematic exercise in the language of the eighteenth century: the language used to evoke religion and the past (*préjugé, barbarie, ignorance*); the belief in the exemplary rather than the spectacular value of literature; and the insistence that truth is a universal category which does not change with the age. On this last point, it is clear that Vernes is in fundamental disagreement with Michaud: the truth of which he speaks is a modern one of which there may have been glimpses during the centuries (the *Discours préliminaire* to the *Encyclopédie* proposes the same analysis); for Michaud, and for the Ultras in general, truth is old. The disagreement, in other words, is over the ideology of progress.

What is the narrative consequence of this programme? The novel opens where *Mathilde* left off, at Mount Carmel. Malek is resurrected in the form of an identical brother, Selim, and Mathilde ('un jeune coeur avec ses dix-huit ans et toute la sensibilité de son âge'), of course falls in love with him. Like Mme Cottin's heroine, she realises that she must convert her lover if their love is to flourish, but it is here that Selim reacts in an unexpected manner: he refuses her premisses and argues for the indifference of institutional religions, the universal truths of reason and love, even the existence of the Supreme Being. Mathilde cannot resist such enlightened instruction delivered by so charming a teacher; their love triumphs over the obstacles raised in its path by a breathless narrative, and they marry, reigning together over a peaceful and tolerant Orient.

The vindication of love against Mme Cottin's vision is conducted in such a way that a whole series of eighteenth-century values are in fact restated at the same time: natural as against institutional religion, the primacy of the moral over the religious. The space which the novel defines is a *laïc* one: religion must not interfere with love, family life, happiness, all of which are conceived as the foundation of virtue. Vernes's prime target in this attack is the monastic institution, which is not only evil for all the philosophical reasons rehearsed above, but also, in Vernes's presentation, because it serves as the last resort of 'parents dénaturés' who wish to impose partners on their children, for reasons of religion or birth.

No less interesting are the echoes of the eighteenth century at a formal level. The *conte philosophique* is present in the form of the Arab who bears truth through a process of relativisation, dismantling the prejudices of the Westerner and building in their place a more tolerant and universal set of values. *Mathilde au Mont-Carmel* is, in some sense, a novel of education. Its form, and the values which it seeks to establish, are a curious foretaste of the ideological formations of Republicanism later in the nineteenth century.

One thing is lost in this reconstruction, however: the story is supposed to be taking place in the Middle East at the turn of the twelfth and thirteenth centuries, and in building this model of modernism Vernes has lost touch with that basic fact. Throughout the novel, in fact, there is a tension between the resolutely progressive vision of history which he is attempting to publicise, and a fascination, terribly reminiscent of Michaud, with the past as spectacle. Describing a massive assembly of Crusaders at St Mark's in Venice, Vernes is carried away by his subject: the Maréchal de Champagne makes a speech

dont les expressions, simples et naïves, peignent mieux que nous ne pourrions le faire l'esprit et les sentiments des temps héroïques de notre histoire. En lisant dans l'histoire des croisades de pareils discours, de pareils faits commandés au nom du ciel, qui ne se sent ému de l'enthousiasme religieux qui les inspirait, et disposé à croire que le ciel en effet les dictait lui-même?

This is the movement of identification mentioned earlier. It is succeeded by the opposite movement:

Néanmoins, à quoi tendaient-ils réellement? à la ruine, à la destruction des peuples paisibles de la Palestine, de l'Egypte, de la Syrie qui adoraient Dieu selon la loi de leurs pères. (vol.2, pp. 308–12)

The judgement of the man of 1822 must carry more weight than any identification with the spirit of the age. Voltaire takes the upper hand. Vernes is faced with a similar problem in his conclusion, but in reverse. Having constructed his happy ending, he must somehow extricate himself from the anachronistic contradiction which has Mathilde and Selim reigning happily over a peaceful kingdom. They die, he tells us, leaving a son who would have been, like them, 'le bienfaiteur des chrétiens', 'si le fanatisme qui renouvelle sans cesse le penchant de l'homme à croire ce qui l'étonne et flatte ses voeux, n'eût rallumé le feu des croisades, et entraîné l'Europe à de nouvelles guerres, de nouveaux malheurs' (vol. 2, p. 329). These are the last words of the *roman du bonheur* which Vernes was so patently seeking to write in answer to Mme Cottin. That quest must pass into the conditional tense and become a Utopia, while the true record, as in Voltaire, remains one of disaster.

La lutte grande et solennelle où la valeur heroïque et le patriotisme français viennent de décider le triomphe du droit des peuples sur un despotisme superstitieux.[51]

This is the phrase with which Vernes greets the events of 1830 in France; it comes from his *L'homme politique et social*, published in Paris the following year, and forming, together with *L'homme religieux et moral* of 1829, and *Seymour, ou quelques notes du bonheur* (1834), a triptych of moralising works. The sense of finality which this evocation of the July days conveys is an apt introduction to the last phase of his career. If *Le Voyageur sentimental en France sous Robespierre* and *Mathilde au Mont-Carmel* demonstrate the use of narrative as a projection of a historical problematic, then the work of Vernes's last years signifies a retreat – or a progression – into a non-narrative manner of imagining the relationship between the subject and history.

Vernes continues, in many ways, to imagine the historical process as an Enlightenment teleology, a struggle between antagonistic principles requiring constant vigilance if it is to beget progress.

Hélas, si nous ouvrons les annales de l'histoire, nous offriront-elles autre chose qu'une déviation constante de ces premiers principes? Ne nous y trompons pas, le fer sanglant de la Saint-Barthélémi n'est point brisé; une religion plus éclairée le repousse d'elle avec horreur; mais le fanatisme humilié pleure en secret sur la rouille qui le couvre.[52]

The Revolution of 1830 has restored mankind to the original integrity of the divine model; 'les peuples' are now 'rendus enfin à l'instinct trop-longtemps étouffé de la dignité de leur nature' and 'offrent le spectacle imposant et sublime de leur marche simultanée vers de plus hautes destinées et une plus noble civilisation'.[53]

But it is precisely this fundamental historical shift which makes it necessary now to call a halt to the march of history. The coming of liberty and Enlightenment is a finite process, and a moment must come when the process is deemed to be at an end, the aims achieved, the battle won. In the tradition of the Girondins and the *directoriaux*, Vernes speaks of 'une véritable aristocratie, celle des vertus et des talents'[54] which is the basis of differences in rank and fortune. Unsurprisingly, the language of sentimentalism proves easily adapted to this new function of immobilism:

Pareils à la lumière du jour, son [God's] amour, sa bonté, sa tolérance se répandent sur l'ensemble entier de ses enfants, sous le chaume comme dans le palais des grands: la larme du humble habitant des hameaux pèse autant aux balances de sa justice que celle des puissants de la terre: et si les uns paraissent avoir été plus favorisés que les autres, cette part inégale de bonheur n'a été que l'effet du cours naturel des lois d'une Providence dont nous ignorons les compensations, mais qui, malgré des inégalités de propriété et de destinée attachées nécessairement à l'état de société et à la différence des moyens individuels, n'en appelle pas moins tous les hommes à satisfaire tant qu'il est en eux, chez leurs semblables, la soif ardente du bonheur qu'elle a allumée au même degré chez tous.[55]

The language of sentimentalism is reunited in this vision with the problematic of the theodicy as it had been posed during the eighteenth century. Happiness and misfortune, virtue and persecuting vice, those fundamental categories around which the narrative dynamic of the sentimental text were organised, are now shifted into a very different set of relationships. Vernes asks the classic question

L'innocence persécutée et le vice triomphant, n'accusent-ils pas [les perfections divines] à nos yeux? O justice, ô sagesse, ô bonté que j'adorais, vous dont l'univers entier m'offre l'image, pourquoi perdons-nous tant de fois vos traces chez les êtres que vous deviez protéger? Le mal doit-il exister devant vous? Quand la vertu malheureuse va pleurer à vos autels, doit-elle trouver la divinité voilée?[56]

To which he proposes an equally classic answer, directly in line with the 'cosmic toryism' of the middle years of the eighteenth century:

Tout est aussi bien dans l'ordre physique que le permettait le principe dont s'est servi le Créateur pour réaliser le plan général de l'univers; et tout est aussi bien dans l'ordre moral que le permet l'usage que fait le genre humain du plus beau don que pouvait lui accorder son Dieu, celui de la liberté morale.[57]

There is not a whisper here of the sentimentalism which proclaimed, however mildly, the injustice of exclusion: it is an error and an act directed against Providence to suppose that some historical dynamic could continue beyond a given point – the point which has now been reached – the work of expunging injustice from the pages of history. Wisdom counsels acceptance. And with this theodicy, an ahistorical, immobile, metaphysical insistence upon the justification of injustice takes over. *Ahistorical*, which is also to say *non-narrative*: the theodicy denies the necessity of narrative; it is by its very nature an attempt to arrest development and questioning, and to reduce discourse to the perfect circularity of Pope's 'Whatever is, is right.' Curiously, these passages are able to coexist, in the same work, with continued evocations of the persecution of virtue by the forces of obscurantism through the ages. In a historical context, the whole narrative celebration of the struggle of virtue against the forces of oppression is still acceptable; but in contexts where the immediate application to contemporary social reality is concerned, narrative stops.

The emergence of the discourse of theodicy within the field of Vernes's sentimentalism is revealing: it is, as it were, the negative imprint which serves to highlight the dominant function of narrative in Vernes's earlier work. Story-telling, for Vernes, has above all to do with the working out over time of conflictual situations in which the misuse of power gives rise to injustice; in radical contrast with the theodicy, the task of narrative here is to operate a realignment of the forces present in such a way that injustice is not justified within the text, but is effaced from it. For Vernes, narrative reaches resolution only when that function has been performed, and transparency restored. In that sense, narrative performs a reforming rather than a conservative function: it is the bearer of denunciations of injustice and claims for reform on the part of individuals and classes.

Pictorial sentimentalism. Jean-Baptiste Greuze: *Le fils puni* (1777), Louvre, Paris. Photo Musées Nationaux. The importance of *tableau* in sentimental texts is discussed below, pp. 75–86.

CHAPTER 2

Towards a model of the sentimental text

In the preceding chapter I looked at some of the central preoccupations which emerge from the work of three minor sentimental authors. My purpose in the present chapter is to draw together these disparate strands, and to sketch out an interpretative model of sentimental narrative, a 'meta-structure' which exists nowhere in a textual form but which can be extrapolated from individual texts and can, on the model of the grammar, be understood as the set of rules which in turn makes possible the realisation of other texts. This attempt at synthesis will inevitably involve a consideration of some of the main aesthetic preoccupations of the period; here, I shall be drawing on much recent work on eighteenth-century aesthetics which, not surprisingly, takes as its focus the towering figure of Diderot.[1] But a second concern will be to examine the place of sentimentalism within the overall culture of the period: I will suggest ways in which the textual patterns of sentimentalism reproduce the patterns of other types of text, and can therefore be said to belong to an overall process of cultural patterning called Enlightenment.

The preceding case-studies make it abundantly clear that the most fundamental category operating in the sentimental text is that of misfortune, *malheur*. Constantly overcome but constantly renewed in a multiplicity of forms (themselves analysable into patterns, as my third chapter seeks to show), misfortune is the founding event of the sentimental narrative, conferring on the person whom it befalls the crucial status of victim. It is that status, closely associated with notions of powerlessness and innocence, which is the basis of the process of sentimentalisation. If sentimentalisation is dependent to a significant degree on procedures which arrest and suspend narrative, narrative nonetheless supplies the fundamental structure without which sentimentalisation could not be achieved. Misfortune must be understood in relation to its function within a narrative dynamic: it is that which disrupts a previous state of happiness, and which must then be overcome as a condition of the re-establishment of an ulterior happiness which will represent the closure of the text, the point where it passes beyond narrative into silence. There are echoes of comedy and of romance here, but the most pertinent analysis is Propp's *Morphology of the Folktale*. The relevance of Propp's analysis is primarily situated at a methodological level: his aim is to proceed inductively from a corpus of texts to the identification of the underlying structure which, beyond the individual variations of motivation and realisation, unites all the texts considered. But, however imprecise the concept, it seems to me that the *primitiveness* of both corpora is a further reason for the relevance of Propp's model to sentimental narrative.

Propp's starting point is the notion of function: 'an act of a character, defined from the point of view of its significance for the course of the action'.[2] Propp's claim is that all the tales of his corpus manifest a single fundamental structure, defined as a sequence of functions: after a preparatory phase, most of the details of which need not concern us, Propp identifies as crucial function 8, in which 'the villain causes harm or injury to a member of the family'. This function, which Propp himself refers to subsequently as 'misfortune', 'is exceptionally important, since by means of it the actual movement of the tale is created. [...] The complication is begun by an act of villainy' (p. 30). This misfortune, the result of the direct agency of a villain, may be replaced by what Propp refers to as 'a situation of insufficiency or lack': this may manifest itself, for instance, as the desire of a hero for love, and, in that it represents the starting point of the quest which is the structural dynamic of the tale, Propp considers that it may be considered as morphologically equivalent to the act of villainy. Only one feature of the preparatory phase leading up to the misfortune or act of villainy needs specific attention, and it is an element which is presented as a 'digression' from the main substance of function 2, 'An interdiction is addressed to the hero'. Propp has this to say:

Further on the tale presents the sudden arrival of calamity (but not without a certain type of preparation). In connection with this, the initial situation gives a description of a particular, sometimes emphasised, prosperity. A tsar has a wonderful garden with golden apples; the old folk fondly love Ivašečka, and so on. A particular form is agrarian prosperity [...] This prosperity naturally serves as a contrasting background for the misfortune to follow. The spectre of this misfortune already hovers invisibly above the happy family. From this situation stems the interdictions not to go out into the street, and others. (pp. 26–7)

It is as though misfortune were inscribed already within this initial state of happiness: happiness and misfortune are inseparable ingredients of the narrative, for the beauty of the tsar's apples and the virtue of Ivašečka require no recounting, and are only the stuff of narrative in as much as they are threatened by some outside force.

Happiness and misfortune remain the main structural features of the extended and complex phase which follows the intervention of misfortune: now, the 'liquidation' of misfortune and a return to the tranquillity of the opening phase are the driving force of the narrative, and the misfortune which was essential to the beginning of the story must be overcome if the story is to abolish itself in its own accomplishment. In respect of the hero whose adventures represent the stuff of this extended second phase of the tale, Propp distinguishes between two types of hero, the 'seeking' and the 'victimised'. Both types interest us for their relevance to the sentimental narrative. The 'seeker' is a hero who undertakes a quest on behalf of the victim of misfortune (or lack), while the 'victimised' hero is himself the subject of misfortune (or lack) and his adventures are on his own account (pp. 36–8). I have insisted on this element because it represents an adumbration of the distinction which is apparent in some sentimental texts between the victim – frequently, of course, a woman – and the agent of her salvation,

which may be another character or indeed the narrator ful-
filling a curious intermediary role between telling the story and
being an actor within it.

Propp also has an extremely interesting passage on
imbricated narratives. During the phase of quest and resolution which extends from the intervention of misfortune to the
end of the tale, further elements may be inserted at any
juncture, with the effect of delaying the final resolution and
extending the suspense.

Any tale element [. . .] can, as it were, accumulate action, can evolve
into a dependent story, or can cause one. But like any living thing,
the tale can generate only forms that resemble itself. If any cell of a
tale organism becomes a small tale within a larger one, it is built, as
we shall see later, according to the same rules as any fairy tale. (p. 78)

Sentimental texts have a constant habit of generating within
themselves further narratives which replicate the structures
and preoccupations of the main stem; in particular, as I shall
show in greater detail below, these imbricated narratives
provide for the repeated initiation of reaction on the part of
beholders.

Many of the functions which Propp identifies in the folktale
must be discarded for the purposes of an analysis of sentimentalism. Often, these are magical sequences, unexpected
transformations and fantastic occurrences characteristic of a
dream world; indeed, it is the marginality of such features to
the present object of study which marks the cultural distance
between the two phenomena, and provides useful qualification
to the remarks above concerning the primitiveness common to
both models of narrative. But Propp's central perception
remains extremely pertinent: on the structural relationship
between the initial state of happiness and the event which
comes to disrupt it are built the dynamic of the narrative, the
sense of meaningfulness and purposiveness which are the basis
of the listener's potential interest in and identification with the
tale.

I am maintaining, then, that sentimentalism has its roots in
narrative, and in a type of narrative which is at heart very
simple. But even a cursory reading of the previous chapter

shows that sentimental narratives are constantly punctuated by *tableaux* of various kinds, which appear to function precisely in a spatial rather than a temporal dimension, and to imply a mode of perception radically opposed to that of narrative. The relations between the two are complex, and much of what I shall have to say about *tableaux* will have to do with elucidating the nature of the relationship; but it might be useful at the outset to state that the fundamental relation is one of inter-dependence, and to offer as an illustration the case of the print as it operates within the narrative framework of a novel. The print cannot be conceived in isolation from narrative: its func-tion is to underscore the meaning of certain crucial scenes, to elaborate on and complement by non-narrative means – pic-torial and spatial – the significance which is latent in particular points in the narrative, but by virtue, precisely, of that narra-tive. In the non-sequential we can read relations which proceed from sequentiality: the *être* of the pictorial represen-tation would have no meaningful existence without the *devenir* of narrative. If the print, and the *tableau*, hold up for contem-plation an intensified and heightened vision, then it is a heightened vision *of* something, and the primary form of that something lies in the narrative mode. Every picture tells a story.[3] (See above, p. 70, Greuze's *Le fils puni*.)

The *tableaux* to which I am referring in the sentimental text are of course textual features, and the use of terms like 'pic-torial' or 'spatial' is a metaphorical one. But that metaphor was of course present in the aesthetic thought of the eighteenth century, and nowhere more so than in the thought of Diderot. The most famous formulation of the notion is in the *Entretiens sur le Fils naturel*, where Diderot proposes the replacement of the *coup de théâtre* by the *tableau*, an arrangement of the char-acters on stage which is conceived as having a particularly strong expressive force. Here, the reference to the world of painting is explicit: 'Je pense, pour moi, que si un ouvrage dramatique était bien fait et bien représenté, la scène offrirait au spectateur autant de tableaux réels qu'il y aurait dans l'action de moments favorables au peintre'.[4] In the textual context, the notion of *tableau* therefore implies the use of certain linguistic procedures the purpose of which is to immobilise the action and to highlight those features which imply a visual perception of the described reality: the relative positions of characters amongst themselves, gesture, facial expression, arrested movement, as well as situational features constituting background or setting. Here, the textual *tableau* may be said to operate in a manner comparable to that of the print: its function is to freeze narrative, to suspend temporal progression so that the set of forces which the narrative has brought together in a particular moment may be allowed to discharge their full affective power.

In some situations, however, the relation between narrative and *tableau* is reversed. The best illustration of this process is the beggar scene, perhaps the sentimental scene par excellence. In these scenes, the *tableau* is frequently the starting point rather than the culmination of a narrative sequence: described initially in an immobilising manner, the beggar represents a 'spectacle intéressant', and it is for that reason that the narrator is moved to enquire about the past of the unfortunate individual, which is recounted in the narrative which the latter provides as proof of his sentimental pedigree and moral worth. In this case, one of the principal textual constituents of the *tableau* becomes explicit and visible: the constitution of a particular description as a *tableau* is dependent upon an explicit or implied relation of looking, on the setting up of a distance between observer and observed. In the *Pensées détachées*, Diderot writes that 'toutes les scènes délicieuses d'amour, d'amitié, de bien-faisance, de générosité, d'effusion de coeur se passent au bout du monde'.[5] Quite apart from describing the distance which is logically implied by a separation between observer and observed, the phrase is suggestive of a remoteness which sometimes characterises the sentimental *tableau*, as of a scene glimpsed through glass (or, in the case of Vernes's narrator, perceived aurally through the physical separation of a wall) in which the participants are somehow suspended in an unreachable time and space. In the context of painting, this sense of remoteness is a close corollary of the absorption which Michael Fried has traced as a crucial theme in the expressive, anti-Rococo aesthetic of the second half of the eighteenth century. In other cases, however, this distance is associated with a process of reification, in the sense that the character is divested of all traces of will and agency: despite the vocation of the sentimental text as a privileged site for the working out of notions of humanity, benevolence, etc., the victim as presented in the *tableau* is characterised by her/his helplessness and vulnerability, as it were the moral attributes of immobility.

I wish to press the notion of *tableau* further. In as much as it is the central imaginative and affective core of a story, the *tableau* operates as a metaphor for the whole, a form of synecdoche. For that reason, it is an easily repeated, reproduced form of the entire narrative sequence, in the way that the print doubles the text. Frequently, in sentimental narratives, a previously narrated scene is quoted, as it were, in its *tableau* form: its function may be to reassert the voice of virtue, to serve as the basis for a moral or moralising reflection on the part of the narrator, or indeed, as in the case of Mme de Condorcet, to initiate an abstract sequence of thought on the subject of the origins of moral feeling.[6] Here, the visual metaphor is stretched to the limit; the repetition in question may indeed be a narrative repetition, in which a previously narrated story is retold to another listener, himself situated within the narrative. But *tableau*, memory and narrative repetition all function within a logic of *reception*. Hence the sustained importance in the sentimental text of phrases which serve to introduce the reaction of a subject to fictive reality. Subjects are constantly described as reacting (usually with tears) 'au récit de', 'au souvenir de' or 'au spectacle de' some moving act or segment of narration. This repetition, this process of internal quotation, has no sense outside the reception framework: it is the reaction of an observing subject which gives sense to the narrative. This activation of the narrative sequence may take various forms: if the most common form is the speechless homage of tears, the impact of narrative on the subject may also be to spur him to virtuous action, or indeed to produce another text, this time an abstract discourse on the theme of humanity, tolerance, benevolence, etc., which the subject (who is frequently also the narrator) is impelled to share with the reader as a result of the overwhelming sentimental and moral epiphany which the original narrative has provoked.

It is in this sense that Jay Caplan speaks of *framed narratives* in Diderot. The central notion of Caplan's very perceptive analysis is that the *tableau* is the basis of an 'aesthetic of sacrifice' in Diderot. The tableau dramatises an incomplete whole, typically a family unit in which a structural element is lacking, and which can only be made complete, resolved, by the sacrifice of the beholder. Narratives are *framed* in such a way that they solicit the beholder, who is called upon to give of himself, to commit a sacrifice which will be the founding act of the régime of virtue.[7] This structure of loss and completion appears to be the counterpart in a spatial, non-temporal dimension of Propp's misfortune or lack: the suspension of the narrative projects onto the plane of immediacy and simultaneity the force which provides the narrative dynamic in the temporal mode. Narrative is linear, stretched over time, *différé*, and therefore appears as resistant to possession; *tableau* holds up the possibility of arresting that constant process of shifting, of allowing the subject to claim a place in the represented world. Diderot formulates the problematic of linearity and simultaneity in a famous passage from the *Lettre sur les sourds et muets*:

Autre chose est l'état de notre âme; autre chose le compte que nous en rendons soit à nous-mêmes, soit aux autres: autre chose la sensation totale et instantanée de cet état; autre chose l'attention successive et détaillée que nous sommes forcés d'y donner pour l'analyser, la manifester et nous faire entendre. Notre âme est un tableau mouvant d'après lequel nous peignons sans cesse: nous employons bien du temps à le rendre avec fidélité; mais il existe en entier et tout à la fois: l'esprit ne va pas à pas comptés comme l'expression.[8]

Diderot is writing here within an expressive framework, but the same tension applies by extension to the problematic of reception and understanding. The tableau provides a model for understanding the way in which narratives are made usable in the sentimental aesthetic; it is when a subject responds to narrative, when the framing device of 'au récit/spectacle de' initiates the manifestation of affection on the part of the subject ('son visage s'inonda de larmes', etc.), that the sequential nature of narrative is resolved for a fleeting moment in the instantaneity of undeferred perception. The *tableau* epitomises the character of the sentimental text: its insistent and repetitive holding up of represented action for contemplation, its constant reaching for a more complete possession of the affective meaning of that action, even its inflationary tendency to inscribe in the tiniest detail the most overwhelming affective and moral significance. In all these respects, the sentimental text declares that its ambition is the affirmation and celebration of the possibility of a common, communicable human experience. The relation between *tableau* and the Enlightenment project of fraternity is a direct one.

Furthermore, the dialogic potential of the *tableau* is closely related to the democratisation of the subject-matter of literature which takes place in the eighteenth century, and which is partly theorised by Diderot (and by Lessing in Germany) in connection with the bourgeois drama. This genre differs from classical theatre in its vocation to represent the 'conditions' of modern life ('l'homme de lettres, le philosophe, le commerçant, le juge, l'avocat, le politique, le citoyen, le magistrat, le financier, le grand seigneur, l'intendant') as well as family relationships in ordinary families.[9] The peasant woman grieving for her dead husband will use the same language, and move us to the same degree, as a woman of superior rank whom the same has befallen.[10] In the *Eloge de Richardson*, it is precisely the democratic representation of the world which is praised, for it is the basis of the recognition which is the condition of sentimentalisation:

Le monde où nous vivons est le lieu de la scène; le fond de son drame est vrai; ses personnages ont toute la réalité possible; ses caractères sont pris dans le milieu de la société; ses incidents sont dans les moeurs de toutes les nations policées; les passions qu'il peint sont telles que je les éprouve en moi; ce sont les mêmes objets qui les émeuvent; [...] il me montre le cours général des choses qui m'environnent.[11]

This similarity is the basis of the illusion of reality which Diderot repeatedly praises in Richardson: as the reader is drawn into the illusion of the text, he (she) identifies with events which could be happening to himself (herself): illusion and identification are bound together. And they are together the condition for the communicative aesthetic which Diderot evokes in a famous passage:

Hommes, venez apprendre de lui à vous réconcilier avec les maux de la vie; venez, nous pleurerons ensemble sur les personnages malheureux de ses fictions, et nous dirons: 'Si le sort nous accable, du moins les honnêtes gens pleureront aussi sur nous'.[12]

If the formulation is not revolutionary in the social or political action which it implies, it clearly articulates the notion that the text, read and wept over, is to be the site of a community of like minds drawn together by their common reaction to a common scene. Lessing's formulation of the notion of the democratisation of subject-matter similarly links it to the possibility of identification. Pity and fear are not felt for the person to whom they occur; they arise from 'our similarity to the suffering person', and are 'for ourselves' (he has read his empiricist philosophy). It follows that 'the misfortune of those whose circumstances are closest to our own must naturally touch us more deeply. And when we have compassion for kings, we have it for them as men, and not as kings.'[13]

If analysis of *tableau* as a formal feature of the sentimental text is a key to understanding the structure and dynamics of enunciation, then the sentimental text's preoccupation with signs points the way for an examination of the processes of signification within the text. The sentimental aesthetic appears to function emblematically; it manifests a general tendency to hypostasise, to hold up for the privileged attention of the reader, features which are significant in themselves, outside the syntagmatic dimension of the narrative. *Tableau* as it has been defined above is part of this tendency, and it operates in the text as a sign: as well as providing the mode of enunciation most apt to establish a dialogic relationship between the different participants in the textual process, it signifies. But investigation of this point must be delayed until two other hypostatisations of the sign in the sentimental text have been analysed.

Three examples drawn from Vernes's *Voyageur sentimental* represent the first type of sign which I shall identify in the sentimental text. The woollen bonnet knitted for the virtuous beggar by Marianne has already been noted, as has the scene in which the narrator comes upon a group of children surrounding the death-bed of their mother, and trying to give the dead woman sweets. The third case, quite Gothic in tone, concerns the story of the lovers Louis and Nina; Louis is driven to madness by the tragic death of his loved one, and finally exhumes her coffin and stands it upright at the side of his bed with a clock on top, so that, every time the clock strikes, he, in his madness, believes that it is Nina speaking to him.[14] In all these cases, it seems that the sign stands for a loss: it stands in place of a loved one who is absent or dead. These passages are reminiscent of the *tableau* in the opening pages of Diderot's second *Entretien sur le Fils naturel* in which a woman is lamenting the death of her husband:

Le mort était étendu sur un lit. Ses jambes nues pendaient hors du lit. Sa femme échevelée était à terre. Elle tenait les pieds de son mari; et elle disait en fondant en larmes, et avec une action qui en arrachait à tout le monde: 'Hélas! quand je t'envoyai ici, je ne pensais pas que ces pieds te menaient à la mort.'[15]

Diderot in fact intends the scene as part of his (Dorval's) demonstration of the expression of heightened emotion through means which bear little resemblance to the traditionally accepted canons of discursive expression; but Caplan, who uses this particular *tableau* as his starting point, shows how the feet are operating as a sign for the absence of the husband.[16] All these examples share a common feature: the sign, often in itself a detail in a *tableau*, arrests the attention and takes on a particularly strong emotional charge as the principal expression both of the absence of the departed figure and of the reaction to that loss on the part of the character most directly involved. Like the overall *tableau*, the function of the sign is to articulate misfortune or loss and the sentimental reaction of a subject.

In some senses, the same is true of the second category of sign which I wish to distinguish. This corresponds more closely to the intended sense of Diderot's analysis in the passage just quoted. The sentimental text – and the melodramatic one, as Brooks shows[17] – constantly insist upon various features and notations which are to be read as signs of the inner life of characters, an inner life which cannot be adequately conveyed to another subject by conventional expressive means such as ordered, discursive speech. The role of the sign in the dialogic operation of the text is here logically prior to the category of sign identified above, in that its role here is simply to externalise inner states which otherwise would not be readable by the beholder. Often, the function of such signs is scarcely distinguishable from the former: the tears of the victim of misfortune, the 'voix entrecoupée', the cries of anguish quickly lead to a sentimental reaction, they are the 'signes du malheur' of which Vernes's narrator says that they attract him more than the signs of happiness. But their nature is less clearly metaphorical than in the previous type of sign; or rather, the metaphorical system to which they belong is one of expressivity, like the notion of the window onto the soul referred to somewhere by Locke in an attempt to evoke the ambition of the empirical philosopher to grasp the inner workings of the human psyche. The *Entretiens sur le Fils naturel*, as is well known, develop an expressive theory of acting in which the key term is *pantomime*, conceived, as in Court de Gébelin, as a kind of universal language of nature from which the conventional techniques of classical French acting represent a divergence. It is passion, the reaction of humans to extreme circumstances, which interests the dramatist (and the novelist), and passion externalises itself in cries, inarticulate sounds, gestures, looks:

à l'exception de quelques sentiments qu'il rend dans le premier accès et auxquels il revient sans cesse, le reste n'est qu'une suite de bruits faibles et confus, de sons expirants, d'accents étouffés que l'acteur connaît mieux que le poète.[18]

Similarly, the true accent of love lies not in the phrase 'Je vous aime', but in the trembling of the voice which says the words and the tears and looks which accompany them. Peter Szondi,

describing the opening scenes of Diderot's *Le Père de famille*, the
purpose of which is to display for the audience the inner state of
the father in the absence of his son, writes that the text
functions as a 'psychograph'.[19]

The problematic of the visibility of the internal movements
of the soul is bound up in sentimentalism with a distrust of
linguistic expression, and an apparent scepticism towards the
very possibility of communication. Sentimentalism is intimately persuaded of the ineffability of sentiment, of the
impossibility of exhausting through language the full depth of
emotion as it is felt experientially. Apart from seeking an outlet
in gesture and facial movement, internal states manifest themselves in interruptions in speech, elisions and, in the strongest
case, in silence. As Caplan points out, elision operates in the
sentimental text as a figure of some inaccessible reality; an
absence on the page or in the sequentiality of discourse, it
points to meanings which are absent at the immediate level of
communication but must, by implication, be present on
another, less directly available plane.[20] The same may be said
of gesture: rather than being a clear representation of an
internal state – for such clarity would ultimately imply the
possibility of translation into discursive language – it hints at
absent meanings, functioning as a pointer rather than a fully
elaborated signifier.[21] Such signs seem to declare the impenetrability of the Other, as in the mysterious encoding of gesture
or the wall of silence which Gorjy's characters manifest. There
is a strange paradox here: it is when characters are most
absorbed in their own emotions, when they appear locked into
their own interiority, that they hold maximum interest for the
sentimental gaze. And yet, explicitly, sentimentalism declares
its project to be the valorisation of feeling, and of the communicability of feeling, as the basis of a regeneration of human
society. The paradox is similar to the one investigated by
Michael Fried in relation to French painting of the middle
years of the century: on the one hand, the culture of paintings
declares that a primary criterion of the success of a painting is
its power to hold the attention of the beholder, to transfix the
attention; and, on the other hand, one of the fundamental

themes of that painting is the evocation of states of absorption in which the represented character is portrayed as indifferent to the beholder, locked in some inaccessible state of internal attention.[22]

The final appeal here is to the notion of imagination. Just as the significance of the *tableau* is that it figures the *prise de conscience* by an observing subject of a segment of the represented world, so gesture, facial expression, elision and silence call on the participation of the reader. The point at which communication through ordered discourse breaks down, threatening a descent into silence and impenetrability, is the point where the imagination of the reader, or of the represented observer, is called into the breach, as in Vernes's narrator who seizes the significance of the dumbshow of the *béquillard* and delivers the meaning to the reader. Imagination as an aesthetic faculty exists as a response to the existence of that internal world which language can only point to, just as it exists in theories of sympathy as the faculty which permits identification between human subjects.

The tension between linguistic and non-linguistic communication has further corollaries, more explicitly related to the role of sentimentalism in the constitution of a moral–philosophical vision. Firstly, the privileged objects of the sentimentalising vision – children, women, the lower classes, the old, those whose misfortune has brought them to the verge of madness – have one thing in common: in the eyes of the observing subject, who implicitly represents the yardstick by virtue of which the comparison is made, they are deficient in intellectual faculties, and, by the same token, moved to a greater extent (than males of the enlightened and cultivated classes) by sensibility. This of course is wholly true of animals: Vernes's cats (see above, pp. 47–8) may stand here as one example of what could be a field of investigation in its own right, the emergence of sensitivity to animal suffering in the eighteenth century. To be moved by one's sensibility is in some sense to operate as an automaton: the subject who is engrossed in an internal world has cut loose of intellection, and thus represents a quintessentially *human* condition. Once again, the paradox is an interesting one, and profoundly revealing of the age: at least in some respects, humanity is seized in its absolute nature when institutions, the historical product of humans living in society, are peeled away to lay bare an underlying stratum of animality.

The second corollary of the preoccupation with the limits of language is an extension of the first. For the eighteenth century, investigation of the workings of human understanding is characteristically an historical or quasi-historical operation: Rousseau's hypothesised state of nature does not claim to be a real historical event, but rather a fiction allowing the philosopher to peel away the layers of the onion. In such investigations, the genealogy of language and the genealogy of sociability finally merge into a single quest. Condillac's *Essai sur l'origine des connaissances humaines* (1746) distinguishes three types of sign, 'naturel', 'accidentel' and 'd'institution', the first of which is the starting point in the creation of human language. He imagines two children 'égarés dans des déserts, avant qu'ils ne connussent l'usage d'aucun signe': in this situation (a familiar one in eighteenth-century anthropology), communication will be the effect first of natural cries and, subsequently, of 'le langage d'action':

Par exemple, celui qui souffrait, parce qu'il était privé d'un objet que ses besoins lui rendaient nécessaire, ne s'en tenait pas à pousser des cris: il faisait des efforts pour l'obtenir, il agitait sa tête, ses bras, et toutes les parties de son corps. L'autre, ému à ce spectacle, fixait les yeux sur le même objet; et sentant passer dans son âme des sentiments dont il n'était pas encore capable de se rendre raison, il souffrait de voir souffrir ce misérable. Dès ce moment il se sent intéressé à le soulager, et il obéit à cette impression, autant qu'il est en son pouvoir.[23]

The origins of language lie in natural cries and gestures, not forming part of any structure of intention but, on the contrary, involuntary: it is the observer who, almost without knowing it, attaches a meaning to these mysterious signs emanating from the other, and who thus participates in the construction of a code. Condillac presents the birth of communication and that of sympathy as consubstantial: the act of imagination which attributes meaning also reacts sympathetically, indeed the sympathetic reaction is prior to any formulation of sense, and both processes take as their starting point pre-linguistic communication. This reproduces exactly the configuration of the sentimental text: an aesthetic feature (the foregrounding of non-linguistic forms of communication) parallels and supports the moralising philosophical project of establishing and celebrating sentiment as the basis of social solidarity.

We can now return to the *tableau*, considered as an ensemble having a signifying function – the *tableau* as the third and most far-reaching case of the sign in the sentimental aesthetic. The signified, here, can only be formulated in terms of discursive abstractions. The *tableau* signifies the encounter of innocence with misfortune; but that signified then enters into another process of signification in which the recognition by the reading subject of an experience which could be his/her own transforms the perception into an affirmation of common humanity, of the wisdom of Nature (or God, or the Supreme Being) in so organising the human being that this sympathetic relation between individuals is spontaneously produced. The tears of the man of feeling, the individual act of charity of the narrator (or indeed of a character represented within the *récit*), refer to a general order of phenomena; they represent a manifestation of abstract and eternal values, and their repetition represents a guarantee that the language of humanity and virtue is a meaningful one. The emotion of the 'homme sensible' provides a coda for understanding the moral universe, or, more accurately, for gaining access to the moral universe from a position within the material world of events, narrative, history.

Peter Brooks has written very convincingly of melodrama as an aesthetic whose central function is to dramatise and make visible the 'moral occult'. Brooks is fundamentally interested in the nineteenth-century novel. For him, melodrama is the 'semantic field of force' which lies at the heart of the universe of Balzac and Henry James. It is an aesthetic which plays upon the tension and the parallelism between the outward world as it is represented in the realist tradition – the social world of human interaction, money, ambition, power – and an overarching system of abstract meanings which structure and give sense to that world. The referentiality of the represented world accounts for the fundamental Manicheism of the genre, its insistence that the struggles taking place in the represented world are in fact between Good and Evil, Virtue and Villainy, Light and Darkness. Now, Brooks's term 'moral occult' suggests forcibly that the relation between the signifier, which manifests itself in material reality, and the moral signified, to which it points, is a problematic one: moral reference in a post-sacred universe has been obscured, occulted, veiled, and the melodramatic is the insistent language in which the link is reasserted, in response to a sense of loss and a rediscovered need for a sacred, transcendent dimension.[24]

The sentimental aesthetic which I am describing is a close relative, an antecedent of melodrama. The melodramatic and the Gothic are certainly inscribed as latent possibilities in sentimentalism: in contradistinction to sentimentalism they require, perhaps, an insistence on the threat posed to virtue by a strongly personified villain, or principle of villainy, and a heightening of the obfuscation of virtue by various narrative devices, notably peripety and deceit.[25] But sentimentalism belongs firmly on the optimistic and triumphant slope of the Enlightenment project; it most certainly operates within the problematic of a desacralised universe, but as a bearer of the message of secularisation rather than an expression of fears concerning the unidimensionality of such a world. The only trace of apprehension might be read in the constant repetition with which the sentimental faith in the coherence of sign and signified is affirmed, but I would be tempted to see this as celebratory rather than reassuring in function. The metaphorical relationship between the visible world and the abstract value systems which are inscribed behind it functions as a substitute transcendence. Morality exists, virtue is not an empty notion, but these categories do not need the guarantee of a traditionally conceived principle of transcendence: they exist as immanent forces in human society, and the only transcendence required is the shift from the individual to the general, from the singularity and experiential authority of

lived experience to a set of abstract categories which demonstrate the universal applicability of the sentimental epiphany.
The processes of signification at work within the sentimental
text operate that shift, celebrate it, refract it outwards through
the multiple prism of the reaction of sentimental subjects.
Rather than reflecting a desacralised universe, the sentimental
text in many respects functions, paradoxically, as the site of a
process of sacralisation: it re-enacts the illuminated communication of the collective religious experience, but this time in a
private, individualised sphere, where the reader experiences
brotherhood through the text, as it multiplies and repeats the
founding act, the primal scene of recognition.

To maintain an 'optimistic' reading of sentimentalism in the
face of Brooks's interpretation, in which melodrama's constant
reassertion of the identity of virtue is seen as a response to the
threat to moral value systems in a world where transcendent
and sacred guarantees have been abandoned, is not to suggest
that the status of moral categories is unproblematic in the
sentimental text. It might well be said of sentimentalism, as it
could be of attempts in the sensationalist tradition to formulate
a 'scientific' theory of sympathy and moral feeling, that such
insistence on the way in which human nature makes possible
such virtuous action is only necessary as a result of profound
changes in the value systems by which society regulates itself:
as self-interest comes to occupy a more central and accepted
place in the representation of human motivation, as the basis of
free competition between economic and social agents defined
in atomistic terms, then it is increasingly important to compen-
sate for this process by an explicit demonstration of the place
which virtue 'naturally' occupies within the new world-view.
In this sense, sentimentalism's affirmation of the immanence of
virtue *is* akin to melodrama's anguished attempts to reassert
the reality of values being occulted by liberalism and capitalism; the difference is that sentimentalism represents the façade
presented by the new values, the claim of the bourgeoisie to
possess the 'feminine' virtues of sympathy as well as the 'masculine' ones of technical prowess and economic vigour. In this
view, sentiment finally becomes the icing on the materialist

cake of capitalism, the aestheticising veil destined to obscure the cracking edifice of an individualist society.[26]

The place of altruism, self-sacrifice, sensitivity to the ills of others in the emerging theory of individualist liberalism is a question which I pursue, from different angles, in chapters 3 and 4. My point here is that, in terms of a process of signification, the individual (person, act, feeling) operates in the sentimental text as a sign, a cypher of abstract, universal categories, and that this is a feature which sentimentalism shares with the philosophy of Enlightenment to which it is intimately related. In the sentimental text, this weeping mother, this unfortunate child, this dying father all refer beyond themselves to the whole of humanity, and the endless repetition of comparable scenarios only serves to heighten the impression that the individual exists in the text as a pointer to the level of abstract discourse which provides statements about Humanity, Generosity, Virtue, etc. This is not to impugn the experiential veracity of the feelings of solidarity which the text simultaneously portrays and seeks to elicit: the important point is the structure. For the same fundamental pattern can be recognised in the concept of universal human nature which triumphs in the Declaration of Human Rights of 1789: the determining relation lies not within and between categories emanating from the social order (the orders, precisely, of the *Ancien Régime*), but between each individual and a universal, natural principle which ignores (theoretically) distinctions of class, power and influence, proclaiming the equal right of each individual to selfhood. The relation of reciprocal dependency between individual and universal constitutes an immanent, secular version of a transcendent morality.[27]

The sentimental text's attempts to inscribe the ideal within the experiential are to be read within the secularising project of Enlightenment. Moreover, in reaching out to pre- and non-linguistic experience, and to those who are the bearers of that experience, and seeking to establish the place of that experience within the ideal world of knowledge, sentimentalism declares and prefigures the pedagogical ambition of

Enlightenment to be a universally recognised explanatory system, a totalising ideology.[28] Vernes's *Mathilde au Mont-Carmel* shows clearly how sentimentalism contains the seeds of this pedagogical project, as he demonstrates to the social subject that his/her experience is to be understood through the categories of Enlightenment abstraction. The Revolution, of course, raises the political and social profile of pedagogy, both through its plans for the creation of an educational system and in the institution of the *fête*. *Le Tour de la France par deux enfants*, that pedagogical classic of the Third Republic, represents a later approach to the same problem: it attempts a secularised moral education of the social subject, based on a linkage between individual experience (narrative) and universal explanatory moral categories.[29]

This chapter began by envisaging sentimentalism as narrative. A long excursion taking in various forms of immobilisation of narrative progression, notably *tableau* and signs raised to the status of emblems, allowed me to analyse in some detail the system of enunciation of the sentimental text and the processes of signification at work within it. I propose to conclude this chapter by returning briefly to narrative, in order to suggest certain illuminating parallels between sentimental and historiographical narrative in the eighteenth century. The fundamental structural similarity which I want to show is, in a sense, simply stated. 'Philosophical' history is the constitution in a sequential, narrative form of the opposition between the forces of obscurantism, associated with the past, and reason, associated with the present; the sentimental text, as we have defined it, organises sequentially an opposition between virtue and villainy, innocence and persecution. The dynamic towards the institution of transparency and 'bonheur' has its equivalent in the historical text's vocation to show how the past brings forth modernity. The processes of identification which, in the case of sentimental narrative, seem clear, have their counterpart in the historical text too: to speak of the production of the present as 'progress' is to identify with that process of change, and indeed the notion of progress may be defined as the constitution of a teleology the culmination of which is the value-system of the historian. In both cases, the dynamic driving the narrative forward is inseparable from the value judgements upon which identification is based: the notion of a 'happy ending' subsumes both these elements.

The philosophical spirit which circulates amidst the darkness of the barbarian past is akin to the sensibility which circulates through the sentimental narrative: each conveys upon the phenomena with which it enters into contact a positive charge, a link between an alien reality and the subject. To take the analysis further, we may say that it is precisely the radical discontinuity between the two terms of the opposition which is the most striking analogy between the two forms of narrative. In *The Open Boundary of History and Fiction*, Suzanne Gearhart analyses the indeterminacy of the two genres in the French Enlightenment. Her analysis of Voltaire's *Essai sur les moeurs* and *Siècle de Louis XIV* shows that enlightenment is always presented as the product of Louis's personal agency, and that this is in contradiction with Voltaire's claim that the progress of humanity, rather than the actions of kings and the outcome of battles, should be the object of history:[30] and yet this radical break between the enlightened figure from the past and the dominant values of his age is necessary for the constitution of reason as reason and unreason as unreason. A process of communication between the two would lessen the definition of each. And the final consequence of such a concession would be that history and reason as Voltaire seeks to constitute them would begin to disappear:

Reason *is* and *is not* present in all of the specific ages which make up history, for if it were simply present in any of them, then each age would be the beginning and the end of history – that is, there would be no history, but only an undifferentiated present.[31]

The sentimental narrative would, similarly, be deprived of its principal motor were the virtue which it so unstintingly celebrates to triumph and vice to be abolished for ever. This is true, of course, in the sense that misfortune and incident are the stuff of narrative, and that utopias and theodicies are in an important way non-narrative, spatialising genres. But it is also true of sentimentalism in the sense that the sentimental text relies on the contiguity, the counterposition of the twin polarities of the narrative for the maximisation of its effect. A passage from Lessing's *Hamburgische Dramaturgie* is a good 'theoretical' statement of this tendency. He is discussing the three degrees of pity or compassion, *Ruhrung* (emotion), *weinende Mitleid* (tears), and *Beklemmung* (anguish) and, in order to compare them, analyses the ways in which a beggar should behave in order to move his audience to tears. 'He draws *tears* from me only when he makes me better acquainted with his good qualities as well as with his misfortunes, and, in fact, with both simultaneously.' Once the primal scene has interested the observer sufficiently for him to invite the beggar's narrative, the linear exposition of misfortune followed by virtue, or of virtue followed by misfortune, will fail to move the observer sufficiently: what the subject must do is

join the two parts of his story; he must say: I was dismissed from office because I was too honest, and thereby turned the minister against me; I go hungry, and with me a sick, lovely wife; and with us our children, who otherwise are full of promise but are languishing in poverty; and will certainly go hungry for a long time to come. Yet I would rather go hungry than be base; my wife and children, too, would rather take their bread directly from God, that is, from the hand of the charitable man, than to know that their father and husband was corrupt, and so on ... For such a story I am always ready to shed a tear. Misfortune and merit are here in equilibrium.[32]

'Joining the two parts of the story' seems to mean uniting the twin poles of merit and misfortune in a single narrative, in which each defines the other; Lessing's example reproduces a familiar sentimental figure in which the text spirals through the polarities, as though it were seeking, as in the *tableau*, to unite them in a single image situated outside time, but were frustrated in this ambition by the ineluctably linear, narrative nature of language.

Three writers whose historical narratives rely at least partially on this principle of structural opposition and contiguity are d'Alembert, Turgot and Condorcet. It is probably more accurate to describe the works in question as *histories of Enlightenment* or texts on the notion of progress than as historical works in which research and factual scholarship are the dominant preoccupations. A passage from d'Alembert's *Discours préliminaire* to the *Encyclopédie* traces the origins of Enlightenment in the Renaissance:

Pendant que des adversaires peu instruits ou mal-intentionnés faisaient ouvertement la guerre à la philosophie, elle se réfugiait, pour ainsi dire, dans les ouvrages de quelques grands hommes, qui sans avoir l'ambition dangereuse d'arracher le bandeau des yeux de leurs contemporains, préparaient de loin dans l'ombre et le silence la lumière dont le monde devait être éclairé peu-à-peu et par degrés insensibles.[33]

The history of Enlightenment is a Manichean combat between opposing forces, with the heroine constituted as the helpless victim.

Two speeches by Turgot, dating from 1750, offer another example of texts in which the organising principle is the struggle for recognition of Enlightenment in the face of the dark, repressive forces of ignorance: *Discours sur les avantages que l'établissement du Christianisme a procurés au Genre humain*, and *Discours sur les progrès successifs de l'Esprit humain*.[34] However, I shall quote from Condorcet's *Esquisse des progrès de l'esprit humain*. This is the opening passage of Condorcet's 'Neuvième époque' ('Depuis Descartes jusqu'à la formation de la République française'):

Nous avons vu la raison humaine se former lentement par les progrès naturels de la civilisation; la superstition s'emparer d'elle pour la corrompre, et le despotisme dégrader et engourdir les esprits sous le poids de la crainte et du malheur.

Un seul peuple échappe à cette double influence. De cette terre heureuse où la liberté vient d'allumer le flambeau du génie, l'esprit humain, affranchi des liens de son enfance, s'avance vers la vérité d'un pas ferme. Mais la conquête ramène bientôt avec elle la tyrannie, que suit la superstition, sa compagne fidèle, et l'humanité toute entière est replongée dans des ténèbres qui semblent devoir être éternelles. Cependant, le jour renaît peu à peu; les yeux, longtemps condamnés à l'obscurité, l'entrevoient, se referment, s'y accoutument lentement, fixent enfin la lumière, et le génie ose se remontrer sur ce globe, d'où le fanatisme et la barbarie l'avaient exilé.[35]

The melodramatic tendencies of this extract are striking. Not only is Enlightenment defined by radical contrast with its opposite, the strength and sharpness of definition being determined by the depth of the discontinuity between reason and unreason: Condorcet seems to attribute intentionality to the forces of darkness, and the virtue of the heroine Enlightenment is made to shine forth more strongly by the process of textual spiralling through a series of epiphanies and obfuscations.

It is in the light of this analysis that the processes of interchange between fictional narrative and historical discourse which have been observed in the work of François Vernes, take on their fullest significance. Not only are there echoes between the two genres, there appears to be a process whereby writing one in some sense constitutes an intervention in the other. This is the theme of Baczko's fascinating book *Lumières de l'Utopie*,[36] which charts some of the interpenetrations between what the French can, conveniently, call *Histoire* and *histoire*. The Revolutionary period seems to mark a high point in this process. If, as I am suggesting, the emergence of 'philosophical' historiography and of sentimental narrative within the same space is to be understood as the expression of a class becoming conscious of its own development, its own past and future, its own role in history, then the particular clarity which the Revolution confers on the phenomenon is scarcely surprising, given that the Revolution is among other things a discursive event. The Revolution perceives itself as the happy ending which crowns the historical narrative, the ultimate establishment of that transparency which we have seen as the ideal informing the dynamics of the sentimental text: in its representations of itself it harnesses all the themes which had informed historical consciousness during the eighteenth century: it is the triumph of enlightenment over the forces of darkness, the vindication of the claims of the virtuous oppressed over the forces of persecution and ignorance.

CHAPTER 3

Love and money: social hierarchy in the sentimental text

In the previous chapter, I was principally concerned with the formal properties of the sentimental text: I outlined a general model of the ways in which it goes about the task of signifying. But if the emphasis of the chapter was in that sense on the aesthetic aspects of the text, the intention was not to suggest that these aspects can be separated from the overall social and historical insertion of the sentimental phenomenon. On the contrary, formal analysis led me to two conclusions directly relevant to the social and historical role of sentimentalism: firstly, that an explicitly imagined readership is crucially important in the hermeneutic of the sentimental text; and, secondly, that the underlying dynamic of the sentimental narrative – its drive to establish happiness through the conquest and elimination of adversity – finds an important parallel in the historical utopianism of Enlightenment.

In the present chapter, I propose to focus more exclusively on the treatment of social questions by the sentimental text – *what* the text signifies in social terms rather than *how* it goes about that process of signifying. Such an analysis should start from notions of social hierarchy, power and domination. We have already seen that the privileged focus of the process of sentimentalisation is the figure of the victim: misfortune and suffering are the primary conditions of sentimentalisation. If one tries to understand this basic prerequisite of the sentimental text in terms of social order, the following hypothesis emerges: the process of sentimentalisation is fundamentally to do with the promotion to centre stage of social categories previously excluded from representation or, more accurately, previously denied a voice of their own within the representational field of literature. Sentimental literature represents the discovery, and above all the popularisation and repeated celebration of the humanity of the excluded, and as such is part of the global project of Enlightenment humanism. What the sentimental text enacts is the recognition of the universal category of humanity in each individual case of suffering encountered: *this* child, *this* mother, *this* destitute old man are exponents of a universal value system, applying equally to all, irrespective of position in the social hierarchy. In this sense, the French Revolution, with its mythic projection of its own function as the final inclusion and recognition of the hitherto excluded, is the ultimate sentimental event, the programme for which is laid down in Sieyès's famous formula:

Qu'est-ce que le Tiers Etat? – TOUT.
Qu'a-t-il été jusqu'à présent dans l'ordre politique? – RIEN.
Que demande-t-il? – A ETRE QUELQUE CHOSE.[1]

Not only that: it appears that one of the structural requirements of the process of sentimentalisation is a more or less explicit denial of the importance of social hierarchy. It is when social barriers are transgressed, when some kind of *déclassement* occurs, when a shift down the social ladder takes place, that true sentimental epiphany is provoked: it is as though the fullest statement of sentimental value – the absolute and unconditional humanity of every individual – were dependent upon a discursive denial of the validity of social hierarchy. Tears flow when social difference is highlighted, and François Vernes speaks for an entire tradition when he says:

J'ai toujours aimé de préférence les Paysans et, en général, ceux que la Nature a bien faits nos égaux, mais que le hazard a mis en sous-ordre; ils sont plus *hommes*; ils m'offrent une nature moins défigurée.[2]

The aim of the present chapter is to look in some detail at the sentimental denial of social hierarchy. How should it be read? To what extent should it be interpreted as a genuine challenge to established order, and, conversely, how much is it to be understood in some kind of figurative sense? Finally – the question is a logical extension of the previous ones, and it brings us back to the dialogical situation of the sentimental text analysed in the previous chapter – who is speaking in the sentimental text, and on behalf of whom?

The chapter is divided into two distinct parts. The first part applies the notion of the transgression of hierarchical structures to the constitution of romantic love in the sentimental text. The second part goes on to look in more detail at the sentimental treatment of poverty and charity, and is thus an extension and generalisation of the questions raised in the treatment of Baculard d'Arnaud in chapter 1.

LOVE

Sentimental or *romantic* love – the etymology is useful in pinpointing the literary roots of the phenomenon[3] – as it is presented, endlessly and repetitively, in sentimental fiction of the eighteenth century, is systematically defined in opposition to social convention; in order to be interesting as narrative, love must be pitted against social barriers, and the most frequent form which such obstacles take is the opposition of parents, frequently qualified by the epithet 'dénaturés', whose preoccupation is with marriage of convention within the correct social group. The economy of these texts, then, is such that experiential authenticity is defined by opposition to external social requirement: the space which we call the heart is created through conflict with a hostile externality, and it is the heart which is seen to transcend class barriers. Sentimental love appears as a figure of democracy: it has only to do with that which the individual feels; the criteria of judgement and choice which it applies are entirely individualised and internalised. The lovers whose love breaks the code of aristocratic society might then be seen as giving voice, precisely, to a message of bourgeois protest at the aristocratic domination of society: the love story is to be read as a figure of ideological values and struggles, and sentiment – the political symbolism is explicit in the case of Vernes's *Mathilde au Mont-Carmel* – is fundamentally democratic.[4] Furthermore, if sentimentalism is envisaged less as a symbolic representation of emerging social forces and aspirations, and more in a *reception* framework which insists on the role of fiction as a form of self-projection and 'self-exploration'[5] on the part of the reader, the fictional treatment of an individualistically defined affection – love – can be seen to be the site of an emerging conceptual and emotional frame: the shift away from extended definitions of the family (particularly in urban centres), the invention of the individual as a unit of affection, decision and social relation, and the concomitant emergence of a domestic space and of the practice of private reading.

If Baculard's *Epoux malheureux* is one of the most reprinted eighteenth-century fictional texts treating the theme of love transcending social barriers, then the most celebrated is *La Nouvelle Héloïse*. There would be no great originality in demonstrating that Rousseau's novel is constructed around a tension between the validation of passion and an imperative of renunciation: 'un rêve de volupté redressé en leçon de morale', to use Lanson's famous phrase.[6] What is interesting is to show how, predominantly but by no means exclusively in its opening phase, Rousseau's novel faithfully reproduces the narrative and linguistic patterns of the standard sentimental discourse, in which romantic love emerges as the experiential truth which is blocked and frustrated by the oppressive forces of a conformist society. An understanding of how Rousseau's starting point in *La Nouvelle Héloïse* is so firmly rooted in the *imaginaire* of his century, allows us to situate more clearly what is at stake in the second phase of the novel, where an attempt is made to defuse the movement of contestation of the first phase, through the internalisation of social demands and conventions which at the beginning of the novel were perceived as external constraints.

The love which unites Saint-Preux, an undistinguished bourgeois, and Julie, daughter of the baron d'Etange, is marked from the outset by its social unacceptability. This sentimental cliché is the fundamental given from which the novel develops and, characteristically, it provides a double logic: on the one hand, the love is defined and rendered more sublime by its extra-social nature; and yet, implicitly, the narrative is articulated around a desire for this deviant love to be recognised by the surrounding society, since such recognition would be the condition of its permanence.

In letter 1,26, in which Saint-Preux announces to Julie that he has taken up refuge at the Meillerie after their enforced separation, the hero laments the injustice of fortune and the curse of possessing a sensitive heart.

Que c'est un fatal présent du ciel qu'une âme sensible! Celui qui l'a reçu doit s'attendre à n'avoir que peine et douleur sur la terre [...] Victime des préjugés, il trouvera dans d'absurdes maximes un obstacle invincible aux justes voeux de son coeur. Les hommes le puniront d'avoir des sentiments droits sur chaque chose, et d'en juger par ce qui est véritable plutôt que par ce qui est de convention.[7]

The revelation of the tragic social contradiction at the heart of their love is somehow simultaneous with the revelation to himself of Saint-Preux's essential humanity:

Sans toi, Beauté fatale, je n'aurais jamais senti ce contraste insupportable de grandeur au fond de mon âme et de bassesse dans ma fortune: j'aurais vécu tranquille et serais mort content, sans daigner remarquer quel rang j'avais occupé sur la terre. (*O.C.*, 2, p. 89)

The social gap, or more precisely the failed attempt to bridge it, operates as the *catastrophe* of which Derrida speaks;[8] it brings to the level of consciousness that which would otherwise have remained obscure. And the imagined solution in this particular letter completes the sentimental structure, in that the future is projected as a sentimentalised rural idyll of love and poverty:

Soyons heureux et pauvres, ah quel trésor nous aurons acquis! Mais ne faisons point cet affront à l'humanité, de croire qu'il ne restera pas sur la terre un asile à deux Amants infortunés. J'ai des bras, je suis robuste; le pain gagné par mon travail te paraîtra plus délicieux que les mets des festins. (*O.C.*, 2, p. 93)

If society's response to their passion is to reject and outlaw it, then they will live out that logic, raising to a moral virtue the opposition between love and social integration which society imposes on them. Poverty, the rejection of the value systems of a hierarchical society, are made to equate with happiness, and the use of 'trésor', operating a shift from the material to the affective–moral plane, is situated firmly in a metaphorical tradition particularly dear to sentimental writers of the period.

Milord Edouard is of course the most explicit exponent of the argument in favour of the free choice of the heart, making two proposals to Julie's father – at the end of the first part, and in letter 2,2, the letter to which Rousseau appended the note on the La Bédoyère case – to establish Saint-Preux in such a way that the difference in social station would cease to exist. The language which he uses in 2,2 is, once again, characteristic: on the one hand *préjugé, tyran, injustice*; on the other *nature, coeurs tendres et bienfaisants, larmes*. Right is unequivocally seen to be on the side of the lovers, and a vision of social order is propounded which can justifiably be compared with the meritocratic discourse of the French Revolution:

Que le rang se règle par le mérite, et l'union des coeurs par leur choix, voilà le véritable ordre social; ceux qui le règlent par la naissance ou par les richesses sont les vrais perturbateurs de cet ordre; ce sont ceux-là qu'il faut décrier ou punir. (*O.C.*, 2, p. 194)

Edouard, too, uses the characteristic metaphorical procedure by which a term denoting an external, social attribute is used to refer to qualities of the soul: speaking to Julie's father in favour of Saint-Preux, he says that the young man possesses nobility, 'non point écrite d'encre en de vieux parchemins, mais gravée au fond du coeur en caractères ineffaçables' (*O.C.*, 2, pp. 168–9).

Nor is this classic opposition between sentimental authenticity and the alienating effects of social prejudice without its more violent expressions. Julie speaks in 1,28 of her father as a 'parent dénaturé' who 'fait de sa fille une marchandise, une esclave'; in 1,63 she writes:

Ah ma cousine, quels monstres d'enfer sont ces préjugés, qui dépravent les meilleurs des coeurs, et font taire à chaque instant la nature? (*O.C.*, 2, p. 177)

But it is Saint-Preux who reserves the harshest treatment for the baron d'Etange, in a fine tirade of excellent sentimental pedigree delivered in response to the baron's threat of a duel:

Quel que soit l'empire dont vous abusez, mes droits sont plus sacrés
que les vôtres; la chaîne qui nous lie est la borne du pouvoir paternel,
même devant les tribunaux humains; et quand vous osez réclamer la
nature, c'est vous seul qui bravez ses lois. [...]

Allez, père barbare et peu digne d'un nom si doux, méditez
d'affreux parricides, tandis qu'une fille tendre et soumise immole son
bonheur à vos préjugés. Vos regrets me vengeront un jour des maux
que vous me faites, et vous sentirez trop tard que votre haine aveugle
et dénaturée ne vous fut pas moins funeste qu'à moi. Je serai malheureux, sans doute; mais si jamais la voix du sang s'élève au fond de
votre coeur, combien vous le serez plus encore d'avoir sacrifié à des
chimères l'unique fruit de vos entrailles; unique au monde en beauté,
en mérite, en vertus, et pour qui le Ciel prodigue de ses dons, n'oublia
rien qu'un meilleur père. (*O.C.*, 2, pp. 326–7)

The first movement of *La Nouvelle Héloïse* – its contestatory
movement – belongs, then, to the tradition of the sentimental
love story which defines love in contradistinction to social
convention. It is worth insisting for a moment on the narrative
aspects of this sentimental affiliation – the dynamic towards a
happy ending, which tends to be obscured by the slow, epistolary, introspective nature of the novel. As I have suggested,
Milord Edouard is the major exponent of this narrative function: it is he who attempts to find ways of reconciling love and
society, thus sustaining the reader's expectation of a possible
happy ending. He not only offers his English country estate to
the lovers, but hatches a plan for Saint-Preux to exercise his
talents in the world of commerce in London, so attaining a
social status which would render him acceptable to Julie's
father, and giving a particularly immediate relevance to the
kind of social promotion referred to in the notion of an 'aristocratie des talents'. As late as letter 3,4, where the ideology of
renunciation is firmly embedded in the narrative and the
appearance of Wolmar on the scene is being prepared, the
possibility of a happy ending is still being envisaged: here
Claire recounts how Saint-Preux's readiness to renounce Julie
(letter 3,2) has so moved Julie's mother that the only obstacle
now remaining is the baron, who, says Claire, could yet be won
over by Saint-Preux's persistence in the ways of virtue and
honesty. The threat of the duel, Saint-Preux's violent letter to

the baron and the scene of the inoculation follow, leading to letter 3,18 in which Julie retraces the history of their love, and tells of the appearance of Wolmar in her life, through the volition of her father, of course. What Julie reveals here – as much to the reader as to the fictional recipient of the letter – is that she has known for some time that the cause of the lovers is hopeless, because of her father's wish for her to marry Wolmar. The two slopes of the novel, in other words, overlap: the dynamic of happiness has actually been subverted from within while it still appeared operative.

If, however, one were to identify a point at which the definitive transition between the two phases of the novel takes place, it would be the account by Julie in 3,18 of the scene in which her father uses the arms of sentiment to persuade his daughter to accept the husband he is offering. The death of the baronne is of course essential in this process, as is the argument deployed by the baron:

Ma fille! respecte les cheveux blancs de ton malheureux père; ne le fais pas descendre avec douleur au tombeau, comme celle qui te porta dans son sein. Ah! veux-tu donner la mort à toute ta famille? (*O.C.*, 2, p. 348)

This is not the only way in which sentimental arms are turned against Julie. The baron explains to her that Wolmar is a man of high birth, but that he has lost his fortune in a recent revolution in his native Russia. The baron is thus faced with a dilemma which in a curious way reproduces the dynamic of the original situation of Julie and Saint-Preux; Wolmar has returned, believing in the good faith of his friend the baron, to marry his daughter: is he now to say to Wolmar 'Monsieur, je vous ai promis ma fille tandis que vous étiez riche, mais à présent que vous n'avez plus rien je me rétracte, et ma fille ne veut point de vous' (*O.C.*, 2, p. 349)? The question is of course rhetorical: to say that would be to renounce all that Julie and her lover have stood for up to this point in the narrative. The tools of sentiment are turned against Julie, and the blackmail works.

This, then, is the confirmation, if not strictly the inception, of the second phase of the novel, in which the former lovers, but particularly Saint-Preux, internalise the necessity of renunciation and develop a new relationship through the mediation of Wolmar, the husband. To what extent should this fundamental shift in discourse be read as a denial of the sentimental ideology of individual feeling as I have analysed it? Does Clarens represent a complete renunciation of the sentimental tradition? Not surprisingly, these questions cannot be answered simply and univocally.

A fundamental symbolic realignment is certainly attempted in the second half of Rousseau's novel: accepted order is to replace the anarchy of individual passion, social insertion and respectability the marginality of illicit love. Saint-Preux, through the agency of Wolmar and indeed of the whole social organisation of Clarens, is to undertake a process of psychological hygiene, in which a love affair taking place in isolation from society is replaced by an open relationship where nothing is hidden from the surrounding society. A particular scene is symptomatic of this change: in letter 4,11 Saint-Preux obtains a key to the Elysée. His intention, it seems, is to recreate an image of the past:

Que d'agréables pensées j'espérais porter dans ce lieu solitaire où le doux aspect de la seule nature devait chasser de mon souvenir tout cet ordre social et factice qui m'a rendu si malheureux! Tout ce qui va m'environner est l'ouvrage de celle qui me fut si chère. Je la contemplerai tout autour de moi. Je ne verrai rien que sa main n'ait touché; je baiserai des fleurs que ses pieds auront foulées; je respirerai avec la rosée un air qu'elle a respiré; son goût dans ses amusements me rendra présents tous ses charmes, et je la trouverai partout comme elle est au fond de mon coeur. (*O.C.*, 2, p. 486)

What in fact happens is that the memory of a reproach made to him by Wolmar the previous day 'a changé sur-le-champ tout l'état de mon âme. J'ai cru voir l'image de la vertu où je cherchais celle du plaisir.' The image of Julie is one in which she is surrounded by her husband, her children, her servants, in fact by the micro-society of Clarens; and this image reveals to Saint-Preux that he was in fact indulging in some kind of masturbatory fantasy – he calls it 'les écarts de l'imagination' –

in which Julie was isolated from her real social insertion so as to be totally available for him. The genius of Rousseau is at work here, in the Proustian analysis of the functioning of the imagination. And what it reveals, through the work on language itself, is the symbolic realignment of which I spoke: the association, in the remembered first phase of the novel, of love with nature, and the concomitant exclusion, or counterposition, of the social, are now superseded by an attempt by Saint-Preux to maintain his love for a Julie who is now a married woman, a mother, a key actor in the micro-society of Clarens. The sentimental utopia of the Meillerie has – should have – no place in this second phase.

This realignment also involves a criticism of the meritocratic theory of society which the sentimental love story articulates. Clarens, it is generally agreed, represents a social model in miniature, an ideal of transparence in which hierarchy and happiness are not mutually exclusive. Letter 5,2 is one of the letters in which the functioning of the economy of Clarens is recounted, in this case by Saint-Preux to Milord Edouard. The writer explains that:

La grande maxime de Mme de Wolmar est donc de ne point favoriser les changements de condition, mais de contribuer à rendre heureux chacun dans la sienne, et surtout d'empêcher que la plus heureuse de toutes, qui est celle du villageois dans un Etat libre, ne se dépeuple en faveur des autres.

Je lui faisais là-dessus l'objection des talents divers que la nature semble avoir partagés aux hommes, pour leur donner à chacun leur emploi, sans égard à la condition dans laquelle ils sont nés. (*O.C.*, 2, p. 536)

Mme de Wolmar's response to this is given at length: in summary, her view is that the argument from individual talent is an abstraction – and, we could add, a political slogan, for it certainly was that in the eighteenth century – disguising a far less attractive social reality, which is that of a scramble for positions of fame and fortune in a society which has lost the ability to regulate itself. The slogan of bourgeois liberation is for her the sign of an urbanised, ambition-dominated culture which has lost hold of its true values: 'On n'a des talents que pour s'élever, personne n'en a pour descendre; pensez-vous que ce soit là l'ordre de la nature' (*O.C.*, 2, p. 537)? The crucial point here is that, once again, and this time in terms which are far more explicitly socio-political in their intention, an aspect of the social organisation of Clarens is actually seen to stand in opposition to the first phase of the novel: an integral part of the challenge to the established order which was represented by the love of Saint-Preux and Julie was, as Milord Edouard clearly identified, precisely this ideology which holds that the place of an individual within a society – and marital status must count as an aspect of that – is to be determined by talent, not by birth. The love story is very clearly a figure of social challenge; and *La Nouvelle Héloïse* attempts to defeat that challenge.

And yet, Rousseau continues, in the latter part of the novel, in the 'Préface dialoguée', in other works such as *Emile*, to speak up for the rights of the heart over social prejudice and matrimonial ambition. In 5,13, Julie writes to Claire, encouraging her to marry Saint-Preux. Foreseeing the objection of the inequality of condition between the prospective partners, she writes:

Quant à l'inégalité, je croirais t'offenser de combattre une objection si frivole, lorsqu'il s'agit de sagesse et de bonnes moeurs. Je ne connais d'inégalité déshonorante que celle qui vient du caractère ou de l'éducation. A quelque état que parvienne un homme imbu de maximes basses, il est toujours honteux de s'allier à lui. Mais un homme élevé dans des sentiments d'honneur est l'égal de tout le monde, il n'y a point de rang où il ne soit à sa place. Tu sais quel était l'avis de ton père même quand il fut question de moi pour notre ami. Sa famille est honnête quoiqu'obscure. Il jouit de l'estime publique, il la mérite. Avec cela fût-il le dernier des hommes, encore ne faudrait-il pas balancer; car il vaut mieux déroger à la noblesse qu'à la vertu, et la femme d'un Charbonnier est plus respectable que la maîtresse d'un Prince. (*O.C.*, 2, p. 633)

Similarly, in the 'préface dialoguée' – a text which confronts head on the arguments concerning the moral impact of novels on readers, and is far from indulgent in its assumptions about the power of the novel to inculcate virtue – Rousseau maintains a similarly uncompromising position concerning the rights of the heart over the dictates of social convention. In line with his analysis in the *Lettre à d'Alembert sur les spectacles*, he accepts that the reading of novels is of no moral use to young people ('C'est commencer par mettre feu à la maison pour faire jouer les pompes'), but he still maintains that the source of moral corruption in sexual mores is to be sought in social attitudes:

Depuis que tous les sentiments de la nature sont étouffés par l'extrême inégalité, c'est de l'inique despotisme des pères que viennent les vices et les malheurs des enfants; c'est dans des noeuds forcés et mal assortis, que victimes de l'avarice ou de la vanité des parents, de jeunes femmes effacent par un désordre, dont elles font gloire, le scandale de leur première honnêteté. Voulez-vous donc remédier au mal? remontez à sa source. S'il y a quelque réforme à tenter dans les moeurs publiques, c'est par les moeurs domestiques qu'elle doit commencer, et cela dépend absolument des pères et des mères. Mais ce n'est point ainsi qu'on dirige les instructions; vos lâches Auteurs ne prêchent jamais que ceux qu'on opprime. (*O.C.*, 2, p. 24)

Emile, too, presents a strong argument in favour of the freedom of the heart: while accepting that, all other factors being equal, partners of similar social condition will enjoy a happier life together than partners of widely differing rank, Rousseau maintains, in the forcefully argued letter to Sophie from her parents, that the inclination of the heart, the voice of nature, must be listened to above all.

La naissance, les biens, le rang, l'opinion n'entreront pour rien dans nos raisons. Prenez un honnête homme dont la personne vous plaise et dont le caractère vous convienne, quel qu'il soit d'ailleurs, nous l'acceptons pour notre gendre. Son bien sera toujours assez grand, s'il a des bras, des moeurs, et qu'il aime sa famille. Son rang sera toujours assez illustre, s'il l'ennoblit par la vertu. Quand toute la terre nous blâmerait, qu'importe? Nous ne cherchons pas l'approbation publique, il nous suffit de votre bonheur. (*O.C.*, 4, pp. 757–8)

The opposition is between natural attributes – ranging from the physical to the moral, from strong arms to virtue – and empty social meaning. The same discourse is at work here as in Saint-Preux's dream of sentimental happiness at the Meillerie, himself and Julie living in simple happiness from the labour of his arms and the sweat of his brow. A few pages later, Rousseau codifies the same basic position more abstractly:

Voulez-vous prévenir les abus et faire d'heureux mariages? Etouffez les préjugés, oubliez les institutions humaines et consultez la nature. (*O.C.*, 4, p. 764)

Where does this leave us in our interpretation of the second phase of *La Nouvelle Héloïse*? Of course, one can maintain that Saint-Preux's and Julie's crime is sexual: in this way, it is possible to preserve intact Rousseau's advocacy of the voice of nature in matters of the heart. But such an interpretation is not really convincing: it is a casuistical reading of a novel which unquestionably articulates a message of renunciation, of internalised authority, even if the attempted internalisation fails and leads, ultimately, to death as the only resolution. Better, then, to accept the contradiction in Rousseau's thought, particularly since the particular contradiction reproduces one to be found in Rousseau's historical considerations on the role of romantic love in the emergence of modern society. Joel Schwartz points out that Rousseau has a positive and a negative interpretation of the historical role of individualised love.[9] The two versions are found in the *Discours sur l'origine de l'inégalité* and in the *Essai sur l'origine des langues*. In the former, Rousseau evokes the moment of transformation when the sexual behaviour of the state of nature – sexual desire seeking satisfaction with the most immediately available partner, no moral or sentimental transaction being involved – is replaced by individual preference. This takes place at the same time as the passage from a nomadic to a settled mode of existence, and is described by Rousseau in the following, typically paradoxical terms:

Un sentiment tendre et doux s'insinue dans l'âme, et par la moindre opposition devient une fureur impétueuse: la jalousie s'éveille avec l'amour; la Discorde triomphe, et la plus douce des passions reçoit des sacrifices de sang humain. (*O.C.*, 3, pp. 168–9)

The *Essai sur l'origine des langues* presents a different picture. Rousseau attributes a fundamental role in the emergence of the social passions to what Eric Zernik calls 'les fêtes fondatrices'. These take different forms in northern and southern countries: in the North, the sociability which develops around the winter fire is the source of the first stirrings of humanity; in the South, on the other hand, the watering-place – again corresponding to the shift from a nomadic to a settled mode of agriculture – is the central focus.

Là se formèrent les premiers liens des familles; là furent les premiers rendez-vous des deux sexes. Les jeunes filles venaient chercher l'eau pour le ménage, les jeunes hommes venaient abreuver leurs troupeaux. Là des yeux accoutumés aux mêmes objets depuis l'enfance commencèrent d'en voir de plus doux. Le coeur s'émut à ces nouveaux objets, un attrait inconnu le rendit moins sauvage, il sentit le plaisir de n'être pas seul. L'eau devint insensiblement plus nécessaire, le bétail eut soif plus souvent; on arrivait en hâte et l'on partait à regret [...] Là se firent les premières fêtes, les pieds bondissaient de joie, le geste empressé ne suffisait plus, la voix l'accompagnait d'accents passionnés, le plaisir et le désir confondus ensemble se faisaient sentir à la fois. Là fut enfin le vrai berceau des peuples, et du pur cristal des fontaines sortirent les premiers feux de l'amour.[10]

The accent is unmistakably different here: the irony of 'le bétail eut soif plus souvent' betrays the tender nostalgia with which the passage is suffused: here is an origin which, in the beginning at least, was innocent and joyful, far removed from the Hobbesian vision suggested by the parallel passage in the second *Discours*.

The *Lettre à d'Alembert sur les spectacles* casts some light on Rousseau's contradictory views concerning individual love envisaged as a challenge to established social hierarchy and conventions. In the latter part of the text, Rousseau proposes dancing festivals as a means of promoting marriage. Such events, far from being immoral as some excessively zealous religious parties have suggested, are 'une inspiration de la Nature', and the effect of the proposed institution would be to introduce an element of individual freedom into the marriage market:

Sans altérer l'autorité des pères, les inclinations des enfants seraient un peu plus en liberté; le premier choix dépendrait un peu plus de leur coeur; les convenances d'âge, d'humeur, de goût, de caractère, seraient un peu plus consultés; on donnerait moins à celles d'état et de biens qui font des noeuds mal assortis, quand on les suit aux dépens des autres. Les liaisons devenant plus faciles, les mariages seraient plus fréquents.

The elders of the town will be called upon to give a prize for the best couple:

Je ne doute pas que cette agréable réunion des deux termes de la vie humaine ne donnât à cette assemblée un certain coup d'oeil attendrissant, et qu'on ne vît quelquefois couler dans le parquet des larmes de joie et de souvenir, capables, peut-être, d'en arracher à un spectateur sensible.[11]

As in many of Rousseau's evocations of *fêtes*, there is already a suggestion of the *fête révolutionnaire*, and indeed of some of the tone of Saint-Just's *Institutions républicaines*, in the attempt to constitute a social ceremony which will combine moral and political rectitude and individual spontaneity in a totally transparent, public form. This projection into contemporary Europe of the imagined historical scene at the water-trough shares with Clarens a desire to reconcile passion with total public transparency.

The description of the dancing festival comes towards the end of a text which expresses all of Rousseau's distrust of the literary representation of love. In his treatment of the representation of love in classical French tragedy, specifically *Bérénice*, Rousseau denounces the preoccupation with individual passion as socially harmful, because it inculcates a fatal lack of masculine virtue, so essential to the functioning of a wholesome republic. Passion is the course of least resistance, the fatal charm which, in the words of the second *Discours*, 's'insinue dans l'âme'; by extension, in this view, virtue is defined as resistance to passion:

Celui qui connut le véritable amour et l'a su vaincre, ah! pardonnons à ce mortel, s'il existe, d'oser prétendre à la vertu![12]

Furthermore, Rousseau specifically rejects the argument that passion is only one element in tragedies such as *Bérénice*, and that the effect of the play will be a moralising one if the plot enacts the triumph of virtue over disordered passion. In Rousseau's view, the identification of the reader remains on the side of passion whatever the plot attempts to show:

Les tableaux de l'amour font toujours plus d'impression que les maximes de la sagesse, et [...] l'effet d'une Tragédie est tout à fait indépendant de celui du dénouement.[13]

Ironically, such a statement opens up the possibility of readings of *La Nouvelle Héloïse* which take no account of the attempted neutralisation of disorderly passion: if readers identify with the text in such a way that it is read as a defence of passion, then that becomes the public meaning of the text. This certainly appears to be what happened in certain politicised circles in the period of the Revolution: as part of the Revolutionary cult of Rousseau, it is precisely the hierarchy-challenging aspects of the novel which are foregrounded, in order to enrol the author under the sentimental-democratic banner of the new era. A play, *La Fête de Jean-Jacques Rousseau*, 'représentée sur le Théatre des Amis de la Patrie POUR LE PEUPLE' on the occasion of the transfer of Rousseau's remains to the Pantheon (11 October 1794), includes the ceremonial installation of a copy of *La Nouvelle Héloïse* on a pedestal at Ermenonville, where the action is set: the ceremony is accompanied by these lines:

> De la sensible Julie
> Quand il nous traça l'ardeur,
> Il combattit la force
> D'un préjugé destructeur.
> Saint-Preux, tes vives allarmes
> Peignent ton coeur sans détour;
> Peut-on résister aux charmes
> Du doux baiser de l'amour?[14]

Similarly, Etienne Dumont insists that the novel expresses 'une antipathie contre les classes élevées et dominantes de la société [...] Le noeud de l'intéret est formé par le préjugé d'un gentilhomme qui sacrifie le bonheur d'une fille chérie plutôt que de souffrir qu'elle déroge en faveur d'un plébéien qui n'a pour lui que son mérite et ses vertus.'[15] Such an interpretation of the novel is of course part of a broader celebration of Rousseau as a precursor of the Revolution *and* a sentimental victim, the two identities being inextricably linked.[16]

In an article which is now over twenty years old,[17] Jean Biou attempted to outline a diametrically opposed analysis of the reception of *La Nouvelle Héloïse*, and one moreover more in keeping with the plot's attempt to subvert and neutralise the message of democratic protest articulated by the first half of the novel. In his view, the novel was the basis for an aristocratic 'idéologie de substitution'. He sees two grounds for such an interpretation: the internalisation of the notion of authority and hierarchy which was discussed above, and, secondly, the authoritarian autarky of Clarens, which he reads as an updating of feudal class relations via a sentimental form of paternalism. The popularity of the novel among the enlightened aristocracy is, according to his hypothesis, a sign that they see sketched out in the work a new way of justifying their position of dominance in society, recuperating the weapons which the bourgeoisie has used against them. Biou enumerates various corpora of documents which might be used to pursue the investigation of his hypothesis, including readers' letters held at the Bibliothèque de Neuchâtel, and expresses disappointment that 'l'intérêt de ces documents relève plutôt d'une autre rubrique: le courrier du coeur'. The reappropriation of a certain sentimental discourse by counter-revolutionary thought after the Revolution is an important phenomenon, but with specific reference to *La Nouvelle Héloïse*, the recent work by Claude Labrosse on the novel's readership seems to confirm Biou's disappointment: identification with the affective experience of the characters, the creation of an imaginative space through the experience of the text, are the dominant features which emerge from Labrosse's analysis.[18] Socially, too, Biou's line of analysis can be criticised: as the second part of this chapter will make abundantly clear, there is no reason to see the sentimental justification of inequality and domination which is effected at Clarens as necessarily aristocratic, given the overall historical nature of the bourgeois social project.

Within a reception framework, Mme de Staël's *Lettres sur les ouvrages et le caractère de Rousseau* offers a coherent model for an understanding of reader response to romantic-sentimental love in which the reader is not forced to choose between the conflicting ideological messages of the text, but responds rather through a kind of poetic totalisation. De Staël's concern, let it be said, is not to defend any ideologically coded reading of *La Nouvelle Héloïse*: on the contrary, she is explicitly concerned with its capacity to instil virtue and devotion to duty (including marriage). In terms of plot, says Madame de Staël, the novel is morally flawed: Rousseau probably was at fault in depicting Julie's sexual relationship with Saint-Preux; in a sense, the novel might be seen as encouraging young women to rebel against the marriage plans of their parents. But what counts in the final analysis is that, depicting love, Rousseau has depicted all of the human heart:

> Mais la véritable utilité d'un roman est dans son effet bien plus que dans son plan, dans les sentiments qu'il inspire, bien plus que dans les événements qu'il raconte. Pardonnons à Rousseau, si à la fin de cette lecture, on se sent plus animé d'amour pour la vertu, si l'on tient plus à ses devoirs, si les moeurs simples, la bienfaisance, la retraite, ont plus d'attraits pour nous.[19]

In a curious way, Madame de Staël is using Rousseau's argument in the *Lettre à d'Alembert*, but inverting it in Rousseau's favour: the plot may appear corrupting, but the identification of the reader with true feeling saves the day. An important element in her analysis is the idea – to which I shall return in chapter 6 – that the virtues of humanity, pity, beneficence, are intimately connected with love in human psychology:

> Quand on s'est accoutumé à ne mettre de valeur à soi qu'à cause d'un autre, quand on s'est une fois entièrement détaché de soi, on ne peut plus s'y reprendre, et la piété succède à l'amour. C'est là l'histoire la plus vraisemblable du coeur.
> La bienfaisance et l'humanité, la douceur et la bonté, semblent aussi appartenir à l'amour. On s'intéresse aux malheureux; le coeur est toujours disposé à s'attendrir: il est comme ces cordes tendues, qu'un souffle fait résonner. (p. 24)

In describing the experiential truth of the life of the emotions, Rousseau is undertaking a task of moral education. Madame de Staël contrasts Rousseau with the ancients and with 'nos romans modernes': the former deal with the idea of fate, the latter with 'l'héroïsme et la galanterie chevaleresque';

mais le sentiment qui naît du libre pechant du coeur, le sentiment à-la-fois ardent et tendre, délicat et passionné, c'est Rousseau qui, le premier, a cru qu'on pouvait exprimer ses brûlantes agitations; c'est Rousseau qui, le premier, l'a prouvé. (pp. 43–4)

In conclusion, Madame de Staël evokes the power of Julie's letter of farewell: the revelation of Julie's continuing love, the knowledge of her impending death, the calm which the letter expresses,

chaque mot de cette lettre enfin a rempli mon âme de la plus vive émotion. Ah! qu'on voit avec peine la fin d'une lecture qui nous intéressait comme un événement de notre vie, et qui, sans troubler notre coeur, mettait en mouvement tous nos sentiments et toutes nos pensées! (p. 46)

In short, Madame de Staël's reading of *La Nouvelle Héloïse* offers a certain freedom with respect to the way in which the social or ideological symbolism of love is worked out through narrative: the text may also be appropriated by the reader as a poetic whole, in which case an important element in the text's interaction with social reality is its role in the reader's activities of self-exploration, and in the imaginary constitution of identity and behaviour models.

This analysis is particularly helpful, it seems to me, as a response to the ideological complexity (or indeterminacy) of certain sentimental texts of the late eighteenth century, which are marked by an apparent contradiction. On the one hand, in their representation of individual love, and in the sentimental aesthetic which underpins that representation, these texts appear to validate individual sentiment in the face of social pressures, and therefore to fit the ideological framework which I am proposing; on the other hand, they explicitly espouse, through plot and at a discursive level, an ideology of sacrifice and renunciation which appears to run counter to the primary sense of the text. One case which has already been examined is that of Baculard, particularly in narratives such as *Euphémie*; but Mme Cottin, Mme de Genlis and the young Chateaubriand also come to mind. In these writers, love remains the imaginative centre of the text, but it is harnessed to anti-Enlightenment values through the symbolism of closure, renunciation and death; and yet, reading these texts, one is left with a persistent feeling that such a direct ideological reading – which contemporaries, like Vernes, were tempted to make – is only a partial understanding. Such texts are marked by a strange ambivalence: they always seem to be saying something other than what they suggest, as though different forces were pulling them in at least two different directions at the same time. Approaching them in the light of Madame de Staël's reading seems to me to clarify at least one important issue here: their total, poetic meaning, the one which is most accessible to reader identification, lies in their sentimentalism. These texts seem to further the cause of individualism in spite of their authors' discursive intentions. It is almost as though the inherited grammar of sentimental writing operates more forcefully in these texts than the language of politics and ideology, which appears as a superficial gloss unable to roll back a constituted set of deep symbolic meanings.

To conclude, then, this treatment of the ideological and social symbolism of individual love in the sentimental narrative, it seems that my opening hypotheses can be maintained, with modifications; at the same time, the preceding pages have thrown up a series of questions which, for the time being, must stand as questions. *La Nouvelle Héloïse*, despite or perhaps because of the strategies which Rousseau deploys to neutralise the threat of disorderly passion, confirms a fundamental symbolic alignment between the representation of individual love and a democratic, meritocratic vision of society. One important qualification needs to be made here, which will be prominent in the second part of this chapter. If the discourse of individual freedom and meritocracy can be read as the discourse of the bourgeoisie in its opposition to the vestigial aristocratic domination of society, we should not conclude that the relation between text and social practice is a mimetic one: the bourgeoisie of nineteenth-century France will not be particularly noted for libertarianism and indifference to considerations of social hierarchy in relation to marriage. The fiction is a discursive practice, not a mimesis; and Lionel Gossmann is right to remind us of the richness and complexity of *La Nouvelle Héloïse*, which, as well as dramatising the ideological conflicts of its time, looks forward to new ones:

> at one and the same time the conflict between feudal order and bourgeois individualism and a foreshadowing of that equally bitter conflict within bourgeois society between the family, the principle of bourgeois law and order, and the individual, the principle of bourgeois freedom.[20]

Secondly, this symbolic system coexists with a related, but logically separate function: the text operates as a site for reader identification, for the fulfilment of personal (or socially shared) fantasies. This is a space in which a whole community of readers participate in the working out and generalisation of a set of cultural models concerning the emotional aspirations of the individual, the notion of the couple and of families; sentimental texts bear witness to the semi-public process whereby a new private space is defined, and to some extent this appears to be the case even if the text in question has no programmatic, discursive attachment to the cause of individualism.

Thirdly, a compensatory dimension is present in the sentimental representation of love. Neither mimesis nor social project, the text in this case represents a space into which the reader may escape. Certainly, the notion of escape implies a prior adherence to the symbolic system into which the escape takes place, and, in that sense, this function is related to the previous one. Nonetheless, Lionel Gossmann's reminder is a useful one:

> literature becomes both the expression and the consolation of modern bourgeois man [sic]. The harmony and totality which his heart, beating in time with the hearts of Julie and Saint-Preux, learns to desire, he finds in the novel itself.[21]

Finally, and particularly in the light of the notion of compensation, difficult questions remain concerning the relation between the sentimental text and social reality and practice. If the compensatory function implies the weakening of a more direct referential or instrumental relation between text and reader, to what extent is this related to what might be termed the autonomisation of the aesthetic, viewed as a characteristic feature of late eighteenth-century European culture? Jochen Schulte-Sasse describes the evolution of sentimentalism in the eighteenth century as a gradual shift in which the element of social criticism inherent in the literary project is diverted into a self-justifying, closed circuit in which referentiality is lost: 'the institutionalization of the aesthetic as a separate, autonomous sphere that compensates for the disenchantment of an increasingly rationalized world necessarily defuses the moral or sociocritical content of each work of art.'[22] Is this a key to understanding the ambivalence of the anti-Enlightenment sentimentalists (Cottin, Genlis, Chateaubriand): that sense of texts which have broken free from their ideological moorings, and are floating freely in an aesthetic realm, the fiction divorced from a social project? Lastly, if sentimental texts are, as I believe, one of the crucial areas in which Enlightenment can be seen shifting towards Romanticism, is this shift located primarily in the complex relationship between fiction, public political discourse, and readers and writers, rather than at a thematic level?

MONEY

The poor are as constantly represented in the sentimental text as are the victims of unhappy love. The sentimentalisation of the poor relies heavily on their representation as victims, and to this end the sentimental text frequently emphasises a set of features – old age or extreme youth, infirmity, bad luck – which constitute the poor as helpless: by virtue of the fact that they are the object of some process or condition which is not of their making and over which they have no control, they are constituted as *deserving*. At this point, the act of charity inter-

venes. Usually, but not exclusively, the giver is also the narrator, and, as I outlined in the previous chapter, a triangular
relationship is thereby set up between the represented person,
the author and the reader, in which the author is in two senses
the giver: not only does he (and as Jay Caplan points out, the
masculine pronoun is nearly always accurate) give money to
the poor, but he also gives the account of that act of humanity
to the reader, together with his own emotional reaction to the
scene in which he is at once actor and spectator; the reader
then becomes the spectator, and in turn reacts (in the form of
tears) to the represented scene and the account of it by the
author. In other words, a discourse is given at the same time as
alms, and it is this conjunction between the representation of
the poor and the articulation of a certain discourse about
poverty, humanity and charity which I wish to pursue in the
remaining part of the chapter. The discussion will be situated
between two poles of interpretation: on the one hand, should
the sentimental portrayal of the poor and of action in their
favour be read, as was suggested in the opening pages of this
chapter, as an attempt to give a voice to the voiceless, to
include the hitherto excluded? Or, alternatively, is the sentimentalisation of the poor to be interpreted, more cynically, as a
discursive strategy through which the enlightened bourgeoisie
states its commitment to values of humanity and justice, and
thereby seeks to strengthen its claims to universal domination?

Marx is savagely ironic about the sentimental presentation
of poverty and charity in his critique of Sue's *Mystères de Paris*
in *The Holy Family*. He is no doubt consciously reductive in his
interpretation of the use of scenes of charity for the purveying
of aesthetic pleasure, but his analysis is still a crucial
benchmark in the understanding of the aestheticisation of
poverty. Speaking of Rodolphe's introduction of the marquise
d'Harville to the joys of charity, Marx writes that

Rudolph has thereby unconsciously expressed the mystery which was
revealed long ago, that human misery itself, the infinite abjectness
which is obliged to receive alms, must serve the aristocracy of money
and education as a plaything to satisfy its self-love, tickle its arro-
gance and amuse it.[23]

For Marx, this sentimentalisation is one of the ways in which the reality of material relations between individuals and classes is masked by discourse: the purpose of his text is to denounce the notion of *mystery* as an idealist obfuscation.

Zola dismantles the sentimentalisation of poverty with pitiless irony in *Germinal*, and his approach must be seen as close to Marx's. The scene in question is one in which the Grégoire family, comfortable bourgeoisie who possess shares in the mine, hand over a parcel of clothes to the Maheu children, children of a mining family who are reduced to hunger precisely because of their economic relation with the class of which the Grégoires are a representative. In other words, the scene of alms-giving takes place within a context where the global economic relationship between donor and receiver is explicit, and indeed much of Zola's purpose is to demonstrate the contradictions between the two relations, and to show how the act of charity simply cements the relationship of exploitation and dependency. It is of course true that what Zola satirises is not a literary representation (a text), but fictional behaviour on the part of characters, but what is striking in his presentation of the scene is that, for the Grégoires, it is actually the playing out of a script: the children have been prepared to play their role, and the whole exercise appears to be designed to procure pleasure to the donors. Thus, the Maheu children who shuffle into the comfortable bourgeois home are described by Mme Grégoire as 'de pauvres mignons', the clothes which are given will suit the children 'à merveille', and the motivation behind the act is revealed as one of representation:

Les Grégoire chargeaient Cécile [their daughter] de leurs aumônes. Cela rentrait dans leur idée d'une belle éducation. Il fallait être charitable, ils disaient eux-mêmes que leur maison était la maison du Bon Dieu.

It is a spectacle which they set up in their own house, and which they then consume as spectators and manipulators. The scene concludes with an improvised gesture from the young Cécile: she gives the children a piece of brioche left over from the family breakfast, et, sous les regards attendris de ses parents, elle acheva de les pousser dehors. Les pauvres mioches, qui n'avaient plus de pain, s'en allèrent, en tenant cette brioche respectueusement dans leurs menottes gourdes de froid.[24]

The scene has not only caused the Grégoires pleasure, in that it has represented to them their own charitable nature: it has also reinforced their position in that the attitude of the recipients is one of respect.

Eighteenth-century sentimentalism is undoubtedly an antecedent of the attitudes criticised by Marx and Zola, and their view does therefore shed some light on my subject. Problems of poverty and vagrancy preoccupied many enlightened thinkers in the latter part of the eighteenth century, culminating in the explosion of concern for the poor which took place under the Revolution.[25] One of the most striking features of the numerous pamphlets devoted to the question of poverty and mendicity is their use of sentimental language and figures. The reason for writing about such a question, and the need to find solutions to what is perceived as an increasingly pressing social problem, are both seen as functions of sensibility and humanity, values worthy of a 'siècle éclairé'. It is as though notions of *bienfaisance, charité*, etc., were the obligatory reference point in such discussions, and the vocabulary is ever-present. At the same time, however, the individual act of charity as celebrated in the sentimental text is frequently criticised in these tracts, on the grounds that such action is basically disorganised and piecemeal in its effect. The recurrent concern of these texts, and, crucially, of the work of the Comité de mendicité of the Assemblée Nationale, is to create structures to replace individual initiative and also, particularly in the Revolutionary phase, to supplant the role of the Church. Rationality is the watchword; but in the passage from the individual to the organised approach to the problem, there is an implicit criticism of the former:

La bienfaisance publique, retenue dans les bornes strictes de la justice, doit encore, dans les moyens qu'elle emploie, considérer l'intérêt général. Différente de l'aumône qui, dans les secours qu'elle donne, peut ne voir que le malheureux qu'elle soulage, la bienfaisance publique doit chercher sans doute dans l'assistance des pauvres le soulagement de ceux qui en sont l'objet, mais considérer avant tout l'intérêt de tous les infortunés, l'intérêt général de la société: ceux qui sont plus près d'elle, ne sont pas plus à ses yeux que ceux qu'elle ignore. Cette bienfaisance n'est pas l'effet d'une sensibilité irréfléchie, elle n'est pas même une vertu compatissante; elle est un devoir; elle est la justice; elle doit en avoir tous les caractères, et se prémunir contre les mouvements si naturels qui pourraient les altérer.[26]

Several important themes are adumbrated in this very revealing passage. A national structure is seen as taking further that which exists only at individual level: there is thus an intensification of the sentimental vision, in the sense that what it presents as charity, the Revolution wishes to proclaim as nothing less than justice. Charity becomes a right, and this already in the early, moderate years of the Revolution. The *plan de travail* of the committee is explicit in this regard:

Cette secourable assistance ne doit pas être regardée comme un bienfait; elle est, sans doute, le besoin d'un coeur sensible et humain, le voeu de tout homme qui pense, mais elle est le devoir strict et indispensable de tout homme qui n'est pas lui-même dans l'état de pauvreté; devoir qui ne doit point être avili, ni par le nom, ni par le caractère de l'aumône.[27]

But if there is a movement of intensification, there is also a movement of criticism in this attitude, which implies more than just an observation of the unsystematised and partial nature of individual charity. Fundamentally, the administrative approach to poverty fears that the individual approach encourages what it chooses to refer to as 'oisiveté': acting out of impeccable motives, such charity may in fact be fooled into thinking that it is giving to deserving cases, when in fact what it is doing is encouraging the shiftless, the criminal and the vicious in their unacceptable ways.

What is happening in this period, then, is a categorisation of the poor according to the basic division: deserving–undeserving. The titles of the tracts dealing with these matters very frequently express the fundamental emphasis as the 'destruction' or 'extirpation' of mendicity; indeed, the official title of the committee to which I have referred was 'Comité pour l'extinction de la mendicité'. So that a policing preoccupation was present from the very start, coexisting perfectly well with the humanitarian language which we have seen. Of course, the dividing line in this categorisation of the poor is *work*: the deserving poor are those not able to work, and the undeserving are those for whom begging is perceived as an easy way of avoiding that universal human destiny. Among these, in a work by the abbé Baudeau published in 1765,[28] are ranged various 'pèlerins mendiants' whose particular claim to charity must be seen to carry no weight: an anticlerical vision can quickly denounce the Church as one of those forces encouraging laziness amongst the populace. The abolition of some of the numerous religious festivals which punctuated the calendar of *ancien régime* France also finds a point of insertion here: the fourth report of the Comité de mendicité suggests, for instance, that nineteen out of the twenty-three festivals celebrated in Paris be moved to a Sunday, in order to step up the fight against mendicity by encouraging work.[29]

For those classed as 'faux pauvres', there is no room for humanitarian treatment. The approach is punitive, ranging from the 'dépôt de mendicité' through placement with an employer to transportation. What all of these have in common, of course, is that work is the essence of the treatment. The abbé Baudeau even imagines a temporal progression in the treatment of these unfortunates: beginning in the 'maison de correction', the prisoner will be forced to acquire a taste for work by the 'Cachot à pompe', a device whereby if he fails to keep turning the handle of the pump, he will, quite simply, drown. This will be followed by agricultural work in uniform, after which deportation to one of the colonies will be perceived as a 'liberation'.[30]

My purpose here is not to be gratuitously satirical. The Revolution, as Alan Forrest has shown, marks a significant advance for the poor, both through the emergence of the notion of a 'droit de subsistence', and through the enormous task of social research and documentation which was undertaken. But the coexistence of a discourse of sentimental

celebration (often marked by a very ambiguous and voyeur-
istic self-righteousness) and, on the other hand, these extremely
punitive attitudes, forces the historian to look closely at the
relationship between them, and at the overall structure within
which the discourse occurs. In the final analysis, this determining frame is an economic one: it is *work* which marks the crucial
watershed between the deserving and the 'false' poor, and
those who can provide work for the latter are celebrated within
the discourse as much as the system which provides subsistence
for the former. The industrialist becomes a philanthropist
within this system of ideas: a telling example which is given is
that of Oberkampf, this 'respectable Suisse' whom we have
seen transform Jouy-en-Josas from

> un misérable hameau en un bourg considérable, le peupler de mille
> habitants, former leurs bras à des arts qui leur étaient inconnus,
> occuper aujourd'hui 900 ouvriers, devenir leur père, les enrichir,
> faire lui-même une fortune immense qu'il n'apprécie qu'autant
> qu'elle lui procure le moyen de faire des heureux.

Job creation, too, can be a narrative of happiness, told in this
case by a Monsieur Dupré, 'négociant, fabriquant, Député de
Carcassonne' in his interestingly titled *Moyens d'exciter l'industrie
nationale et de détruire la mendicité*.[31]

The distinction between the deserving and the undeserving
poor, and the corresponding split between a charitable and a
repressive approach, together constitute a structural feature of
socio-political treatments of poverty throughout the latter part
of the century; and, despite the intensification which occurs in
the Revolutionary period, during which the notion of the
inalienable rights of the poor emerges, the repressive aspect
remains a feature of Revolutionary discourse too. How then
should the absence of the discourse of repression from certain
fictional sentimental texts be interpreted? Of course, the
charity of Vernes or Gorjy may be seen as precisely that
unstructured, unreflective form of alms-giving which the
rational approach seeks to supersede; and yet the fact that
Gorjy can on the one hand pen sentimental representations of
the act of charity, and on the other recommend the measures
laid out in the *Mémoire sur les dépôts de mendicité*, suggests another

interpretation. A certain category of texts is marked by the fact that the repressive aspects of social practice are removed from view in favour of a rosier and more celebratory form of discourse. If such an interpretation can be applied to fictional representations of poverty and alms-giving, it is also relevant to the *fête du Malheur* proposed by Barère as the celebratory climax of the ambitious programme of outdoor relief set up in Year 2. The title of the festival, referring as it does to one of the central categories of the sentimental vision, is in itself worthy of note. The persistence of various features inherited from the sentimental text is striking: those who will step forward to receive the first instalment of relief belong to certain privileged and nature-given categories, intimately related to age and sex:

Combien touchante et auguste sera la cérémonie dans laquelle le Malheur sera honoré, puisque les deux extrémités de la vie y seront réunies avec le sexe qui en est la force! Vous y serez, vieillards agricoles, artisans invalides, et à coté d'eux vous y serez aussi, mères et veuves chargées d'enfants! et ce spectacle est le plus beau que la politique puisse présenter à la nature, et que la terre fertilisée puisse offrir au ciel consolateur.

Représentants du peuple français, voilà les premiers pas vers la destruction de la misère et l'amélioration du sort de l'espèce humaine.[32]

At the same time, this text on the *fête du Malheur* shows how certain aesthetic features connected to the notion of *tableau* can easily be transferred to the context of the *fête révolutionnaire*: here also is a scene which brings together a set of relationships which have developed over time and in different spaces, and holds them up as a *representation*, the function of which is to move and educate the spectator. The difference, of course, is that what is celebrated now is not the individual charity of one man, even if that refers outwards to abstract and universal notions, but the virtue of the Republic itself, which becomes the principal actor in the *tableau*. In this ceremony, 'la reconnaissance publique s'acquittera envers les vieillards et les mères, les infirmes, les non-valides, les cultivateurs et les artisans'. Like the celebration of individual charity, however, this celebration obscures from view the repressive side of the enlightened attitude to poverty: the undeserving poor are not on the platform.

So far, I have been dealing with a relatively narrowly defined theme: the representation by the sentimental text of the poor, and of certain types of charitable transactions between the poor and dominant society. But this is not the only context in which the poor figure in the sentimental text, and I now wish to extend the analysis to what I take to be a wider, and less immediately mimetic framework of meaning. Money, power and status – in short, the material realisations of systems of social value and hierarchy – in fact occupy an extremely ambiguous place in the process of sentimentalisation. The beggar is sentimentalised, fundamentally, because he has no money; at the very least, it seems possible to say that the act of giving money represents the resolution of the sequence of narrative in which he appears. In principle, then, the structure appears to be simple: the text seeks to establish happiness, and the key to doing so is to provide cash. The bourgeois implicitly admits by such a process that money is happiness; the same rules apply to donor and receiver, the only difference being that only one actually possesses the money and, by extension, the power to decide whether to confer it on the other. But, returning to the romantic narrative structure which was the subject of the first half of this chapter, it will be remembered that the source of sentimentalisation was precisely the gesture which expresses disdain for money, wealth and status: it is the baron d'Etange, La Bédoyère senior, Marianne's father in Vernes's narrative, who attach importance to these things, and that judgement brings down on them the opprobrium of the text. On the other hand, thwarted love expresses its sublime, class-transcending qualities by its disdain for worldly wealth: Saint-Preux suggests that he and Julie go live in poverty, eating only that frugal but rarified fare which he can earn by the sweat of his own brow. Marianne summarises the overall structure when she says to her father, of the husband whom he intends for her: 'Il est riche, dites-vous, mais qu'est-ce que l'or? Peut-il nous rendre heureux, quand nous l'arrosons de larmes?' (see above, p. 50).

Mercier's *L'Indigent* (1772) provides a particularly clear illustration of some of the contradictions involved here. On the one hand, the brother and sister Joseph and Charlotte are presented as victims of injustice: their poverty is no fault of their own, but the result of the financial ruin of their father, a virtuous 'cultivateur'. The injustice of their situation is only highlighted by the schemes of the rich and lubricious de Lys, who seeks to take advantage of Charlotte's poverty in order to seduce her. In this sense, the whole drive of the narrative seems to be in the direction of a challenge to injustice; but this is only one aspect of the sentimentalisation at work here, for the heroes only achieve their full sentimental status when their disdain for worldly wealth is articulated fully and coherently. Recalling the days when they were in a pauper's prison with their father, Charlotte and Joseph have the following exchange:

Charlotte

Je pleurais de joie en le voyant manger; et lui, mon frère, comme il regardait ses enfants! comme il nous bénissait! ... ah! n'étions-nous pas alors tous trois satisfaits?

Joseph

Oui, Charlotte, oui, nous l'étions, je me rappelle ces moments. Je ne demande pas d'autre faveur au ciel ... Dans le coin d'une prison, assis sur de la paille; oui, nous avons tous trois pleuré de tendresse ... Il n'y a que les malheureux qui sachent aimer.

Later, the father reappears, and rebukes the vicious de Lys in the following terms:

Riches malheureux, gardez votre or indigne, et laissez-nous la volupté des larmes.[33]

This uncompromising valorisation of poverty is a repeated sentimental *topos*. Vernes's 'ils sont plus *hommes*; ils m'offrent une nature moins défigurée' has already been quoted, and, as we have seen, it is a favourite line with Baculard: 'S'ils sont plus riches que moi, je suis plus heureux qu'eux avec tout leur étalage et leurs filles d'opéra [...] Je me plais à sentir mon coeur, Monsieur' (see above, pp. 96 and 20). Sentimental authenticity is constituted in opposition to worldly criteria of status and success. The absence of all externality is conceived as the condition of experiencing to the full the joys of the internal life: the more the trappings of wealth are pared away, the more obvious are the heart and soul which constitute essential humanity. If, as I have suggested, some form of social shift or transference is a frequent narrative device in sentimental texts, then that shift is typically a downward one.

In *La Nouvelle Héloïse*, Julie offers Saint-Preux the following advice about strategies for spiritual survival in the city:

Si vous voulez donc être homme en effet, apprenez à redescendre. L'humanité coule comme une eau pure et salutaire, et va fertiliser les lieux bas; elle cherche toujours le niveau, elle laisse à sec ces roches arides qui menacent la campagne, et ne donnent qu'une ombre nuisible ou des éclats pour écraser leurs voisins. (*O.C.*, 2, p. 304)

Rousseau is of course the indispensable reference for this valorisation of the humble in eighteenth-century France, and I propose now to investigate in some detail the discourse of social marginality in Rousseau. This will lead me to look also at his treatment of the act of alms-giving. It will become apparent that, as with the role of sentimental love in *La Nouvelle Héloïse*, Rousseau's relation to sentimentalism in the area of poverty and marginality is a double one: his work is at the same time the fountainhead for many of the sentimental stereotypes which became current in the last third of the century, and a yardstick which reveals the gap between genius and derivative popularisation.

Jean Starobinski has described brilliantly the way in which withdrawal from society and identification with the poor represent for Jean-Jacques a discursive position from which to denounce social corruption.

En se singularisant au vu de tous, en revêtant le rôle du pauvre, le moraliste solitaire cherche à donner une leçon universelle. [...] Sa vie de gagne-petit, il ne se contente pas de la subir: il la revendique, pour prouver à ses lecteurs fortunés qu'en l'état présent de la société une existence digne et moralement justifiée n'est possible qu'au confins de l'indigence [...] Il proclame l'alliance permanente, le lien nécessaire de l'infériorité sociale et de la supériorité morale.[34]

Bronislaw Baczko has spoken, too, of Rousseau's 'denunciatory marginality'.[35]

In the fourth and last of the *Lettres à Malesherbes*, in which he traces the origins of his withdrawal from polite society, Rousseau expresses the moral differential between rich and poor in a direct comparison which could be read as programmatic for late eighteenth-century sentimentalism:

> J'estime moi les paysans de Montmorenci des membres plus utiles de la société que tous ces tas de désoeuvrés payés de la graisse du peuple pour aller six fois la semaine bavarder dans une académie. (*O.C.*, I, p. 1143)

Social displacement is structurally important to Rousseau's intellectual project. It confers upon him the status of a privileged and more trustworthy observer of humanity than those observers who view society from a position in the social hierarchy, as a famous passage from the *Ebauches des Confessions* makes clear:

> Sans avoir aucun état moi-même, j'ai connu tous les états; j'ai vécu dans tous depuis les plus bas jusqu'aux plus élevés, excepté le trône [...] N'étant rien, ne voulant rien je n'embarrassais et n'importunais personne; j'entrais par tout sans tenir à rien, dînant quelque fois le matin avec les Princes et soupant le soir avec les paysans. (*O.C.*, I, pp. 1150-1)

In *Emile*, this vision of a humanity transcending social conditions is adapted to an educational end when, in the crucial opening section of Book IV, Rousseau maps out Emile's first steps towards moral knowledge:

> Voulez-vous donc exciter et nourrir dans le coeur d'un jeune homme les premiers mouvements de la sensibilité naissante et tourner son caractère vers la bienfaisance et vers la bonté? n'allez point faire germer en lui l'orgueil, la vanité, l'envie par la trompeuse image du bonheur des hommes; n'exposez point d'abord à ses yeux la pompe des Cours.

On the contrary, Emile is to be exposed to a vision of humanity reduced to its barest essentials, which is nothing other than the vision which Rousseau's lack of a condition enabled him to see:

Les hommes ne sont naturellement ni Rois, ni Grands, ni Courtisans, ni riches. Tous sont nés nus et pauvres, tous sujets aux misères de la vie, aux chagrins, aux maux, aux besoins, aux douleurs de toute espèce; enfin tous sont condamnés à la mort. Voilà ce qui est vraiment de l'homme; voilà de quoi nul mortel n'est exempt. Commencez donc par étudier de la nature humaine ce qui en est le plus inséparable, ce qui constitue le mieux l'humanité. (*O.C.*, 4, p. 504)

Displacement, non-belonging, the rejection of rank, are the first step to seeing humanity for what it is, and, for the educationalist, allowing the young to see it.

It is clear, of course, that for Rousseau the rejection of hierarchy as a mode of perception of humanity is inseparable from a radical critique of society: Clarens, as we know, represents a limit to his egalitarianism, but it remains the case that the movement which detects humanity in the lowest common social denominator is also the foundation of a theory of social and political legitimacy based on the people: 'C'est le peuple qui compose le genre humain; ce qui n'est pas le peuple est si peu de chose que ce n'est pas la peine de le compter' he writes a few pages later in Book IV of *Emile* (*O.C.*, 4, p. 509). His hatred for the rich, expressed so forcibly in the fourth *Lettre à Malesherbes*, has its counterpart in his conviction of the goodness of the people, their fidelity to the voice of nature. In the Second *Discours*, Rousseau proclaims that Pity is (or, perhaps more accurately, could be) the basis of society, the voice of nature which has only been silenced by the corrupt state of present social organisation. He imagines the *philosophe*, whose abstract rationalisations enable him to resist the call to aid his suffering fellows, and contrasts this with the spontaneous charity of the people:

On peut impunément égorger son [the philosopher's] semblable sous sa fenêtre; il n'a qu'à mettre ses mains sur ses oreilles et s'argumenter un peu, pour empêcher la Nature qui se révolte en lui, de l'identifier avec celui qu'on assassine. L'homme sauvage n'a point cet admirable talent; et faute de sagesse ou de raison, on le voit toujours se livrer étourdiment au premier sentiment de l'Humanité. Dans les Emeutes, dans les querelles des Rues, la Populace s'assemble, l'homme prudent s'éloigne: c'est la Canaille, ce sont les femmes des Halles, qui séparent les combattants, et qui empêchent les honnêtes gens de s'entr'égorger. (*O.C.*, 3, p. 156)

Whatever limitations should be placed on Rousseau's egalitarianism, for instance in the light of the social vision of Clarens, it is true that his rejection of hierarchy does not lead to any facile or complacent aestheticisation of the poor. In the letter quoted a little earlier, Julie also advises Saint-Preux:

C'est dans les appartements dorés qu'un écolier va prendre les airs du monde; mais le sage en apprend les mystères dans la chaumière du pauvre. C'est là qu'on voit sensiblement les obscures manoeuvres du vice, qu'il couvre de paroles fardées au milieu d'un cercle. (*O.C.*, 2, p. 303)

Similarly, Rousseau writes in *Emile*, just after the passage already quoted in which he argues that the people is everything, that 'le peuple se montre tel qu'il est, et n'est pas aimable; mais il faut bien que les gens du monde se déguisent; s'ils se montraient tels qu'ils sont, ils feraient horreur' (*O.C.*, 4, p. 509). No easy sentimentalisation here, no urge to surround the poor with an aura of picturesque sanctity. They are not uniformly good, and even less charming, but they are at least authentic and true.

What of Rousseau's treatment of pity, *bienfaisance*, alms-giving? A large part of the Book IV of *Emile*, up to the *Profession de foi du vicaire savoyard*, is devoted to Emile's education in pity and *bienfaisance*, evidently conceived as key elements in the development of the adolescent's 'reason and passions', and as crucial in the building of a bridge between the individual and the society in which he must live. Rousseau repeats here what he had already affirmed in the Second *Discours*, that pity is a natural movement of the human mind in the face of the suffering of fellow human beings. The development of conscience is the extension into the 'ordre moral' of 'affections primitives' provoked by the sight of suffering, and it is the educationalist's job to guide this development. Already in Book II, Rousseau had insisted that 'avant d'oser entreprendre de former un homme, il faut s'être fait homme soi-même'; the tutor is advised:

Déclarez-vous hautement le protecteur des malheureux. Soyez juste, humain, bienfaisant. Ne faites pas seulement l'aumône, faites la charité; les oeuvres de miséricorde soulagent plus de maux que l'argent; aimez les autres et ils vous aimeront; servez-les et ils vous serviront; soyez leur frère et ils seront vos enfants. (*O.C.*, 4, pp. 325–6)

Now, in Book IV, Emile is to be introduced to charity in his own right. As the imagination develops, the young man is able to comprehend the sufferings of others: 'C'est alors que le triste tableau de l'humanité souffrante doit porter à son coeur le premier attendrissement qu'il ait jamais éprouvé.' Since the child is incapable of identification with others before the development of the imagination – the standard sensationalist analysis – and since Emile has not been taught the social graces, that is to say the external signs of emotions which society considers to be appropriate in set circumstances, 'la même insensibilité qu'il a dans le coeur est aussi dans ses manières'. The first task of the tutor will be to expose him to objects which will move him internally and develop his conscience. The first maxim which Rousseau offers to guide this process is a revealing one:

Il n'est pas dans le coeur humain de se mettre à la place des gens qui sont plus heureux que nous, mais seulement de ceux qui sont plus à plaindre.

This is of course perfectly consonant with sentimentalism's predilection for the victim, and for downward social displacement in the sentimentalising process: it is the spectacle of misfortune which is crucial for the formation of the moral sense. The pupil must also be made aware that the misfortune which is depicted before his eyes is not simply the misfortune of others, but may easily befall him one day: he must be given an awareness of the fragility of fortune. 'Apprenez-lui à ne compter ni sur la naissance, ni sur la santé, ni sur les richesses, montrez-lui toutes les vicissitudes de la fortune, cherchez-lui les exemples toujours trop fréquents de gens qui d'un état plus élevé sont tombés au-dessous de ces malheureux.' Finally, Rousseau insists that the pupil must be taught to value all human beings equally, independently of class: otherwise, the sufferings of the poor will leave him unmoved, and only the downfall of the great will have the power to affect him.

En un mot, apprenez à votre élève à aimer tous les hommes et même ceux qui les déprisent; faites en sorte qu'il ne se place dans aucune classe, mais qu'il se retrouve dans toutes: parlez devant lui du genre humain avec attendrissement, avec pitié même, mais jamais avec mépris. Homme, ne déshonore point l'homme. (*O.C.*, 4, pp. 504–10)

Within this framework, the pupil is to be exposed to spectacles of suffering, but only according to a strictly controlled method. 'Il ne s'agit pas de faire de votre élève un garde-malade, un frère de la charité, d'affliger ses regards par des objets continuels de douleurs et de souffrances, de le promener d'infirme en infirme, d'hôpital en hôpital', for, as with doctors and priests, excessive exposure to suffering only hardens the heart. 'Un seul objet bien choisi, et montré dans un jour convenable, lui donnera pour un mois d'attendrissement et de réflexion', and it is this internal reworking of the scene – 'le retour sur ce qu'il a vu' – which is important in the educational process. That may be taken as a very accurate formulation of the project of the sentimental text, as it re-enacts for the reader a scene of suffering and charity. (*O.C.*, 4, p. 517)

Rousseau is not blind to the dangers of an excessive sentimental education. Towards the end of this long development, he evokes the work of justice and charity which the pupil will undertake:

Combien d'opprimés qu'on n'eut jamais écoutés obtiendront justice quand il la demandera pour eux avec cette intrépide fermeté que donne l'exercice de la vertu; quand il forcera les portes des grands et des riches; quand il ira, s'il le faut, jusqu'aux pieds du trône faire entendre la voix des infortunés à qui tous les abords sont fermés par leur misère, et que la crainte d'être punis des maux qu'on leur fait empêche même d'oser s'en plaindre.

But then, embarrassed by the flight of fancy, he satirises his own discourse:

Mais ferons-nous d'Emile un chevalier errant, un redresseur de torts, un Paladin? Ira-t-il s'ingérer dans les affaires publiques, faire le sage et le défenseur des lois chez les grands, chez les magistrats, chez le Prince, faire le solliciteur chez les juges et l'avocat dans les tribunaux? Je ne sais rien de tout cela.

Emile will possess a sense of proportion to know what lies beyond his power and grasp, and to moderate his desire to intervene in favour of all the victims of the earth. The other restriction which Rousseau places on this education in the ways of pity is the requirement for a sense of justice which will mitigate the excesses of a purely affective sense of pain at the sufferings of others. As Emile's knowledge of the world grows, pity will become generalised into justice, a virtue which considers the whole of humanity, and not just the victim who is nearest to hand.

Il faut par raison, et par amour pour nous, avoir pitié de notre espèce encore plus que de notre prochain, et c'est une très grande cruauté envers les hommes que la pitié pour les méchants. (*O.C.*, 4, pp. 544–8)

Pity, then, plays an important role in Emile's moral development: the relation between the growing social subject and the surrounding society is envisaged to a considerable extent through the cognition, internalisation and transformation of the spectacle of suffering humanity. This is consistent with what Rousseau tells us, for instance in the Second *Discours*, about the crucial role of pity as the natural foundation of the just social order. Rousseau is, however, aware of the dangers of sensibility: the need to educate Emile for action is articulated on the uselessness of 'cette pitié stérile et cruelle qui se contente de plaindre les maux qu'elle peut guérir'.

As Jean Starobinski has shown,[36] the nature and meaning of the act of giving preoccupied Rousseau, and he analyses it, most notably, in the sixth and ninth *Rêveries*, as well as in the fifth part of *La Nouvelle Héloïse*. In letter 5,2, Saint-Preux recounts his disagreement with Julie over the question of giving alms to beggars. Saint-Preux's line is without a doubt the standard enlightened attitude:

Je lui représentai que ce n'était pas seulement un bien jeté à pure perte, et dont on privait ainsi le vrai pauvre; mais que cet usage contribuait à multiplier les gueux et les vagabonds qui se plaisent à ce lâche métier, et, se rendant à la charge de la société, la privent encore du travail qu'ils y pourraient faire.

Julie's reply explicitly avoids deciding on the merits or demerits of the philosophical denunciation of alms-giving; but it is unambiguous in its support for the practice. As in the second *Discours*, the *philosophes* are seen as seeking to 'étouffer dans le coeur la pitié naturelle et l'exercer à l'insensibilité'. While admitting that it is 'au Souverain de faire en sorte qu'il n'y ait point de mendiants', she gives because she cannot 'sans une inexcusable dureté leur refuser le faible secours qu'ils me demandent'. She cannot run the risk that the person she refuses is 'cet honnête homme prêt à périr de misère', and giving is a small sign that one shares their hardship, 'une sorte de salutation qu'on leur rend'. It is also a way of 'rendre honneur à l'humanité souffrante ou à son image, et de ne point s'endurcir le coeur à l'aspect de ses misères'. Julie's arguments are not couched in terms of social utility: she argues at the level of psychological and moral hygiene, and her arguments are by no means devoid of Christian echoes, for instance when she refers to beggars as 'mes frères' (*O.C.*, 2, pp. 538–40). Julie's attitude stands in isolation from the standard economic analysis: it may be the business of the state to 'extirpate' begging, but in the meantime, she will continue to give to those people who present themselves at her door. This reproduces the structure suggested by Starobinski: a split between, on the one hand, institutionalised, state responses to the problem of poverty, and, on the other, individual charity undertaken for reasons which may be either aesthetic or moral:

Ce qui avait passé par des formes d'acte donateur désormais déconsidérées comme anciennes et perverses devient l'affaire soit de la *subjectivité individuelle* autonome, soit de la *collectivité*, tenue pour responsable à l'égard du concept générique de *société* ou d'*humanité*, – à l'égard, par conséquent, de sa propre cohésion et de son devenir historique.[37]

Starobinski's very suggestive analysis is based primarily on the sixth and ninth *Rêveries*. The ninth *Rêverie* contrasts two scenes: the first takes place at La Muette, and involves Jean-Jacques and Thérèse paying for a game of *oublies* for a party of young girls out with their governess; the second takes place at a party given by Monsieur and Madame d'Epinay at La

Chevrette, where fistfuls of spice buns are thrown to a crowd of peasants, apparently for the pleasure of seeing the comic battle for possession which results. Jean-Jacques compares the innocence of the first form of giving with the manipulatory nature of the second:

quelle sorte de plaisir pouvait-on prendre à voir des troupeaux d'hommes avilis par la misère, s'entasser, s'étouffer, s'estropier brutalement, pour s'arracher avidement quelques morceaux de pain d'épice foulés aux pieds et couverts de boue?

The first form of giving, on the other hand, seems to Jean-Jacques to have no such manipulatory characteristics. He minimises the possibility that the delight which the scene caused him was enhanced by the fact that he was the author of the girls' joy: rather than being attributable to a 'sentiment de bienfaisance', it was due to 'le plaisir de voir des visages contents. Cet aspect a pour moi un charme qui bien qu'il pénètre jusqu'à mon coeur semble être uniquement de sensation.' He compares this to the pleasure afforded by the sight of happy faces at a rural festival. But then he goes on to question the notion of 'sensation': no, the pleasure afforded by happy faces is not purely sensational, it partakes too of the moral, for

ce même aspect au lieu de me flatter, de me plaire, peut me déchirer de douleur et d'indignation quand je sais que ces signes de plaisir et de joie sur les visages des méchants ne sont que des marques que leur malignité est satisfaite. La joie innocente est la seule dont les signes flattent mon coeur. (*O.C.*, 1, pp. 1090–4)

In other words, it is a matter of *signs*: an affective transaction is taking place, in which that which passes on the face of the receiver is a faithful expression of the inner state, and in that sense, the act of giving is, for Rousseau, a form of communication with a fellow human. The touching account, at the end of the ninth *Rêverie*, of not daring to offer money to a war veteran, stands as proof of the communicative meaning of the act of giving for Jean-Jacques.

Clarens, however, adds a further dimension to our understanding of the act of giving in Rousseau's thought, and brings us back to the denunciatory analyses of Zola and Marx. Letter

5,2 recounts Julie's model treatment of a representative of the lower orders. Often, Wolmar 'rencontre dans ses tournées quelque bon Vieillard dont le sens et la raison le frappent'. The old man is brought home, treated to dinner, after which Julie

passe [...] dans sa chambre, et en rapporte un petit présent de quelque nippe convenable à la femme ou aux filles du vieux bonhomme. Elle le lui fait offrir par les enfants, et réciproquement il rend aux enfants quelque don simple et de leur goût dont elle l'a secrètement chargé pour eux.

The full meaning of the invitation to dinner, and of the gifts exchanged, becomes clear when the old man returns to his *chaumière*. He recounts his evening, passes on the gift from the masters, and the whole household bathes in the honour which has been paid to its head.

Tous bénissent de concert cette famille illustre et généreuse qui donne exemple aux grands et refuge aux petits, qui ne dédaigne point le pauvre et rend honneur aux cheveux blancs. Voilà l'encens qui plaît aux âmes bienfaisantes. (*O.C.*, 2, pp. 555–6)

Here, the act of giving serves very clearly as a form of discourse directed by the masters at the lower orders. The sentimental relation naturalises and masks a hierarchical one; as Starobinski puts it, 'l'essence de l'égalité consiste dans le sentiment d'être égal'.

This use of the act of giving is entirely consistent with the overall project of social management represented by the fictional world of Clarens. Wolmar rules from the centre, all-seeing but unseen. Master and mistress direct the estate in such a way that the workings of an economic and social system appear to be the workings of nature itself. Relations between employer and employee, between dominator and dominated, are cemented by the sentimental relation, by the act of giving as an act of communication. Wolmar, like God in his universe, 'ne songe pas à amplifier ses possessions, mais à les rendre véritablement siennes par les relations les plus parfaites et la direction la mieux entendue'. Thus,

Son Domestique lui était étranger; il en fait son bien, son enfant, il se l'approprie. Il n'avait droit que sur les actions, il s'en donne encore sur les volontés. Il n'était maître qu'à prix d'argent, il le devient par l'empire sacré de l'estime et des bienfaits. (*O.C.*, 2, p. 467)

As a result of such a strategy, the servants 'pensent vouloir tout ce qu'on les oblige de faire', and 'louent Dieu dans leur simplicité d'avoir mis des riches sur la terre pour le bonheur de ceux qui les servent et pour le soulagement des pauvres' (*O.C.*, 2, p. 460). The act of giving is entirely consonant with the dream of social immobilism which Clarens represents: a society in which each individual is happy to accept his or her place, and which is therefore spared the frenetic race after promotion and success which is the mark of the meritocratic society whose birth Rousseau witnessed.

In sum, it would appear that Rousseau's thought operates within the same tension as the sentimental model which I have defined: at one end, the inclusion of the excluded, and radical definition of humanity as a hierarchy-transcending category; at the other, a discursive manipulation of the marginal, in which they become counters in the bourgeoisie's claims to enlightened domination. Robert Mauzi's description of the aestheticisation of poverty states the case against the sentimental manipulation in the strongest terms:

Le double jeu de la pensée bourgeoise est ici manifeste. Elle se sert des humbles contre les grands, mais ce n'est pas pour leur remettre les fruits de la victoire, puisque le peuple est a priori déclaré heureux. La tactique consiste à condamner les grands, au nom de l'idéal moral que le peuple est censé incarner, puis à intercepter les bienfaits de l'opération. Bien loin de modifier la condition des humbles, il faut les fixer dans leur essence, les enfermer dans le halo magique de la frugalité heureuse. Ils sont trop précieux, tels qu'ils sont, comme justification mythique des revendications bourgeoises.[38]

If Mauzi's analysis comes close to a conspiracy theory, it has the merit of stating clearly what is at stake politically in sentimentalism. Can the contradictions be reconciled? Is it possible, or indeed desirable, to get sentimentalism off the hook? It seems to me that Mauzi's denunciation must stand, but that the whole tension must be understood in the wider framework of the history of ideas.

I argue in chapter 2 that sentimentalism stands in a close relationship to the dialectically related notions of individualism and universalism as propounded and practised by the French Revolution. The Declaration of Human Rights, the legal framework which emerges from the Revolution and the Napoleonic period, go about the task of constituting a uniform, national space by thinking of all men and women, and all human situations, as ultimately interchangeable. The individual is, in this project, always perceived as a case of the general, the abstract, the universal. The sentimental text is part of the constitution of this world-view. In it, the individual victim is always called upon to signify suffering humanity in general, just as the general notion of humanity, together with concomitant terms such as virtue, *bienfaisance*, etc., are present as the horizon against which individual events and acts are to be understood.

Now, this interdependency of individual and universal is both a strength and a weakness. On the one hand, the abstraction which considers individuals as equal and interchangeable is directly related to one of the fundamental contradictions of the Revolution. If the Revolution, in its opening phase at least, claims to act in the name of the Tiers Etat, that term masks as much as it proclaims: behind a universal notion, a particular class is at work. Indeed, the universal individualism of which I am speaking facilitates certain forms of social domination, best understood through the example of employment and trade union legislation. The Revolution disbands the old trade corporations, and the Le Chapelier law of 1791 bans trade union activity and organises an economic framework based on liberalism. In this case, the consequence of an abstract definition of universally interchangeable individuality is that employer and employee are falsely constituted as equal partners, and the relationship of domination and dependency which exists at the economic level is rendered invisible.

On the other hand, the strength of Revolutionary universalism lies in the historically demonstrable fact that a message of liberation has continued to reverberate across the continents and across the intervening years, appealing to social groups far wider than the original beneficiaries of the Revolution.[39] In the light of this, denunciations of the bourgeois revolution as *only* a bourgeois revolution are insufficient, as is a rejection of sentimentalism as being irremediably tainted by a discourse of manipulation. The democratic project of the eighteenth century and the will to power of a certain class may share a common root, but that should not prevent us from hearing what that project has to say to us today.

CHAPTER 4

Sentimentalism in the rhetoric of the Revolution

The French Revolution has made a number of somewhat fleeting appearances in these pages, and it is essential now to draw the different threads together, and to propose a deeper and more nuanced analysis. What has been said so far? On the one hand, the Revolution appears as a butt to the sentimental vision: for both Gorjy and Vernes, although in different ways, sentimentalism becomes enmeshed with a hostile reaction to the perceived excesses of the Revolution, notably the Terror. Something similar will be seen in chapter 6: the turmoil of the 1790s is probably a decisive factor in Mme de Staël's espousal of pity as a political value fundamental to liberalism. On the other hand, in the previous chapter, I looked at two aspects of the Revolution: firstly, I examined its attitudes, discourse and action in the area of poverty and mendicity, culminating in the decrees of floréal Year 2 which established the *livre de bienfaisance nationale* and the *fête du Malheur*; and I concluded, at a much higher level of generalisation and abstraction, that sentimentalism belongs to the Revolutionary project by virtue of the manner in which it envisages the relationship between the individual and the universal.[1]

I would like, firstly, to develop this last point in just a little more detail. Individual and universal are the twin poles of meaning in the sentimental text: in *this* weeping child, *this* grieving mother, *this* father repenting his cruelty to his daughter, we are encouraged to read the sufferings of *humanity* as a whole, just as the individual act of generosity towards the victim figures the universal virtues of *bienfaisance* and *sensibilité*. Moreover, the reaction of an observer to the sufferings of the individual victim functions as a sign, an indication, a proof of the existence of that universal category, for it is humanity, sensibility which are perceived as the bridge between the two individuals; they are the condition of a humane social order. In this sense, we are dealing with an immanent moral system: the principles by which society must live are none the less universal for being situated within the lived experience of each individual: on the contrary, it is that which makes them universally generalisable, the essential and irreducible humanity of each individual, whatever his or her social position, being the guarantee of this infinite mirroring and extension. It is here that the internal–external axis can be seen to relate to the individual–universal one. In rendering visible and therefore communicable the lived moral experience of the subject, the sentimental text in fact takes the first step towards a shared system of immanent values: from the tears of a child can be constructed a moral system, for those tears are comparable to those of the perceiving subject, are understandable in terms of that subject's own inner experience. The social and moral space is an outgrowth from, and penetrates into, the inner experience of each individual.

I propose now to turn to a series of Revolutionary texts, with a double view. In the first part, I shall examine some texts from the early period of the Revolution, in order to show how the language of sentimentalism is used, practically, in articulating the claims of the excluded. After that, using Marat as a transitional figure (*l'ami du peuple* exploited again), I want to extend the analysis to the problematic period of 1793–4, showing how the language of sentimentalism finds a place within the dissensions and internal rifts which mark that crucial period.

The common characteristic of this first set of texts, belonging to the first phase of the Revolution before the appearance of serious internal conflict, is that in them, the sentimental denunciation of injustice is not complicated by the discursive strategies of party politics or the life and death struggles of 1794. These texts are about the inclusion in the field of humanity of the excluded, they constitute an appeal in favour of a marginal social group whose claims have not hitherto been heard.

The abbé Grégoire's *Motion en faveur des juifs* is the text of a speech to the National Assembly calling for full citizenship and freedom of worship for the Jews. The *Motion* follows his *Essais sur la régénération physique, politique et morale des juifs* of 1788. It is above all the opening phase of Grégoire's argument which is marked by a sentimental accent, as though the audience were to be won over by an appeal to the basic notion of injustice before the arsenal of historical and legal arguments is brought into play. Grégoire thus pictures the penury imposed on the Jew by the special tax régime, in the following terms:

> Dans son triste galetas le pauvre Israélite étouffant les soupirs d'une âme consternée, et condamné à vivre, pourrait invoquer la mort avec plus de sincérité que le bûcheron harassé [...] Communément bon père, il retranche à ses enfants avec serrement de coeur quelques bouchées d'une chétive nourriture, recout quelques lambeaux de plus à son vêtement délabré, économise quelques deniers de misère pour fournir à l'avidité des harpies qui mangeraient même sa table.[2]

The Jews are a people excluded from the community and from history: 'Quand rendrons-nous à l'humanité ce peuple outragé par nos persécutions, [...] sans rang dans la société, ne voyant autour de soi que l'opprobre, et traînant partout des fers baignés de ses larmes?' (p. 12) Returning to the language of sentiment in a concluding appeal, Grégoire combines an explicitly Christian notion of *charité* with the secular notion of sensibility; here, the reaction of the perceiving subject to the spectacle of the injustices inflicted on the Jews is hypostatised in typical fashion, mobilising the self-image of the listener as a man of feeling:

> voilà à notre porte les rejetons de ce Peuple antique, des frères désolés, à la vue desquels on ne peut se défendre d'un déchirement de coeur [...] Tant qu'ils seront esclaves de nos préjugés et victimes de notre haine, ne vantons pas notre sensibilité [...] Telle est leur déplorable situation, que pour n'en être pas profondément affecté, il faut avoir oublié qu'ils sont hommes, ou avoir soi-même cessé de l'être. (pp. 43–4)

Another text by Grégoire, his *Lettre aux philanthropes, sur les malheurs, les droits et les réclamations des Gens de couleur de Saint-Domingue, et des autres îles françaises de l'Amérique* (1790), concerns the mixed-blood people of the colonies. If the black slaves must be led only gradually to freedom, those of mixed race are 'le support des colons', and their claim must therefore be satisfied immediately. The precise object of Grégoire's protest is the decree of 12 October 1790, which envisaged the freedom of the *mulâtres* only upon consent of the colonists. Comparing this injustice unfavourably with St Bartholomew's Day, he argues that the decree is contrary to the principles upheld by the National Assembly, which grant all men 'le patrimoine in-aliénable de la liberté', and contrary to humanity: 'Si votre âme n'est pas fermée à la pitié, écoutez les sanglots de quarante mille malheureux dont les droits sont inconcussibles, dont les maux sont incontestables.' And he refers to the reaction of a deputation of mixed blood people who were present in the National Assembly when the decree of 12 October 1790 was pronounced:

J'ai vu des infortunés de cette classe à la galerie, le jour où l'on prononça leur nullité civile, leur réprobation politique; ils fondirent en larmes, quand ils ouïrent ce préambule de décret, qui laisse des millions de victimes sous le glaive des sacrificateurs! Et l'on ose parler de justice, de religion, de charité![3]

A similar rhetoric can be found in texts defending the cause of the slaves: Mirabeau, who was chosen by the *Société des amis des noirs* (founded in 1788 by Brissot, Clavière and others) to be their spokesman in the debates in the National Assembly in early 1790, had a model of a slave ship built, which he was in the habit of using in his demonstrations of the inhumanity of the trade. Such an aid is perfectly consonant with sentimental-ism's predilection for the visual: it provides speaker and audi-ence with a common *spectacle* upon which a reaction can be based:

Voyez le modèle d'un navire chargé de ces infortunés, et tâchez de ne pas détourner vos regards. Comme ils sont entassés les uns sur les autres! [...] Voyez comment le vaisseau qui roule les meurtrit, les mutile, les brise l'un contre l'autre, les déchire par leurs propres chaînes et présente mille supplices dans un seul tableau.[4]

Thomas Clarkson, the British campaigner against slavery, came to Paris soon after 14 July 1789 to support the efforts of the French society; in a letter to Mirabeau he describes the seizure of slaves in their country of origin:

La mère qui va de nuit puiser de l'eau pour ses enfants et qui est emportée par les voleurs aux aguets; la famille qui est réveillée par des cris occasionnés par le feu et par l'épée, et qui est mise aux fers et ensuite transportée vers des régions inconnues.[5]

Brissot's *Mémoire sur les noirs* (1789) describes what he learned about slavery and its abolition from his journey to America, where, particularly in Quaker Pennsylvania, experience proved that abolition, as well as being desirable on humanitarian grounds, was economically justified, since the free man is infinitely more motivated to work than the slave. These economic and social arguments form the heart of Brissot's case, with the language of sentimental indignation being relegated to the background. The passages which contrast the lax husbandry of the southern states with the tidy productivity of Pennsylvania do however resort to idealised pictures of family harmony against a natural backdrop: the well-cultivated fields, the good clothes of the freed slaves, the loghouse in which they live, their numerous children 'les font remarquer des Européens voyageurs, et l'oeil du Philosophe se plaît à considérer ces habitations où la tyrannie ne fait point verser de pleurs'.[6] Moreover, not all is perfect even in Pennsylvania: Brissot argues for the reform of the original Act of 1780, which does not allow for the retroactive freeing of those who were slaves before the Act, and here the tone begins to rise:

Quoi! L'enfant d'un Nègre esclave en Pennsylvanie peut espérer de jouir un jour de la liberté [...] Et le malheureux père est à jamais privé de la liberté! – Son fils qui n'a pas comme lui senti la douleur, le désespoir d'être enlevé à sa Patrie, à sa famille, à tout ce qu'il y a de plus cher pour l'homme, son fils qui n'a pas été déchiré par ces tourments si communs avant la révolution actuelle, son fils est favorisé par la loi! Et cette loi partiale condamne le père à être infortuné toute sa vie! – Non, cette injustice ne peut souiller long-temps le code des lois, dans un pays où la raison et l'humanité se font entendre. (pp. 21–2)

Olympe de Gouges was also committed to the anti-slavery campaign, and her play *L'Esclavage des Nègres, ou l'Heureux Naufrage* given at the Théâtre de la Nation in December 1789, is a sentimental tale serving a political cause. Zamore and Mirza, black slaves, are lovers. Zamore has murdered a white man who tried to take Mirza away from him, and they flee to a desert island, where they save some French people whose ship has been wrecked in a storm. Zamore and Mirza are caught, taken back to the colony, and sentenced to death as an example to others, and not even the pleas of those whom Zamore and Mirza saved from the seas can temper the severity of the law. At the last moment, the wife of one of those saved by Zamore comes to ask the governor for clemency; the governor recognises a daughter born in France of a clandestine marriage, and the tears of this long-lost daughter finally swing the balance in favour of humanity: Zamore and Mirza are pardoned and marry.[7]

The pro-slavery lobby did not miss the fact that the language of sentiment was being enlisted against them. The *Journal politique et national* scoffed at the anti-slavery campaign in the following terms:

Il est bien extraordinaire que des [...] géomètres qui n'ont jamais rien aimé, tels que MM Duport et Condorcet, veuillent nous persuader qu'ils ont calculé les larmes des Nègres et que leur sort les empêche de fermer l'oeil. Est-ce qu'en politique on parle de sensibilité? [...] Gardons nos larmes pour nous.[8]

Similarly, in a letter to the *Journal de Paris* on 28 December 1789, a Monsieur Mosneron de Launay argued that it was 'inutile de s'attendrir sur des individus qui ne connaissent pas le bien que vous leur offrez', while, in the very act of reforming the slave trade, the anti-slavery lobby would cause untold damage to the domestic economy and consequent hardship to the people of France.[9] Charity begins at home.

Olympe de Gouges's sentimental pen was also used in other causes. Arguing in 1789 for a 'caisse patriotique' to alleviate the suffering of the rural poor, she describes the countryside deserted, the peasants eating food fit only for pigs; 'le peuple ne demande que du pain: il veut même l'acheter à la sueur de son front, mais qu'il puisse au moins le manger sans l'arroser à la sueur de ses larmes'.[10] And her *Le Couvent, ou les Voeux forcés*, produced in October 1790 in a climate of anticlericalism, takes up the old sentimental theme in the defence of the freedom of the heart against the depredations of monasticism and tyrannical parents: 'Songez, declares a good priest, que le droit de se choisir librement une place dans la société appartient, par la nature, à tout être pensant, et que le premier de tous les devoirs est d'être utile.'[11]

My last example will be Lequinio's *Les Préjugés détruits*. Jean-Marie Lequinio is a curious figure. A Breton landowner and Montagnard deputy, he was an ardent dechristianiser, and when he was despatched to the West of France by the Comité de Salut Public in autumn 1793, such was his excessive anti-clerical zeal that he had to be called to order by the committee. Dominique Godineau points out that he stands practically alone among male writers of his time in having a perspective on feminism marked by a notion of male domination and 'lutte des sexes'.[12] His writing is particularly turgid; reading him, one has the sensation, as with some other sentimental writers, that the thinking subject is caught up in the discourse, which begins to take on a life of its own and to dictate the positions which the writer will take up. The extended 'Dédicace' is addressed to the various categories of readers who should heed his message: 'Venez ... venez ...' Among these groups are the

simples habitants des hameaux, [...] vous qui, chez toutes les nations, fûtes asservis par ceux que vous alimentiez de vos sueurs et de vos peines; [...] vous dont la vie laborieuse et frugale force toutes les nations à l'estime, et qui jusques ici fûtes négligés par tous les peuples, abandonnés par les rois, et pressurés par mille tyrans; vous que ces injustes oppresseurs voudraient couvrir encore du manteau de l'ignorance et des superstitions sur lesquelles ils établirent le despotisme que vous osez à peine secouer.[13]

'Le sexe aimable' should also heed him: 'enchaîné jusqu'à ce jour à tous les torts de vos époux', it is up to them to break the force of prejudice in their own minds, 'vous dépouiller des fantômes dont votre imagination se remplit', for, in an analysis which recurs more than once in Lequinio's book, and which marks a significant break with sentimentalism, liberation will come from the oppressed subject understanding that his or her oppression is at least partly the product of his/her own consent, and that the first stage in its destruction is to imagine oneself as a free individual. In this, Lequinio seems to me to be closer to Marat than to the moderate constitutionalists of the opening years of the Revolution. Thus, speaking of the equality of the poor, Lequinio writes, in a sentence which seems to echo a sentimental commonplace, that 'ce n'est ni dans les meubles, ni dans les habits qu'elle peut consister, c'est dans le coeur'; but he immediately adds 'et tel est l'égal d'autrui, sitôt qu'il ose s'estimer autant' (pp. 99–100). What is more, this independence of mind will be encouraged in the poor by the awareness that the rich, as the sentimentalists have always maintained, depend on the poor: but Lequinio takes the argument a significant stage further, encouraging the poor to draw active consequences from that dependence, and to threaten to withdraw their services. But Lequinio is not consistent: having sketched out this quite radical position, he can happily go on, in the chapter on 'les domestiques', to praise the example of the enlightened employer, 'cet agriculteur, ce bon père de famille' who eats at the same table as his servants, giving them his own virtue as an example to follow and treating them 'en égaux, en frères'. In a concluding phrase which takes us straight back to the model of Clarens, Lequinio writes that 'je dois [...] à mon serviteur, outre le prix de l'échange, un sentiment de reconnaissance qui ne peut être le même envers tant d'autres individus qui ne me vendent ou ne me louent que des fadaises' (pp. 118–19). The inequality of the transaction, in economic terms, is compensated by a charge of feeling flowing from the employer to the employee; equality is feeling free, in another, much more conservative sense.

Inevitably, the illusion of a univocal, unproblematic Revolution is shattered: a shift of point of view from sentimentalising to sentimentalised subject is enough to remind us that relations of social domination can be masked in the process of sentimentalisation. It is to Marat, the people's friend, the indefatigable denouncer of domination, that I propose to turn now: what place does sentimentalism occupy in his political rhetoric?

Charlotte Corday gained admittance to Marat's apartment, after two failed attempts, with the statement: 'Je suis persécutée pour la cause de la liberté; je suis malheureuse, il suffit que je le sois pour avoir droit à votre protection.' During the trial, Fouquier-Tinville picked up on this phrase: 'Comment avez-vous pu regarder Marat comme un monstre, lui qui ne vous a laissé introduire chez lui que par un acte d'humanité; parce que vous lui aviez écrit que vous étiez persécutée?', and Corday replied 'Qu'importe s'il se montre humain envers moi, si c'est un monstre envers les autres?'[14] Whatever the logic of her reply, Corday's strategy was well chosen, for it plays upon one of the functions which Marat fulfilled during his political career in the Revolution, that of a kind of advice centre for the people. Walter tells us that the offices of his newspapers were besieged by people seeking redress for their wrongs, and that their complaints sometimes found their way into the pages of Marat's newspapers.[15] One such episode, published in *L'Ami du peuple*, 5 January 1790, is interesting because it reproduces one of the classic scenes of sentimental literature in the eighteenth century: the chance meeting with the deserving subject, as illustrated by Vernes. Having bewailed the fact that 'soir et matin le pauvre ami du peuple est assailli par une foule d'infortunés et d'opprimés qui implorent son secours', the author goes on to recount the arrival of a certain 'soeur Catherine' accompanied by an older woman. The two are practically obliged to force the door in order to gain access, but then the established form takes over. First, outward description of the subject: 'Son air ouvert et naif, le ton de douleur qui animait sa voix et son ingénuité qui annonçait une âme simple et honnête, m'inspirèrent de l'intérêt.' The visual signs lead the observer to solicit a narrative, the function of which will be to explain the history behind the present state: 'Je lui demandai

la cause de ses malheurs; elle m'apprit que ...' It is the story of
a nun persecuted by her superiors because of her patriotic
views: the classic opposition to the monastic institution ('ces
tristes demeures, où tant de femmes sensibles sont forcées de
consumer leurs beaux jours') is combined with a new criterion
of virtue and villainy, fidelity to the Revolution being the
dividing line here.[16]

If the echo of sentimentalism is predominantly formal in the
episode of sister Catherine, there is no doubt about Marat's use
of the full vocabulary of sentimentalism in his denunciations of
injustice and tyranny. But, if we take *Les Chaînes de l'esclavage* as
our starting point, it is clear that sentimentalism here has
already undergone at least some of the transformations which
lead to melodrama. The subterfuges and secret mechanisms
whereby tyranny seeks to lead humanity into error, to pervert
natural virtue and counter the attempts of the oppressed to
gain control of their lives – in short, tyranny's unfathomable
will to perpetuate its own reign – is the subject of the book, as
the subtitle makes clear:

Ouvrage destiné à développer les noirs attentats des princes contre les
peuples; les ressorts secrets, les ruses, les menées, les artifices, les coups
d'état qu'ils employent pour détruire la liberté, et les scènes sanglan-
tes qui accompagnent le despotisme.[17]

Marat's language in *Les Chaînes de l'esclavage* is peppered with
the vocabulary of sentimentalism: public representatives must
be men who 'se montrèrent toujours les protecteurs de l'innocence opprimée' (p. 16); he evokes with indignant eloquence the sordid fate of the beggar picked up by the police
('Séjours de désolation où le malheureux, nourri d'aliments
malsains et dégoûtants, couche dans l'ordure, respire un air
infecte, gémit sous le fouet d'un gardien féroce, et où tous les
maux qui affligent l'humanité viennent l'assaillir à la fois'
(p. 337)), and contrasts the harshness of the English prison
régime with the overriding preoccupation of members of
Parliament with the protection of their hunting rights: 'tandis
qu'ils laissent sans pitié leurs malheureux concitoyens gémir
sous le poids de la plus cruelle oppression, et que le peuple

affamé leur demande du pain, ils n'ont pas honte d'employer le temps à renouveler les *lois qui leur assurent le droit de chasse* (p. 338; Marat's italics). Marat's vision, in short, is structured around the opposition between the innocent oppressed and the tyrannical persecutor; but the important transformation is the importance attached to the *intention* of persecution. More than simply an impersonal and anonymous force (chance, history, fortune), persecution is actively willed by tyrants, and therefore the people must be eternally vigilant if they are to triumph over the universal conspirator. Even in a chapter on Ignorance, the notion of intentionality remains. Whereas one Enlightenment vision – illustrated by d'Alembert's *Discours préliminaire* or Condorcet's *Tableau* – defines the forces of darkness and ignorance principally in negative terms, as an absence of their opposite, Marat personifies ignorance, making it an agent of tyrants:

C'est elle qui, tenant le bandeau sur les yeux des peuples, les empêche de connaître leurs droits. [...] C'est elle qui, leur cachant les noirs complots, les sourdes menées, les profonds artifices des princes contre la liberté, leur fait donner dans toutes les embûches, et se prendre perpétuellement aux mêmes pièges. (p. 171)

But if this melodramatisation enhances the activity of the oppressor, it does the same for the victim. Marat is not content to evoke the powerlessness of the people in the face of tyranny: on the contrary, the dynamic of his work is to drive the people to resistance. This, too, leads to certain transformations of the sentimental vision. On poverty, for instance, there is no trace of the aestheticisation which we have seen in Baculard or Vernes: only in the case of nations where 'l'amour de la pauvreté est inspiré par les institutions sociales' (he is thinking of the ancient republics, or of nations where the wealth of the state is confined to its territory and the land is distributed more or less equally among the population) does poverty cease to be a force which 'abat le coeur et le plie à la dépendance' (pp. 27–30). 'Je serai toujours gueux, se dit à lui-même l'homme qui n'a aucune propriété, l'homme foulé d'impôts'.[18] On religion, he is ruthless: all religions 'prêtent la main au despotisme', but Christianity does so more than any other, by encouraging an

attitude of resignation and acceptance which bears a strange
resemblance to the attitude of the sentimental victim:

Sans défiance, sans crainte, sans artifice, sans colère, sans désir de
vengeance, un vrai chrétien est à la discrétion du premier venu.
L'esprit du christianisme est un esprit de paix, de douceur, de charité
[...] *Quand on les frappe sur une joue, ils doivent présenter l'autre* [...]
Quand on les persécute, ils doivent bénir leurs persécuteurs [...]
Toujours résignés, ils souffrent en silence, tendent les mains au ciel,
s'humilient sous la main qui les frappe [...] Comment repouss-
eraient-ils par la force leurs oppresseurs? comment combattraient-ils
les ennemis de la liberté? comment payeraient-ils de leur sang ce
qu'ils doivent à la patrie?[19]

In Marat, the sentimental phase typically gives way to a
discourse of vengeance. Thus, in a *Discours au peuple* of September 1789, he writes: 'O ma patrie, à l'aspect des malheurs qui
t'accablent, et te menacent, mon coeur se fend de douleur, des
larmes de sang coulent de mes yeux', but the sentimental phase
gives way to one of action, in which the remedy to the ills in
question is proposed – in this case, the committees must be
purged of all suspect and dangerous men.[20] The same progression marks his *Supplique de dix-huit millions d'infortunés*, a plea to
the National Assembly for the abolition of the distinction
between active and passive citizenship, published in *L'Ami du
peuple*, 30 June 1790. The poorest section of the nation is the
one which has made the greatest sacrifices for the Revolution,
giving its labour freely while the rich remained hidden in their
'souterrains'. 'Quel sort affreux est le nôtre! Pour nous le Ciel
fut toujours de bronze, et aujourd'hui, comptés pour rien dans
toutes vos dispositions, l'espoir même nous est enlevé; vos
entrailles seraient-elles fermées pour nous?' Various arguments
are used in the development of this piece: the common good,
the unity of the Revolution. But the concluding tone is one of
threat: if, because of our poverty, you deny us our civil rights,
we will take away your wealth; you depend on us,

pour vous mettre à votre place, nous n'avons qu'à rester les bras
croisés. Réduits alors à vous servir de vos mains et à labourer vos
champs, vous redeviendrez nos égaux; mais moins nombreux que
nous, serez-vous sûrs de recueillir les fruits de votre travail?[21]

The similarity with the discourse glimpsed in the work of Lequinio is apparent: but Marat makes systematic this transformation of the language of sentimentalism, exploiting its function as a denunciation of injustice, but adding to it a crucial dimension of action, of revenge, which is nothing else than a *prise de parole* on the part of the sentimentalised subject, a full entering into history. This discourse continued, of course, after Marat's death. In the hours following his assassination, the epitaph which appeared on the door of his home in the rue des Cordeliers read:

> Peuple, Marat est mort. L'amant de la patrie,
> Ton ami, ton soutien, l'espoir de l'affligé,
> Est tombé sous les coups d'une horde flétrie;
> Pleure, mais souviens-toi qu'il doit être vengé![22]

The radicalisation of the Revolution, of which Marat is perhaps the first and most consistent advocate, is the ground for another metamorphosis of sentimental discourse, related to Marat in that it maintains the possibility of associating the discourse of pity with that of revenge, but more complex because it is intricately bound up with the interrelating and conflicting ideologies which mark the Revolution from the fall of the monarchy onwards. This transformation is a complex structure which I propose to unravel step by step; what the structure bears witness to, however, is that the language of sentiment, and crucially the notion of pity, becomes a central symbolic *enjeu* of Revolutionary debate at this point in the Revolution.

The structure can be seen emerging in debates in the Convention during the trial of the king at the very end of 1792. The immediate issue is not the guilt or innocence of Louis, but rather the sentence, and more particularly the method of determining that sentence: one group (the Montagne, more or less) argues for a sentence of death imposed by the Convention, and another group, with certain Girondins prominent in it, argues for a popular consultation, *l'appel au peuple*. It appears that anything falling short of an immediate verdict of death is dismissed as misplaced sensibility by the radical group. Saint-

Just speaks of Louis's 'fausse sensibilité': he 'disait n'être heureux que de leur [his subjects'] bonheur, n'être malheureux que de leurs peines', but this was subterfuge, his actions speak louder than his words, he must die. 'En songeant combien il outragea la vertu par sa fausse sensibilité, on rougira de paraître sensible'.[23] Lequinio speaks also of a 'pitié factice et criminelle frappant à tous les coeurs sensibles pour les égarer, dissolvant la République dans ses bases, et nous reportant au royalisme directement' (p. 873). But it is Robespierre who develops the theme in all its complexity, putting sensibility at the heart of the debate. The first objective of Robespierre's intervention is to adjudicate between the competing claims of pity and rigour.

Je partage, avec le plus faible d'entre vous, toutes les affections particulières qui peuvent l'intéresser au sort de l'accusé. Inexorable, quand il s'agit de calculer d'une manière abstraite le degré de sévérité que la justice des lois doit déployer contre les ennemis de l'humanité, j'ai senti chanceler dans mon coeur la vertu républicaine en présence du coupable humilié devant la puissance souveraine. La haine des tyrans et l'amour de l'humanité ont une racine commune dans le coeur de l'homme juste qui aime son pays; mais la dernière preuve de dévouement que les représentants du peuple doivent à la patrie, c'est d'immoler ces premiers mouvements de la sensibilité naturelle au salut d'un grand peuple et de l'humanité opprimée. La faible sensibilité qui sacrifie l'innocence au crime est une sensibilité cruelle; la clémence qui compose avec la tyrannie est barbare. C'est à l'intérêt supérieur du salut public que je vous rappelle. (p. 876)

Trahard points out that Marat had been arguing as early as 1789 and 1790 against a 'fausse humanité', which prevented the Revolution from taking drastic but necessary measures in the public interest: better to sacrifice a limited number of counter-revolutionaries now than to allow such a false sense of humanity to cause the death of many more innocents.[24] This is indeed Robespierre's argument here: he opposes individual feeling and overarching common good, in a movement which turns sentimental commonplaces on their head by applying adjectives such as 'cruel' and 'barbare' to 'sensibilité' and 'clémence'. This is of course partly a barb aimed at the Gironde, and which did not fail to sting: 'la clémence qui compose avec la tyrannie' is no small accusation. But the whole development is certainly more than that, in the sense that the *salut public*, and the practice of the Terror which it justifies, will have to find discursive ways of coming to terms with the apparent contradiction between the reality of political practice and the humanitarian theory which, even as it wheels out the guillotine, the Revolution continues to proclaim as its philosophical and psychological bedrock.

Secondly, Robespierre is concerned with the correct alignment of the discourse of pity: who is the true victim? As against Louis's claims of humanity and concern for his people, he raises the spectre of the massacre of the Champ-de-Mars, 'le sang des meilleurs citoyens, le sang des femmes et des enfants coula pour lui sur l'autel de la patrie' (p. 876). That very people, including 'la proportion la plus nombreuse, la plus infortunée et la plus pure de la société, celle sur qui pèsent tous les crimes de l'égoïsme et de la tyrannie' – the equivalence through juxtaposition of misfortune and purity should be noted – wants the death of Louis. And this fixing of sentimental categories very firmly on the people is then turned on the Girondins in the form of an attack: the complaints of the people are nothing other than the 'cris douloureux du patriotisme outragé par l'excès de la perfidie', and all the Gironde can do is to interpret these reactions as an act of rebellion. This is proof of their 'fausse sensibilité', for they thereby demonstrate their inability to distinguish the true victim from the false.

Robespierre's speech is a sustained attempt to mobilise the language of sentimentalism for the radical cause. The Girondin case is argued far more sparsely. Salles defends the 'appel au peuple' on very much the same grounds that Mme de Staël will use in her analysis in the *Considérations sur la Révolution française*:[25] the Revolution should do everything in its power to keep the high moral ground, and avoid exposing itself to accusations of inhumanity by its opponents, who will unerringly attempt to 'apitoyer le peuple sur le sort de son ci-devant roi'. This would be pure hypocrisy on their part, since the 'chefs de parti affecteront de le plaindre lorsqu'il ne les gênera plus' (p. 860); but, sincere or not, this strategy would, like

Robespierre's, be an attempt to harness the sentimentalisation of a victim to a political cause. Vergniaud, for his part, turns the language of sentiment back on the Montagne when, on 31 December 1792, he pictures the desolation which will result from the policies of the Montagne, and appeals to the people, the site of virtue and industry, the generators of wealth and civic happiness, but who will be the first to suffer the consequences of their leaders' errors:

> Que deviendriez-vous? quelles seraient vos ressources? quelles mains essuyeraient vos larmes et porteraient des secours à vos familles désespérées?
> Irez-vous trouver ces faux amis, ces perfides flatteurs, qui vous auraient précipités dans l'abîme? [...] Vous leur demanderiez du pain, ils vous diraient: Allez dans les carrières disputer à la terre quelques lambeaux sanglants des victimes que nous avons égorgées: ou voulez-vous du sang? prenez, en voici. Du sang et des cadavres, nous n'avons pas d'autre nourriture à vous offrir.[26]

These exchanges demonstrate the extent to which the language of sentimentalism is a structuring force in some of the key debates of the Revolution. Accusation and counter-accusation, appeal and counter-appeal seek to appropriate legitimacy through the manipulation of a grammar the terms of which are suffering and persecution, virtue and villainy, pity and callousness. It is as though, at the heart of the Revolution's discourse about its own legitimacy, lay a network of images and values which I have defined as those of sentimentalism.

Confirmation and development of what I am saying comes from debates which took place a year later, in the winter of 1793–4. The Girondins have gone, the decree 'Lyon n'est plus' is being put into effect, Desmoulins is publishing *Le Vieux cordelier*, the *loi des suspects* of 17 September 1793 is in operation and the decrees of ventôse will come soon. The problem which constantly exercises the Convention now is the application of the Terror, its justification, its limits, and how to determine when a suspect has been falsely accused and should be released. Such problems arise, for instance, in the case of the repression of the federalist movement in Lyon. On 26 brumaire (16 November) the representatives sent to Lyon, Collot d'Herbois

and Fouché de Nantes, write to the Convention. Their justification of the violence of the repression recalls exactly the
debates of a year previously:

Convaincus qu'il n'y a d'innocent dans cette infâme cité que celui qui
fut opprimé ou chargé de fers par les assassins du peuple, nous
sommes en défiance contre les larmes du repentir; rien ne peut
désarmer notre sévérité [...] Nous devons vous dire, citoyens collè-
gues, l'indulgence est une faiblesse dangereuse.[27]

Their conclusion: the demolition of the city must continue, the
pace be stepped up, 'il faut des moyens plus rapides à l'im-
patience républicaine'. On 30 frimaire (20 December) a petition of the citizens of Ville-Affranchie, as Lyon was now
called, is read out in the Convention. The original decision to
execute the leaders of the conspiracy was an 'arrêté à la fois
juste, ferme et humain', but the Revolutionary committee set
up by Collot d'Herbois to perform summary executions goes
beyond that original act. The 'mitraillades' which figure in
Vernes's *Voyageur sentimental en France sous Robespierre* attract the
particular attention of the petitioners, the treatment reserved
for the expressions of human pity being considered very
shocking:

La pitié même d'un sexe faible et sensible a semblé un crime: deux
femmes ont été traînées au carcan, pour avoir imploré la grâce de
leurs pères, de leurs maris et de leurs enfants. On a défendu la
commisération et les larmes. La nature est forcée de contraindre ses
plus justes et ses plus généreux mouvements sous peine de mort.
[...] Ah! par cette pitié gravée dans le coeur de tous les hommes,
mais qui dans celui des hommes publics doit être plus puissante et plus
active, parce qu'ils ont plus de larmes à essuyer et plus de bienfaits à
répandre, représentants du peuple, pères de la patrie, ne soyez pas
sourds à la voix d'une ville plus infortunée encore que coupable.[28]

The petition was referred to the Comité de salut public.
    During the same session, a deputation of women appeared at
the bar of the Convention, seeking a response to their petition
of 22 frimaire. They are 'citoyennes, mères et épouses, filles ou
soeurs de citoyens en état d'arrestation', and their petition
began with the words 'Citoyens législateurs, vous voyez devant

vous des épouses malheureuses . . .' Once again, the sex of the
petitioner is mobilised in the appeal. Robespierre proposes a
decree, which is adopted, to the effect that the two committees
will appoint commissioners to investigate the cases of 'des
patriotes qui auraient pu être incarcérés', but then goes on to
make a speech in which he questions the case which the women
are making. It is inconceivable that so many errors should have
been made, and the petition is therefore a sign of 'modéran-
tisme, aristocratie'. Robespierre then homes in on the play
which is being made of the petitioners' sex: 'Des femmes, ce
mot rappelle sans doute des idées touchantes et sacrées', but
the perilous situation of France does not allow these women
the luxury of 'oublier leurs qualités de citoyennes pour ne se
rappeler que celles d'épouses, de soeurs, de parents'.[29] A few
days later, in his report on the application of the law of suspects
of 17 September, Barère develops this theme of the separation
of public and private, political and private virtues. He denounces one of the strategies of the aristocracy: it 'ameuta des
femmes avec des pétitions et mit leur sensibilité à contribution
pour rendre à la patrie des flots d'ennemis'. In a lesson to such
women, he quotes the example of the mother of the Gracchi:
when told that her sons are dead, her only reply to the mess-
enger is 'Eh! vil esclave [. . .] t'ai-je demandé si mes enfants
vivent? dis-moi que la bataille est gagnée et courons au
Capitole en rendre grâce aux dieux.'[30] Republican heroism is
thus a transcendence of pity and sympathy, and is a particularly laudable virtue in a woman, whose whole nature, as
the Revolutionaries continued firmly to believe, inclines her
towards the private, domestic virtues which are the privileged
ground of sentimentalism.

This report by Barère is the one in which he responds to the
famous tirade in No. 4 of Desmoulins's *Vieux cordelier* on the
echoing proliferation of the term *suspect*. The point must be
made that *Le Vieux cordelier* is peculiarly devoid of sentimental
figures and language: its chosen idiom is much more that of the
witty, allusive pamphlet. This is important, because Desmoulins, like the Girondins, has been constituted by subsequent
historiography as a sentimental victim seeking only to defend a

humane Republic against the monsters of the Comité de salut public.[31] Certainly Desmoulins is not without his sentimental moments. In No. 4 of *Le Vieux cordelier*, in which Desmoulins calls for the setting up of a *comité de clémence*, he asks, rhetorically: 'à ce mot de comité de clémence, quel patriote ne sent pas ses entrailles émues? car le patriotisme est la plénitude de toutes les vertus, et ne peut pas conséquemment exister là où il n'y a ni humanité, ni philanthropie, mais une âme arride et desséchée par l'égoïsme', and, similarly, in the 'crédo politique' of No. 7, he declares that

notre liberté, c'est l'inviolabilité des principes de la déclaration des droits, c'est la fraternité, la sainte égalité, le rappel sur la terre, ou du moins en France, de toutes les vertus patriarchales, c'est la douceur des maximes républicaines, c'est ce *res sacra miser*, ce respect pour le malheur, que commande notre sublime constitution.[32]

Nevertheless, the overall tone, if not sparse, is not sanctimonious. In the same way, the famous last texts of the Girondins are striking in their restraint. They may, as Pierre Trahard suggests, be models of sensibility and nobility in the most desperate of circumstances, but there is a purity and genuineness about them which is not compatible with sentimental inflation. Pétion's 'Epître dédicatoire à mon fils' even finds considerable room for a powerful and dark message of vengeance.[33] Aulard is right to caution that these militants should not be transformed mythically into 'je ne sais quelles victimes douces, sentimentales, éplorées'.[34] The real experts in the use of sentimental and melodramatic figures, at least among the leading figures of the Revolution, appear to me to be the Montagnards, even if part of their message is, as we have seen, a limitation of the sentimental rights of the victim in the name of public virtue.

Saint-Just's reports of ventôse Year 2 which led to the decrees of the same month make ample use of the notion of false sensibility. Do the enemies of the Revolution have any time for clemency, asks Saint-Just? 'Insensés que nous sommes, nous mettons un luxe métaphysique dans l'étalage de nos principes, et les rois, mille fois plus cruels que nous, dorment dans le crime.' Saint-Just presses the logic of pity further: the advocates of clemency have argued from nature, but is this argument applicable to the enemies of the Republic? 'Les fripons, et les tyrans, et les ennemis de la patrie sont-ils donc à vos yeux dans la nature, ô vous qui réclamez en son nom pour eux?' Again, an opposition between the public and private sphere is suggested: 'vous n'avez le droit ni d'être cléments, ni d'être sensibles pour les trahisons; vous ne travaillez pas pour votre compte, mais pour le peuple'. And, as in the debates of December 1792, the people as victim is the counterweight to the dismissal of the claims of humanity on behalf of the enemies of the Revolution:

Abolissez la mendicité qui déshonore un état libre; les propriétés des patriotes sont sacrées, mais les biens des conspirateurs sont là pour tous les malheureux. Les malheureux sont les puissances de la terre; ils ont le droit de parler en maîtres aux gouvernements qui les négligent.

Saint-Just's conclusion sets his text firmly in the sentimental–melodramatic mould:

ne souffrez point qu'il y ait un malheureux, ni un pauvre dans l'état: ce n'est qu'à ce prix que vous aurez fait une révolution et une République véritable: eh! qui vous saurait gré du malheur des bons et du bonheur des méchants?[35]

The decree of 8 ventôse, as well as providing for the liberation of wrongly imprisoned patriots, stipulated that 'les biens des personnes reconnues ennemis de la République seront séquestrés au profit de la République', and a decree of 13 ventôse went on to stipulate that all *communes* would draw up a list of 'patriotes indigents' and that the Comité de salut public would produce a report on 'les moyens d'indemniser tous les malheureux avec les biens des ennemis de la révolution'.[36] This linkage of the deserving patriot and the undeserving enemy of freedom through confiscation and redistribution is not entirely new: in a sense, it is present in the sale of *biens nationaux*, although the beneficiaries of that process were scarcely needy patriots; and Soboul notes that the confiscation of the property of counter-revolutionaries for the benefit of the needy is being discussed in sans-culotte circles back in May 1793.[37] But the development of the idea in the decrees of ventôse is revealing, because it represents a concrete, legislative manifestation of the discursive opposition between the undeserving counter-revolutionary and the deserving patriot: the nexus of ideas which we saw emerging during the trial of the king takes on real social meaning. The report promised in the decree of 13 ventôse is none other than Barère's report of 22 floréal, proposing the setting up of the *livre de bienfaisance nationale* and the celebration of the *fête du Malheur* (see above, pp. 123–4).

I have already noted how the legislation of floréal Year 2, and particularly the *fête du Malheur* which it proposes, use the language and *dramatis personae* of sentimental texts. What is of particular interest in the present context is the way in which the legislation concerning poor relief fits into the wider discursive context: the struggle for the future direction of the political life of the country is conducted in terms of the correct attribution of the categories of villainy and innocence, and this polarity finds concrete expression in the twin institutions of the guillotine and a public celebration of the deserving poor. I would not wish to push this too far, at the risk of slipping into melodrama myself: the Revolution is much more than can be contained in this simple dichotomy. But the parallels remain striking, and, at the very least, it seems that the legislation of floréal, while fitting into the well-established framework of social investigation and assistance which was pioneered by the Revolution, also performs a compensatory function, reassuring the citizen, and perhaps even more the legislator, that the Revolution has not lost touch with its sentimental roots.

Perhaps Robespierre's rise to fame can be partly explained by his unshakeable faith in the validity of the sentimental categories of vice and virtue, persecutor and victim, evil and purity: he provided the moral grid which was needed. When he declares at the Jacobins on 21 November 1793, in his offensive against dechristianisation,

L'athéisme est aristocratique. L'idée d'un grand Etre, qui veille sur l'innocence opprimée et qui punit le crime triomphant, est toute populaire. (*Vifs applaudissements.*) Le peuple, les malheureux m'applaudissent; si je trouvais des censeurs, ce serait parmi les riches et parmi les coupables.[38]

Robespierre is affirming that History can be a sentimental narrative, or rather that the social subject should be allowed to imagine History in those terms. 'Nature' and 'humanité': 'Je soutiens, moi, ces éternels principes sur lesquels s'étaie la faiblesse humaine pour s'élancer à la vertu'.[39] One of the most striking features of his famous report of 18 floréal (four days prior to Barère's report), on 'les rapports des idées religieuses et morales avec les principes républicains, et sur les fêtes nationales', is its uncompromising Manicheism. 'Le vice et la vertu font les destins de la terre: ce sont les deux génies opposés qui se le disputent.' These categories expand to fill the entire space available to mankind: 'Le méchant voudrait dans son coeur qu'il ne restât pas sur la terre un seul homme de bien, afin de n'y plus rencontrer un seul accusateur'. Once again, atheism is the object of his analysis: it suggests that 'une force aveugle' presides over human destiny 'et frappe au hasard le crime et la vertu'. Error! cries Robespierre, invoking the sentimental witness of humanity:

Vous qui regrettez un ami vertueux, vous aimez à penser que la plus belle partie de lui-même a échappé au trépas! Vous qui pleurez sur le cercueil d'un fils ou d'une épouse, êtes-vous consolés par celui qui vous dit qu'il ne reste plus d'eux qu'une vile poussière? Malheureux qui expirez sous les coups d'un assassin, votre dernier soupir est un appel à la justice éternelle! L'innocence sur l'échafaud fait pâlir le tyran sur son char de triomphe: aurait-elle cet ascendant, si le tombeau égalait l'oppresseur et l'opprimé? Malheureux sophiste! De quel droit viens-tu arracher à l'innocence le sceptre de la raison, pour le remettre dans les mains du crime?[40]

The function of the transcendent dimension which Robespierre is projecting is to guarantee the distinction between good and evil, even if it appears to be ignored and turned on its head by fortune. That transcendent dimension is only really a projection forward of the moral superiority which is conferred by the status of victim, and of the internal affective activity suggested by the words 'regrettez', 'pleurez', 'soupir': it is a transcendence imagined in immanent, sentimental terms.

The significance, then, of some of these debates of the period 1793–4 as far as my purpose here is concerned, is that beyond the internal fractures which have opened up within the Revolution – indeed, precisely *because* of their existence – the figures of sentimentalism take on a pivotal role. The discursive constitution of deserving victims, and of the speaker as their most fierce defender, becomes a statement of Revolutionary legitimacy, just as the correct and incorrect use of pity become an indicator of political position. These conflicts confirm, in my view, the interlocking of sentimentalism and the Revolution: they intensify and in some cases transform a symbolic and discursive association which was culturally available because of the place of sentimental narrative in the Revolution's beginnings.

What of the *fête révolutionnaire*, which is one of the major themes of Robespierre's report of 18 floréal? Thematically, the *fête* reproduces many of the preoccupations of sentimentalism, which are the social and moral preoccupations of the period. A glance over the list of *fêtes* proposed by Robespierre in the same report is ample proof of the sentimental credentials of the institution:

A l'Etre suprême et à la Nature. Au Genre humain. Au Peuple français. Aux Bienfaiteurs de l'humanité. Aux Martyrs de la liberté. A la Liberté et à l'Egalité. A la République. A la Liberté du monde. A l'Amour de la Patrie. A la haine des Tyrans et des Traîtres. A la Vérité. A la Justice. A la Pudeur. A la Gloire et à l'Immortalité. A l'Amitié. A la Frugalité. Au Courage. A la Bonne foi. Au Désintéressement. Au Stoïcisme. A l'Amour. A la Foi conjugale. A l'Amour paternel. A la Tendresse maternelle. A la Piété filiale. A l'Enfance. A la Jeunesse. A l'Age viril. A la Vieillesse. Au Malheur. A l'Agriculture. A l'Industrie. A nos Aïeux. A la Postérité. Au Bonheur.[41]

Abstract moral qualities and virtues, on the one hand, and the salient stages and functions of human life in the family seem to form the major part of this list. Similar conclusions could be drawn from Saint-Just's *Institutions républicaines*, which imagines a series of public celebrations which will characterise republican society. Recalling that 'le respect de la vieillesse est un culte dans notre patrie', Saint-Just describes a *fête de la vieillesse* in which 'les hommes qui auront toujours vécu sans reproche' will present themselves at the temple at the age of sixty and, 'si personne ne les accuse', will be allowed to wear a symbolic white sash. The *fête de l'égalité* reproduces very closely a common-place of sentimental narrative:

> Tous les ans, le premier floréal, le peuple de chaque commune choisira [...] un jeune homme riche, vertueux et sans difformité, âgé de vingt et un ans accomplis et de moins de trente ans, qui choisira et épousera une vierge pauvre, en mémoire de l'égalité humaine.

The age restrictions are precise, the affective symbolism unbounded. Finally, Saint-Just's 'déclaration annuelle de ses amis au temple' celebrates friendship: those who declare that they have remained united in friendship all their life, will be buried together, but 'celui qui dit qu'il ne croit point à l'amitié ou qui n'a point d'amis, est banni'.[42]

The Revolutionaries' model for the *fête* is, of course, Rousseau, popularised any number of times. What they dreamed of as they planned their *fêtes* was the kind of un-mediated, transparent society which Rousseau had seen in the country *fête*, bypassing the alienation of an urban existence lived in the eye of the other. As Starobinski says, the dream of the *fête révolutionnaire* is a dream of the reciprocal communi-cation of social subjects. A text such as David's plan for the *fête de l'Etre suprême* testifies to the force of this dream. If the text begins life as a set of stage directions, the desire to capture the fullness of the imagined unanimity leads to what is finally a much more novelistic form of text. This is seen in the provision of an opening sequence which goes clearly beyond that which can be controlled by a stage-manager:

> L'aurore annonce à peine le jour, et déjà les sons d'une musique guerrière retentissent de toutes parts, et font succéder au calme du sommeil un réveil enchanteur.
>
> A l'aspect de l'astre bienfaisant qui vivifie et colore la nature, amis, frères, époux, enfants, vieillards et mères s'embrassent, et s'empres-sent à l'envi d'orner et de célébrer la fête de la Divinité.

This in fact continues for some paragraphs: what is apparently being described is not the event itself, but the city waking up on the morning of the *fête*. The mother is plaiting her daughter's hair, with a baby at the breast ('sa plus belle parure'); meanwhile, the son is preparing himself for the ceremony, but insists on receiving the baldric from his father; 'le vieillard, souriant de plaisir, les yeux mouillés des larmes de la joie, sent rajeunir son âme et son courage en présentant l'épée aux défenseurs de la liberté'.[43] The boundary between this microcosmic scene-setting and the *fête* itself is somewhat unclear, but, after a few paragraphs, it becomes apparent that the discourse is no longer that of novelistic description, but that of a programme, a set of stage directions. However, when the climactic point is reached at which 'tous les ennemis de la félicité publique', together with the figure of atheism, are consumed in flames, another discursive shift takes place, integrating the affective life of the spectators and the metaphorical meaning of the natural setting:

Du milieu de ces débris s'élève la Sagesse au front calme et serein; à son aspect, des larmes de joie et de reconnaissance coulent de tous les yeux; elle console l'homme de bien que l'Athéisme voulait rendre au désespoir. La fille du Ciel semble dire: Peuple, rends hommage à l'auteur de la nature; respecte ses décrets immuables. (p. 153)

Similarly, the singing of the hymn by M.-J. Chénier concludes with another passage describing the reaction of the people:

Tout s'émeut, tout s'agite sur la montagne; hommes, femmes, filles, vieillards, enfants, tous font retentir l'air de leurs accents. Ici les mères pressent les enfants qu'elles allaitent; là, saisissant les plus jeunes de leurs enfants mâles [...], elles les présentent en hommage à l'auteur de la nature. [...] Au même instant, et simultanément, les fils, brûlant d'une ardeur guerrière, tirent leurs épées, les déposent dans les mains de leurs vieux pères; ils jurent de les rendre partout victorieuses; ils jurent de faire triompher l'égalité et la liberté contre l'oppression des tyrans. Partageant l'enthousiasme de leurs fils, les vieillards ravis les embrassent, et répandent sur eux leur bénédiction paternelle. (p. 155)

These passages suggest that there is a formal bond between the text of the *fête* and sentimental narrative. Judith Schlanger has written that the *fête* uses a 'présent intemporel', a tense which simultaneously states the planned execution of a programme and describes an event which is actually being witnessed.[44] In a sense, the text of the *plan de fête* therefore appears as a narrative which has slipped from the descriptive to the prescriptive mode, in a movement which confirms what Jean Starobinski has described as the enormous voluntarism of the *fête*.[45] The text becomes a hybrid, adding to the programme in the strict sense of the term a set of other notations: natural description, scene-setting, evocation of the supposedly spontaneous reaction of a group of spectators, abstract reflections on the moral to be drawn from the ceremony. In other words, it is as *text* that the programme comes nearest to its aim of evoking the experience of social community, of a society united in its affections and in its commitment to a set of abstract ideals.

One of the functions which such a text shares with sentimental narrative is to externalise inner emotion, to render communicable the life of the sentiments. Thus the descriptive accretions noted above. Thus also the power of the word, in Saint-Just's declaration of friendship, which translates itself into the honour of a common burial or the shame of banishment. The other function is the setting up of a line of communication between the individual and the universal, partly corresponding to the pair concrete–abstract. It is above all here that Starobinski's notion of the voluntarism of the *fête* is useful: the ceremony, as we have seen, very often derives its meaning from an abstract, universal concept, and its task is to represent that concept. The aim is a moral pedagogy: what has been conceived by reason must now be made effective, the people must be brought to an understanding of the new values, so that they read the world and their experience through them. The *fête* seeks to impose a new moral grid on the experience of a people, to diffuse throughout the national space a universal system of values. The paradox of texts such as David's plan or Saint-Just's *Institutions républicaines* is that the more they try to bring together in one simultaneous, undifferentiated, unifying perception – as does the *tableau* – abstract concepts and the emotions of the individual subject, the more they cry out the separation between the two. Their desperate desire for reality to mould itself to the model proposed by the Revolution leads the Revolutionaries to produce the most manipulative of texts, and to reproduce the fundamental vice which Rousseau had denounced in the theatre and which had led him to put forward the *fête* as a social model free of the alienating effects of representation.

CHAPTER 5

Sentimentalism and 'idéologie'

In thermidor and fructidor Year 3, the *Décade philosophique* carried an anecdote entitled 'Le Bourg et le hameau', which it placed under the heading 'Morale appliquée à la législation'. The context of the story is the law of 17 nivôse Year 2 establishing the equal division of inheritances, and more specifically the decision to cancel the retroactive application of the legislation to cover all inheritances established since 14 July 1789. The anecdote is recounted by a primary narrator on his return from a botanical tour of the Auvergne, during which he was accommodated in a small town (the 'bourg' of the title) under the roof of one Dennet. The citoyen Dennet is the eldest sibling who, in the face of opposition from his ambitious and avaricious wife, has been obliged by the law to share his inheritance with his younger brothers and sisters. The contrast articulated by the title is between the self-interest of the townsfolk and the humanity and generosity of the inhabitants of the country, exemplified by Jacques Pinard, an inhabitant of one of the outlying hamlets. Before the law of 17 nivôse even came onto the statute book, he had refused to accept his legal rights as elder brother, and had shared out his inheritance with his siblings. This shining example, predictably enough, prevails: when the retroactivity of the law is cancelled, Dennet refuses to go back on the equal division of the inheritance, which had provided his sister with a precious dowry. In the office of the notary who had drawn up the legal document formalising this noble gesture, a tender scene of family reconciliation takes place:

166

Les frères se regardèrent, s'émurent et se jetèrent dans les bras les uns des autres; ce fut un moment d'ivresse que les spectateurs eux-mêmes ne purent s'empêcher de partager, et je t'avouerai que pour mon compte j'en fus attendri jusqu'aux larmes.

The moral is now pointed in terms which consciously and precisely echo debates under the Directory over the nature of the relationship between legislation and morality:

Quel est l'homme qui en interrogeant son coeur, ne trouve qu'il applaudit à cette conduite? Le sentiment intime nous dit que c'est là de la probité, de la vertu [...] Nos profonds politiques auront beau dire que les successions doivent se régir par les lois de l'état, et non par celles de l'équité et du sens commun, qu'autre chose est le droit naturel, autre chose le droit civil: je croirai toujours vrai ce que nous avons souvent dit ensemble; que les meilleures lois positives sont celles qui se rapprochent le plus de la loi naturelle, celles dans lesquelles on retrouve la raison écrite et la morale sanctionnée.[1]

Earlier in Year 3, the *Décade* published a story probably by Jean-Baptiste Say, entitled 'Lévald et Amélie'. The author's purpose is to 'montrer comment les lois ont une grande influence sur les moeurs des nations', and the form of an anecdote is used because 'ce ne sont pas les discours spéculatifs, quelque forts qu'ils soient, qui feront haïr les mauvaises lois; ce seront les exemples des maux qu'elles entraînent'.[2] The laws in question are none other than the power of the church under the *Ancien Régime*, and, specifically, the institution of the celibacy of the clergy. Amélie is a virtuous orphan who has been brought up by Bonnefond, a 'cultivateur aisé'; Bonnefond wishes her to marry Saint Léger, but she systematically refuses out of love for another, who is none other than Lévald, the priest. Her love for him is reciprocated, and he complains at the injustice which places obstacles in the way of their pure and virtuous love: 'Préjugés barbares! Par esprit de parti, par fanatisme, des hommes ont dit: Il faut étouffer les mouvements de la Nature, et ils ont enchaîné leurs successeurs!'[3] The true villain of this moderately Gothic piece is, however, neither Bonnefond nor Saint Léger, but the bishop ('un homme de cette caste appelée dans ce temps-là *la noblesse*') who, in collaboration with the *intendant*, is plotting to seduce Amélie, his own daughter by a villainous liaison with Denise, Bonnefond's virtuous and long-suffering housekeeper and, according to the official version, Amélie's wetnurse. Lévald is finally removed from the scene by means of an episcopal summons, and is locked away in a cell by 'des sbires en soutanes, créatures de l'évêque'. From his cell, Lévald writes to Amélie:

'La petite fenêtre qui m'éclaire, donne sur la rivière Eure qui passe au pied des murs de ma prison; au-delà de la rivière, est un autre quartier de la ville, un faubourg; et comme l'endroit que j'habite est très élevé, j'aperçois la campagne par-dessus les toits des maisons; je ne vois pas Vaucresson, mais il est de ce côté-là. Embrassez pour moi votre papa et la bonne Denise.'

Amélie trempa cette lettre de ses larmes, la lut à sa mère, la relut cent fois; son coeur sensible y voyait, à travers un calme apparent, la douleur d'un homme qui souffrait pour elle.

Her reply is pure sentimentalism: nothing can come between them, even his captivity ('ils peuvent te ravir la liberté, ils ne pourront jamais te ravir mon coeur'); her happiness is to be at his side:

je n'en peux plus goûter que lorsque mon imagination me transporte à tes côtés, lorsque je pense, en idée, essuyer les larmes qui coulent de tes yeux.

Amélie leaves in the hope of catching a glimpse of Lévald through the window of his cell, but finds him drowned on the banks of the Eure, clutching to his breast her last letter to him.

Voilà donc ô ciel! les désastreux effets du célibat forcé d'une classe de citoyens [...] Un homme aimable et sensible réduit à se donner la mort! Une femme douée de toutes les qualités qui font le charme de la vie, une femme destinée par la Nature à rendre heureux dans cette vie un époux et des enfants, consumant ses jours languissants dans les larmes.[4]

It appears, then, that the *Décade philosophique*, which from the Directory through to the beginnings of the Empire represented the cause of moderate, bourgeois republicanism, and defended the heritage of Enlightenment, particularly in the form of the thought of the *Idéologues*, did not consider that the tools of sentimentalism were inappropriate to the defence of the Revolutionary heritage. Marc Régaldo confirms that the *Décade* allotted a considerable place in its pages to such sentimental narrative:

S'agit-il de prêcher la bonne entente entre époux, la pacification, la tolérance, le partage égal des biens paternels entre les enfants, vite Andrieux, Say ou Duval troussent une nouvelle émouvante à souhait. Persécutée ou reconnue, la vertu y est toujours attirante; triomphant ou puni, le vice toujours odieux. Fiancés modèles, femmes indulgentes, bons fils, pères tendres, frères affectionnés, quelle galerie de belles âmes, avec, de loin en loin, pour le contraste, quelque 'traître' bien noir.[5]

The case for an examination of the role of sentimentalism in the work of the *Idéologues* does not rest solely on the use of sentimental anecdotes by the *Décade*. There are in fact two related reasons for the investigation undertaken here. The first has to do with the relationship between sentimentalism and the sensationalist-empiricist philosophy which the *Idéologues* inherited and sought to develop and popularise. I argued in chapter 2 that such a relationship exists at two levels. Firstly, at a mimetic level, sentimental texts manifest a preoccupation with the problem of the notation of the inner life of the observed subject: the moral and affective life of the Other is perceived empirically through a series of material signs – notably gesture, expression, tears – which correspond to pre-linguistic stages in the sensationalist genealogy of language and sociability. Secondly, within the broader economy of the relationship between text, author, reader and society at large, sentimentalism reflects an empiricist *construction* of morality out of experience: hypostatising the primal scene of the Other's misfortune, the text enacts a process of signification in which that founding experience is refracted out into the individual and collective imagination, building a system of social responsibility from the raw materials of the *vécu*. Given the *Idéologues'* commitment to a fundamentally sensationalist and rationalist politics, the first question is this: does the work of the *Idéologues* contain elements of sentimentalism, and, if so, what is its mode of coexistence with their sensationalism and rationalism?

The overall context and character of the Ideological project provide a second and broader justification for the investigation which will be undertaken in this chapter. Not only are the *Idéologues* self-conscious inheritors of Enlightenment; they seek to apply that inheritance to the social and political situation of post-Thermidorian France, and their avowed aim is to establish the moral, intellectual, philosophical and (through education) social base for a régime of moderate republicanism. For them, intellectual production must serve social and political praxis, and, if sentimentalism has a place in their work, then they represent something of a test case: where does sentimentalism fit into the theory of political and economic liberalism which, on the threshold of the nineteenth century, the *Idéologues* propose?

I propose to look first at the relationship between sensationalist philosophy and sentimentalism. In 1798, the *Classe des sciences morales et politiques* of the *Institut* – itself a creation of post-Thermidor – put up for competition the question 'Quels sont les moyens de fonder la morale chez un peuple?' No submission was deemed worthy of the prize, and two years later the question was reformulated as 'Quelles sont les institutions les plus propres à fonder la morale d'un peuple?' One of the texts generated by this competition was an essay by Destutt de Tracy, *Quels sont les moyens de fonder la morale chez un peuple?* The arguments advanced by Tracy lie close to the heart of the *Idéologues*' view of the nature of social morality. The text is utterly dismissive of innate ideas as the source of morality: 'C'est une erreur bien ancienne et bien absurde de croire que les principes de la morale sont comme infus dans nos têtes, et qu'ils sont les mêmes dans toutes; et d'après ce rêve, de leur supposer je ne sais quelle origine plus céleste qu'à toutes les autres idées qui existent dans notre entendement.' Any rational analysis must, on the contrary, accept the proposition that 'la morale est une science que nous composons comme toutes les autres des résultats de nos expériences et de nos réflexions'.[6] It follows from this that education must play a primary role in the construction of morality, since the science of morals is the result of a process of reflection and combination of ideas; and it also follows from this that, if the first notions of morality are known and acknowledged by all, the more complex reaches of the science are not spontaneously known to the multitude, any more than they are to the 'savage' in the state of nature. Morality, in other words, is unambiguously represented as a virtue of social and not natural origin, if by the latter is meant the notion that the rules by which human beings interact in society are inscribed in all hearts by some agency possessing more or less divine attributes. It would seem that such a starting point is profoundly anti-sentimental: out goes the conception of morality as an ontological given waiting to be acknowledged; out too goes the myth that the lower orders in some way have privileged access to moral feeling, that lowliness and purity are related qualities.

Tracy speaks the language of moral realism. 'Le législateur qui veut que nous aimions notre prochain précisément comme nous-mêmes, et celui qui veut que nous vivions exactement isolés, nous prescrivent deux choses également impossibles' (p. 12). Social coexistence means conflict of interests, and the task of the legislator is to recognise, manage and minimise that conflict. The means to that end, in Tracy's view, is the use of social institutions, rather than a voluntarist faith in the capacity of human beings either to see the ultimate good and strive towards it without guidance, or indeed to act upon well-intentioned moral instruction and advice.

Vous aurez beau prêcher la fidélité à l'amitié et le respect dû à l'innocence, la loi n'a qu'à favoriser les dénonciations et admettre les confiscations, vous verrez se multiplier les trahisons et les condamnations injustes. (pp. 24–5)

Abstract and concrete are opposed: moral values expressed as universal categories are of little weight in the face of institutional determination. Two conclusions are to be drawn. Firstly, there can be no hope of moral improvement until a society's laws are reformed in such a way that all its members are given the means to develop as moral individuals: here, a thorough-going programme of republican legislation is outlined, covering political equality, divorce, freedom of industry and trade, the right to lend and borrow money for interest, and strict limitations on the power of the church and freedom of inheritance. Secondly, the art of the legislator is to act on the members of the society without their knowledge, to be the strings which make the puppets move:

Quand il est question d'agir sur des êtres animés, rien de ce qu'on veut opérer directement ne réussit. *Disposez les circonstances favorables, et ce que vous désirez arrive sans que vous ayez l'air de vous en mêler.* (p. 33)

The power of the institutional framework within which human societies operate is determining, and only when that framework is right will morality flourish. Once that point has been reached, however, a certain spontaneity returns to Tracy's representation of morality: the legislation of economic liberalism, described as the 'complément de la liberté naturelle', will unleash the natural industriousness of the nation, encourage the circulation of wealth, and the result of this is presented in a utopian cameo where we see a people rendered 'laborieux, modeste, sensé, heureux, jouissant de l'aisance' by its new economic circumstances. Now, in contrast to the scathing dismissal of any belief in the spontaneity of moral values or the usefulness of moral preaching, the moral appetite of this industrious people has been whetted: a people of proprietors will, miraculously, perceive the need for education where a people subject to the yoke of feudalism and absolutism will not. In short, the establishment of rational legislation marks the watershed between two systems of meaning in Tracy's text. In an unreformed economy, the appeal to spontaneous values springing from nature is to be rejected as a pure naivety; but in the utopian phase of the text, the appeal to nature, to spontaneity, to human agency which does not need to be the object of a decomposing, scientific attention, once again becomes possible.[7]

Jean-Baptiste Say's *Olbie, ou Essai sur les moyens de réformer les moeurs d'une nation*, published in Year 8, was submitted to the same *Institut* competition as Tracy's *Quels sont les moyens?* It can more accurately and completely be described as utopian in the sense that, after a theoretical introduction, it examines the functioning of the society of a mythical country, Olbie, fifty years after the establishment of political liberty on the ruins of an absolute monarchy. Say shares with Tracy a set of explicit philosophical suppositions about the nature of morality: it is a science, since not all the rules of behaviour in society are of 'institution naturelle', but are, on the contrary, learnt in the same way that a language is learnt. Secondly, as in Tracy, one of the basic premises of that science is that virtue is not to be defined as sacrifice: moral behaviour must include an important element of self-interest properly understood, in other words the task of the legislator is to make virtue and happiness compatible, and to create social institutions which go with the inclination of human nature rather than seeking to mould it to a strict and unrealistic definition of what is virtuous. 'Il faut chercher les moyens de fonder de bonnes moeurs dans le coeur de l'homme. Il ne faut pas vouloir qu'on fasse: il faut faire qu'on veuille'.[8] If human beings are offered a realistic means of pursuing virtue, they will follow that path in their pursuit of happiness.

This, then, is the content of the introductory essay. The function of the utopian phase of the text is to imagine the moral character of a society which has undergone legislative and institutional reform. Part of the technique is to juxtapose images of the reformed society with their equivalents from Olbie's *ancien régime*: the worker who drinks, beats his wife and dies in squalor is compared to the one who lives a life of frugality and honour, accumulating regular savings which in their turn produce interest – Say's Protestant consciousness is more than evident – and allow our hero to spend his last years 'au sein d'une famille active qu'il a rendue heureuse, et dont il est adoré' (pp. 5–6). Similarly, in a passage on the moralising influence of the institution of the savings bank, Say writes:

on ne voyait plus, comme auparavant à Olbie, les cabarets pleins d'ivrognes abrutis, chantant et jurant tour-à-tour: mais on rencontrait fréquemment dans les campagnes qui entouraient la ville, un père, une mère et leurs enfants, tous animés d'une gaîté tranquille, celle du bonheur, et qui marchaient vers quelque rendez-vous champêtre pour s'y réunir avec d'autres amis de même état qu'eux. (p. 34)

The sentimental tableau is unmistakable, and is characteristic of the tone in which Say evokes the happiness which is the result of rational reform. Not surprisingly for the future author of the *Traité d'économie politique*, economic considerations are crucial in the constitution of this ideal republic: a free market creates an atmosphere of responsibility in which saving, enterprise and access to property are the foundation of public happiness; but it is a public happiness made up of a series of private, family idylls: the inhabitants of Olbie 'cherchaient leurs plaisirs les plus chers dans la société de leur famille et d'un petit nombre d'amis; [...] vivant plus sobrement, leur humeur fut plus égale, leur âme plus disposée à la justice et à la bienveillance qui sont mères de toutes les autres vertus' (p. 27). Reading, self-improvement through education, become crucial values in this economy; and the entrepreneur who gives work, and therefore the possibility of self-advancement, to those who would otherwise be unemployed, is celebrated, not for the first time, as a man accomplishing a labour of *bienfaisance*.

The particular role reserved for women in the economy of Olbie is worthy of particular note. Women possess moral virtues to a greater degree than men, referred to in the text as 'nous'. 'Elles sont plus accessibles à la pitié, plus fidèles dans leurs engagements, plus dévouées dans leurs affections, plus patientes dans l'infortune.' It is scarcely surprising, then, that the Olbiens have decided to use these sentimental virtues of women in a socially fruitful way, by entrusting them with the charitable works of the nation. A comparison with the age of chivalry is used: the Olbiens 'mélèrent [...] l'amour honnête à toutes celles de leurs institutions qui purent l'admettre; et, s'il faut l'avouer, ils prirent quelques conseils à nos siècles de chevalerie' (p. 46). Thus,

ce fut aux femmes que le gouvernement confia l'exercice de la bienfaisance nationale; il protégea les associations que plusieurs d'entre elles formèrent en faveur des filles à marier, des femmes en couches; associations louables qui présentent le touchant tableau de la faiblesse généreuse, faisant cause commune avec la faiblesse infortunée. (p. 47)

This insistence on the pre-eminence of weakness, a development of sentimentalism which is particularly favoured during this period and not by any means exclusively in the politically progressive camp, is characteristically expressed in the formula 'L'empire de la femme est celui de la faiblesse sur la force.' Part and parcel of this happy development was that working-class women forsook the world of work 'pour se consacrer plus à la famille' (p. 48).

The insistence on the learnt, constructed nature of moral ideas which we have seen in Tracy and Say is undoubtedly characteristic of *idéologie* as a whole. It is linked to the militant sensationalism of the whole group, which met at the salon of Mme Helvétius in Auteuil, and it forms the intellectual base of much of their thought about political economy. There is a self-conscious reductivism in this philosophical approach, a discourse, which *idéologie* clearly shares with eighteenth-century materialism, which is ready and keen to deflate what it perceives as myth, pipe-dream, unnecessary dressing up of a fundamentally material reality: human beings can be explained, taken apart and reassembled, *un point c'est tout*. And yet the evidence of the preceding analysis suggests that this discourse – 'anti-sentimental' at least in the sense that its aim is a deflating one – is quite able to coexist with narrative and linguistic features belonging to literary sentimentalism: the tableau of family happiness, the pre-eminence of women, the narrative structure which, through reform, provides for a happy ending, and the sense that, once reform is in place, it is possible once again to rely on resources in the make-up of humanity which are in some sense 'natural' and spontaneous.

Bernardin de Saint-Pierre was one of those who took issue with what he saw as the reductivist sensationalism of the *Idéologues*, and defended the cause of innate ideas. A member of the class of moral and political science of the *Institut*, he was given the task of reporting on the various submissions for the competition 'Quels sont les moyens de fonder la morale chez un peuple?' at the session of 3 July 1798. His report ended with a solemn statement of his belief in certain religious principles and, according to the account given by Aimé Martin, Cabanis protested at Bernardin's statement of faith with the words 'Je jure qu'il n'y a pas de Dieu et je demande que son nom ne soit pas prononcé dans cette enceinte.'[9] In his report, Bernardin observes that the authors of the memoirs upon which he is called to comment have spoken at length about the effects of morality, but 'se sont trouvés dans un grand embarras pour en asseoir les fondements. Les uns les ont placés dans l'éducation, les autres dans les lois; ceux-ci, dans des fêtes et des spectacles; ceux-là, dans notre propre coeur si versatile' (p. 329). His object is to show that there are two types of morality, one originating in the human passions, a 'morale terrestre' which varies from country to country and epoch to epoch, and a 'morale céleste': this latter morality is equated with the 'morale de la raison', 'le sentiment des lois que la nature a établies entre tous les hommes' (p. 332). It is this which binds together brothers, husbands and wives, parents and children, as well as cementing the links between tribes and nations, and between nations and humanity at large. Bernardin then embarks upon an invocation of this lofty ideal, which is couched in familiar terms:

C'est cette morale céleste, innée dans chacun de nous, qui seule nous fait supporter l'ordre social, lors même qu'il nous opprime. Elle éloigne des jouissances corrompues du monde la jeune fille laborieuse, et en la revêtissant d'innocence et de pudeur, la rend bien plus digne d'être aimée que celle que le vice couvre de diamants. (p. 333)

Morality and virtue are defined here by their radical opposition to fortune and self-interest. Where Tracy and Say speak of ways of making virtue and self-interest coincide, Bernardin is interested only in a definition which raises the moral stakes by placing the two sets of terms in contradistinction. He then appeals to the category of misfortune: the virtue of which he speaks is the feeling which drives the North American Indian to

offrir sa cabane hospitalière à l'Européen, qui là baigna dans le sang. Mais quand la politique des puissances invoque la patrie pour détruire les patries; quand la morale de leurs passions a sanctionné leurs crimes par des religions corrompues; quand les infortunés sans défense semblent n'avoir plus d'espoir, la morale céleste fait entendre leur voix. Toutes les âmes sont émues, toutes les tyrannies sont ébranlées. Le fil de la pitié, touché par elle, a des secousses plus rapides que le fil électrique agité par la foudre. (p. 333)

Again, virtue and power are opposed: the characteristic inflation of sentimentalism seeks to conjure great moral qualities out of the most abject weakness. In contrast with the discourse of Tracy and Say, the Christian resonances are obvious. Bernardin concludes with an anecdote concerning a young woman who is driven to madness by the injustice of a father who takes away all the fruits of her labour, promising to recompense her with a gold cross which he never produces. A doctor attempts to cure her by effecting a family reconciliation:

La fille émue, verse des larmes, lui tend la main, l'embrasse, et en peu de temps recouvre sa santé. Ainsi le père retrouva sa tendresse dans le malheur de sa fille, et la fille sa raison dans l'amour de son père, et tous deux baignèrent de leurs larmes la main du sage qui les avait guéris. (p. 341)

Bernardin, in conclusion, addresses the materialists:

laborieux naturalistes, orateurs diserts, philosophes profonds qui remontez aux sources de la pensée et qui cherchez à en perfectionner les signes, [...] une femme timide, éloquente des seules formes de la nature, va, d'un sourire, troubler votre logique, ou la renverser avec ses larmes. (p. 342)

Bernardin was not the only person to defend the cause of innate ideas in post-Thermidorian France. François Picavet has shown that, as early as 1794, both Grégoire and Sieyès were interested in introducing the philosophy of Kant in France as a means of combating the materialism and atheism which, in their view, had so nearly triumphed in the Jacobin experience. The main focus of the debate about Kant was the question of what force or institution was to guarantee the application of moral values in the real world, and Kant was seen as a thinker who had introduced a source of immediate experiential authority into the moral sphere, a point of certainty where the philosophy of the eighteenth century had created only doubt.[10] This was clearly the tenor of a number of interventions made at the *Institut* by Louis-Sébastien Mercier between Year 8 and Year 10: 'Mémoire sur les idées innées' (7 and 17 ventôse Year 8); 'Mémoire sur la philosophie de Kant' (2 brumaire–17 frimaire Year 10); 'Mémoire sur la philosophie de Kant comparée à celle de Fichtey [sic], savant d'Iéna en Saxe' (27 frimaire Year 10); 'De l'acte du moi, ou le fumeur' (14 floréal Year 10).[11] These interventions have left few written traces, but what has survived does suggest that Mercier's position was close to Bernardin's. A manuscript commentary by Mercier on one of his *Institut* interventions makes clear the alignment of opposing forces:

J'entre en lice en faveur de la philosophie de *Kant*; [...] Je serai clair, vif et rapide; ouvrez-moi l'arène, je tiens en main le jugement et la condamnation des Empiristes; nous appelons ainsi les idéologues qui ne s'étayent que sur les sens de l'homme et qui ne se fondent que sur les expériences matérielles. Il est temps que l'on entende une doctrine digne de la pensée de l'homme, une doctrine éclairée et sentimentale qui chasse les nuages impurs de l'encyclopédisme, ce monstrueux assemblage d'un savoir pire que l'ignorance; il est temps de rétablir la moralité, de réclamer en faveur du beau, du bon, absolu et idéal.[12]

'De l'acte du moi, ou le fumeur' was delivered in response to a *mémoire* by Tracy read on 7 floréal Year 10, entitled 'De la métaphysique de Kant, ou Observations sur un ouvrage [...] de J. Kinker'. Tracy contrasts the speculative, imprecise and unrealistic nature of German thought with the precision and objectivity of 'l'idéologie française'.[13] Mercier's own summary of his intervention was published in the *Magasin encyclopédique*. His argument is that the *moi* is a moral entity capable of acting in opposition to the promptings of self-interest:

C'est mon *moi* qui développe les sentiments moraux par le monde physique; et cela est si vrai, que, malgré le plaisir sensuel ou la douleur physique unie à une sensation, je suis obligé de reconnaître souvent dans la douleur un *bien* et dans le plaisir un *mal*. Et quel rapport y a-t-il entre le jeu de toutes les fibres et fibriles, et l'admiration que j'éprouve au récit d'un grand sacrifice fait à l'auguste image de la vertu? [...] le *moi* intérieur s'élève souvent dans toute sa dignité au milieu des bourreaux; et souffrir dans la cause de la vertu, ce n'est plus que renforcer ce plaisir intime que donne le calme de la conscience. On a vu le martyr attaché au pieu fatal, lancer sa pensée dans les cieux, devenir tout céleste, et les flammes le dévorer sans qu'il participât à la douleur physique.[14]

As in Bernardin, the type of narrative segment which is being used to support the claims of a spontaneist vision of moral feeling belongs to the strongest tradition of sentimentalism, of the type which, in purely literary terms, undergoes the transformation into melodrama and Gothic. Mercier's text places in contiguous opposition the virtuous victim and the tormentor, and it is the contiguity which is seen as the reinforcement of the claims of virtue. The alignment between sentimentalism and an anti-sensationalist defence of innate ideas is clear.

Two texts expressly concerned with the origins of sympathy suggest that this alignment is not the whole story, and confirm the existence of important structural links between the sensationalist theory of sympathy and the sentimental aesthetic. These are Sophie de Condorcet's 'Huit lettres sur la sympathie', addressed to her brother-in-law Cabanis and published with her translation of Adam Smith's *Theory of Moral Sentiments* in 1798, and sections of Roederer's *Cours d'organisation sociale*, delivered at the Lycée in 1793.[15] Both authors (Mme de Condorcet for obvious reasons) take as their starting point the work of Smith, which provides them with a basic theory of the origins of sympathy as a spontaneous and unreflective reaction to the inner life of others (although, paradoxically, this spontaneity is a materialist one); both then develop this in a rationalist direction, insisting on the role of self-interest and of reason in the transformations of basic sympathy which take place in moral behaviour and in social institutions.

Mme de Condorcet's is a very elegant work, in which the language of sentiment is counterpoised by a very rationalist approach: the overall tone is one of restrained optimism and of faith in the notion of progress. The high moral tone of sentimentalism is always present: in the first letter, she addresses parents, insisting that sensibility and benevolence must form a central part of their children's education:

Que vous êtes coupables, si vous êtes plus pressés des succès de vos enfants que de leurs vertus; si vous êtes plus impatients de les voir plaire dans un cercle, que de voir leurs coeurs bouillonner d'indignation à l'aspect de l'injustice, leurs fronts pâlir devant la douleur, leurs coeurs traiter tous les hommes en frères! [...] Que la douce habitude de faire le bien leur apprenne que c'est par le coeur qu'ils peuvent être heureux, et non par leurs titres, par leur luxe, par leurs dignités, par leurs richesses!

Sensibility and self-interest are opposed. Moreover, the author insists that it was the example of her mother which first taught her the importance of sensibility:

Oui, c'est en voyant vos mains soulager à la fois la misère et la maladie; c'est en voyant les regards souffrants du pauvre se tourner vers vous et s'attendrir en vous bénissant, que j'ai senti tout mon coeur, et que le vrai bien de la vie sociale, expliquée à mes yeux, m'a paru dans le bonheur d'aimer les hommes et de les servir.[16]

Elsewhere, she speaks with enthusiasm of the educational value of the 'école de l'infortune et de l'adversité' (p. 317), and sees human sensibility, the urge to run to the assistance of misfortune, as a principle of balance and harmony: 'Bénissons ce rapport sublime qui se trouve entre les besoins moraux de quelques hommes et les besoins physiques de quelques autres, entre les malheurs auxquels la nature et nos vices nous soumettent, et les penchants de la vertu, qui n'est heureuse qu'en les soulageant' (p. 337).

And yet, the rationalist Mme de Condorcet has no doubt that this capacity is a function of physical sensibility: its origins lie in the the fact that local pain generates 'une impression douloureuse dans tous nos organes', which can continue after the disappearance of the local pain; and, once experience has taught us to recognise the *signs* of pain in others, the idea of that pain can generate in the beholder a similar generalised pain (p. 315). After this point, self-interest and the more or less rational combination and comparison of ideas take over. Although habit may obscure the fact, it is self-interest which makes us act upon the promptings of original sympathy, either in the sense that we act in order to relieve the pain that we *ourselves* experience at the sufferings of others, or in the sense that virtuous behaviour is a source of self-satisfaction (pp. 382–3). As for processes of rationalisation, their role is to develop and generalise the urge to relieve the sufferings of others, so that notions of *justice* emerge out of notions of *bien*, and benevolence situated within an immediate, direct context can be transformed into more abstract notions of social well-being. Almost by virtue of a mathematical model, that which is more generalised, that which applies to a wider range of individual cases, is superior in moral and social worth: the universal is an outgrowth of the individual. The familiar correlate of this is that informed benevolence is more socially useful than well-intentioned but possibly short-sighted spontaneity (as in enlightened criticisms of individual alms-giving). Furthermore, in direct opposition to a certain sentimental *topos*, Mme de Condorcet believes that country people, because less self-conscious, are *less* given to compassionate action than town dwellers. Inescapably, education, one of the aims of which is to develop the capacity for general ideas, for conceptualisation, becomes a central social institution (pp. 388–95).

The overall form of Mme de Condorcet's theory of social sympathy is the key to understanding the links with the sentimental aesthetic. The process of elaboration and construction which she describes has its inception in an original founding scene where the human subject – spontaneously, indeed involuntarily, but no less miraculously – recognises the pain of the Other and reacts with sympathy. That scene of recognition has its equivalent in any number of sentimental narratives; and the process of intellectual and social elaboration which is then set in train mirrors the repetition, refraction and internal quotation by which the sentimental narrative magnifies the original scene, making it available as the basis of a moral system. In Mme de Condorcet, imagination, reflection, the combination of ideas are operations executed on an original sign; they take the original moment where the pain of the other impinges on the observing subject, and re-project, re-present it in an ever-widening chain of development. Mme de Condorcet's text clearly shows the crucial formal similarities between a sensationalist theory of morality and the sentimental aesthetic:

both figure, in a different language, the emergence of social morality from individual experience.

Roederer's *Cours d'organisation sociale* predates Mme de Condorcet's work by five years. Roederer is aware of two different visions of the social virtues: a radically materialist theory of benevolence, exemplified by Helvétius, and a theory of sympathy which he traces to Hume and Smith. He seeks to occupy a middle ground, sketching out the familiar view that a spontaneous movement of sympathy is the foundation of more elaborate, rational forms of behaviour. It is Roederer's treatment of the original movement of sympathy which particularly interests me here. Roederer is very attracted by the analysis, taken from Smith, which suggests that the power of sympathy is such that it can transport us inside the skin and psyche of another human being. He in fact reconsiders his position on this metaphor in the 'Observation' added subsequently to the text of the *Cours*, stating that this idea of interpersonal penetration

est en opposition avec ce que nous savons de l'origine des idées et par conséquent de l'origine des passions. Il suppose, ou que nous pouvons avoir le sentiment de la douleur sans en avoir l'idée, ou que nous pouvons en avoir le sentiment ou l'idée par les organes d'autrui, et que, sans avoir éprouvé par moi-même ce que c'est que souffrir, je l'éprouverai en voyant souffrir un autre, par communication, par affinité secrète. Cela nous jetterait dans le magnétisme, dans les fluides de Messmer, etc.[17]

This rethinking is part of a hardening of attitudes between the first version of the *Cours* and the 'Observation'. But there is no reason to suppose that this calls into question what is in a sense a very materialist section of the *Cours*, where Roederer reflects on the visibility of the passions and the role of this visibility in the emergence of sympathy. Sensitivity to the affections of others has a double origin:

Elle vient de deux choses: premièrement de la faculté de voir et de discerner dans les autres les signes de nos propres douleurs et de nos propres plaisirs; deuxièmement dans [sic] l'extrême visibilité, dans l'apparence très sensible, dans l'évidence très frappante de nos douleurs ou de nos plaisirs, et, si je puis le dire, dans l'*extériorité de nos signes*. (pp. 192–3, my italics)

This 'visibilité des passions' is more marked in humans than in other animals, for a whole series of reasons:

Le rire et les larmes, la rougeur et la pâleur, sont des indices de l'état de notre âme et de l'état de notre corps, dont la réunion ne se trouve dans aucune espèce animale. Ajoutez à ces circonstances la puissance de la parole, la science du langage, qui nous sont aussi particulières et qui donnent du corps ou du moins du son à tous nos sentiments, à toutes nos affections; et vous concevrez sans peine comment l'homme dont l'état se manifeste continuellement par tant de signes extérieurs, peut en donner l'idée à son semblable. (p. 193)

The visibility of the human soul is thus the product of a whole series of signs which deeply interest the *Idéologues*: speech and language, laughter and tears are part of the same structure and fulfil parallel functions. Cabanis, for instance, writes

La sympathie morale exerce son action par les regards, par la physionomie, par les mouvements extérieurs, par le langage articulé, par les accents de la voix, en un mot, par tous les signes.[18]

But it is the transparency of the skin which particularly interests Roederer here. In his opening remarks, he had announced the theme in a lengthy and enthusiastic passage, enumerating the different transformations of the skin and suggesting that 'la seule transparence de la peau humaine a servi à l'exercice, au développement, à la perfection de la bienveillance raisonnée' (p. 136). Now, he attempts a strange gradation of different categories of human being by the transparency of their skin:

La transparence de la peau humaine est tellement un principe de sociabilité, que les affections sociales sont, ce me semble, très-sensiblement graduées, je ne dirai pas sur la peau des hommes, mais du moins comme ces différences, et par conséquent paraissent en emprunter quelque chose. (p. 193)

The hierarchy which he sketches is this: 'le nègre; un homme hâlé; un homme frais et rasé; une femme brune et ridée; une femme jeune et fraîche; une brune foncée; une blonde; un enfant'. He insists that what he is classifying is simply the facility with which different types of people command instant attention by virtue of the visibility of their passions (they 'saisissent' more, but they do not 'intéressent' less).

The strange reductivism of Roederer's approach is interesting on two counts. By focussing on a *specific* physiological feature, and raising it to pre-eminent status in the genealogy of moral feeling, Roederer echoes the sentimental text's very explicit concern with the externalisation of the inner life. Secondly, and despite his disclaimers, it is striking that his physiological gradations reproduce in large part the hierarchy of sentimentalisation in which women and children attain privileged status as objects of sentimental regard.

Incidentally, the problematic of the inner and the outer also finds expression, in inverted form, in certain descriptions of the power of society over the individual:

il faut qu'outre le tribunal institué qui jugera les actions répréhensibles, il s'en élève de toutes parts qui soient toujours en fonctions, qui soient présents à toute la vie des citoyens, qui les suivent dans leur conduite publique et dans l'intérieur de leurs familles; qui assistent, pour ainsi dire, à toutes leur pensées mêmes, et décernent à chacun la récompense ou la peine qui lui est due [...] ce ne pourra être que l'opinion publique bien éclairée, bien vertueuse, bien unanime, bien moralisée. (p. 228)

This worrying vision of clandestine social control, it should be remembered, is not that of some closet Jacobin, but of a man who went into hiding immediately after 10 August for his opposition to the imprisonment of the royal family and what he saw as the beginnings of mob rule.[19]

Beyond disagreements about the innate or the constructed nature of moral feeling, which appeared to mobilise certain aspects of sentimental language in favour of innate ideas, these texts by Mme de Condorcet and Roederer confirm formal and structural parallels between sensationalist discourse and sentimental narrative: on the one hand, sensationalist theory is, like sentimentalism, concerned with the problematic of the inner and the outer, and its impact on moral feeling. On the other, the construction and combination of signs and complex ideas which is involved in the genealogy of morality according to the *Idéologues* represents a formal echo of the sentimental text, in which scenes of pain and pity are juxtaposed, repeated and refracted. It is worth emphasising the formal nature of the relationship which is being suggested: rather than being a programmatic application of philosophical ideas, the fictional text belongs to the philosophical world by virtue of shared formal characteristics.

Turning away from the *Idéologues'* sensationalism and preoccupation with the origins of moral feeling, I propose to conclude by looking at some texts which suggest the kind of relationship which exists between the inherited language of sentimentalism and the theory of liberalism – in an economic but also a broader social sense – which the *Idéologues* develop. I have chosen to deal with two themes analysed at length in chapter 3: poverty, and love and marriage.

Cabanis's 'Quelques principes et quelques vues sur les secours publics' was the fruit of his work as a member of the Parisian 'Commission des hôpitaux' from 1791 to 1793. A passage from the opening section of the work offers a fair summary of Cabanis's analysis.

Sous un bon régime, tout homme en état de travailler ne manque jamais d'ouvrage: les moeurs générales flétrissent la fainéantise et sollicitent l'industrie; elles établissent dans les familles un esprit et des sentiments qui repoussent toute idée d'abandon d'un père, ou d'une mère infirme, ou d'un enfant au berceau; elles inspirent à la fois l'horreur du métier de mendiant, et la touchante compassion qui s'empresse de secourir la misère. Quand ces sentiments et ces habitudes n'existent point, c'est toujours la faute des lois.[20]

Cabanis's economic liberalism is much in evidence in his analysis of poverty. Mendicity is the consequence of two factors: the unnatural distribution of wealth which characterises an aristocratic society based on privilege, and the non-circulation of wealth which is blocked by various other obstacles in such a society. Since poverty is the product of human causes ('le mal est produit par art'), legislative reform is the fundamental solution: a programme including the abolition of privilege, a just tax system, meritocracy ('ces loix fraternelles qui appellent également tous les hommes à tous les emplois') and reform of inheritance law would soon reduce the gap between rich and poor (pp. 19–20). His liberalism has as its philosophical foundation the belief that self-interest is a powerful and legitimate motivator of human beings considered as individuals. People enjoying the basic freedom to pursue their self-interest will help themselves: Cabanis evokes a situation in which

> chacun se trouve placé dans sa sphère propre [...], chacun peut n'obéir qu'à des impulsions personnelles, s'isoler dans le but de ses travaux, et disposer à son gré de ses fruits [...] C'est du sein de la vie privée, où d'ailleurs ils sont le plus heureux, que [les hommes] concourent encore le plus efficacement au bonheur public. (p. 29)

The effect of rational reform will be to reduce the problem of poverty, and therefore to limit the occasions when society as a whole is called upon to provide assistance for the deprived. Nevertheless, and particularly in the short term, society must offer a safety net:

> quand des malheureux manquent du plus indispensable nécessaire, il faut le leur fournir; quand des malades sont privés chez eux de tout secours, il faut leur en donner; toutes les théories et tous les calculs cèdent au cri de la nature, au devoir de l'humanité. (p. 10)

This response is a sentimental one: it requires no rationalisation, it is spontaneous and immediate, as the recourse to the notion of the 'cri de la nature' in particular shows. But Cabanis is not to be diverted from his firm resolve to limit public assistance and promote what today is called 'community care': where work is to be given to the able-bodied poor, it is always desirable that this be done within the private sector, since this represents the least possible disruption of the natural equilibrium of the economy; and in the case of the old, the sick, 'secours à domicile' is preferable, not least because of its unifying and pedagogical effects, evoked here in sentimental tones:

> C'est par les soins mutuels que l'esprit de famille se conserve, que la bonté se cultive, que les moeurs se perfectionnent. Un malade à garder, à servir, est un spectacle utile, une leçon vivante d'humanité: c'est le moyen de réveiller efficacement dans le coeur une foule de sentiments précieux. Quand ce malade est un père, une mère, un frère, une soeur, un fils, une fille, combien les soins qu'on lui rend ne resserrent-ils pas les liens naturels! Presque toutes les vertus humaines

sont fondées sur la bienveillance réciproque: et c'est par le malheur surtout que les hommes se rapprochent; c'est en recevant ou en donnant des secours, qu'ils apprennent à se chérir. Une créature aussi faible devait trouver dans sa faiblesse même, et dans les maux qui en découlent, la source de sa principale force et de ses plus douces affections. (pp. 44–5)

The family, already identified as the private space within which individual industry flourishes best, is also the privileged site of sentimental epiphany. It is almost as though the familiar boundary separating one individual from another – the boundary, in other words, between the inner and outer spheres – had been redrawn, to define on the one hand the family, the primary unit within which the laws of sympathy operate without restriction, and, on the other, the political economy, where the mode of articulation between individuals/units is one of competing self-interests; although of course that process of competition is seen as resulting naturally in a state of harmony, situated this time at the level of the whole economy.

If these are the structures of classic economic liberalism, then I believe that they are also apparent in the *Idéologues'* attitude to romantic and marriage relations, although the demonstration is necessarily more complex in a less directly economic field. Certain texts would seem to justify the view that the *Idéologues'* attitudes in this area are fundamentally at one with sentimental narrative. In a passage from his *Cours d'organisation sociale* which refers specifically to Revolutionary legislation on divorce, the age of majority and parental authority, Roederer seems to view the work of the Revolution as a direct continuation of the cry of protest raised by the sentimental novel of the eighteenth century.[21] In an extensive examination of the place of the family within society, he argues that women should not be granted political rights because the contract instituting civil society is between families, the basic unit of domestic society, and the head of that unit is the man; he goes on to challenge the notion of absolute paternal authority, which he sees as an extension of absolutism into the domestic field; and then comes to the argument in favour of divorce, which he defends as the means of guaranteeing love as the basis of marriage. Some have criticised the institution of divorce as a measure calculated to institutionalise libertinage, and it is in response to this argument that he launches into a dramatised and rhetorical passage rich in the language and concepts of sentimentalism:

C'est la licence insolente de la tyrannie domestique qui a appelé libertinage les douces réclamations de l'amour contrarié, affligé, tourmenté par nos institutions. Toutes ces plaintes douloureuses dont nos romans, nos poésies, nos drames sont remplis; ces plaintes si pénétrantes, qu'on dit être si dangereuses pour la jeunesse, ne le sont que parce qu'elles sont justes, fondées, parce qu'elles tirent une force extrême des droits de la nature, et qu'elles trouvent en nous autant de points sensibles qu'il y a de fibres dans notre organisation. Et, après tout, les romans ne se réduisent-ils pas tous à dire ce que la loi a récemment consacré: 1 que les parents n'ont pas le droit d'empêcher le mariage de leurs enfants; 2 qu'ils n'ont pas le droit de contraindre leurs enfants à des mariages auxquels ceux-ci répugnent; 3 que l'union du mariage ne doit pas être plus durable que l'union des coeurs [...] Nos romans, je ne parle pas de ceux qui sont lascifs ou indécents, sont la véritable déclaration des droits des coeurs aimants. Ce sont eux qui ont établi la liberté d'aimer, cette première des libertés, qui repose dans le plus inviolable sanctuaire, le coeur. Nos romans ne sont contraires qu'à nos vieilles et coupables institutions; nos romans ne sont funestes aux coeurs sensibles que comme l'exposition des droits de l'homme l'était autrefois aux esprits ardents et libres, en les froissant entre les volontés de la nature et les aspérités de nos tyrannies sociales. Eh! on appelait aussi libertinage, on punissait aussi de peines cruelles ces engagements toujours cachés et jamais secrets des femmes malheureuses avec des hommes sensibles, ce recours des coeurs opprimés à l'amour protecteur et consolateur; combien de malheureuses n'a-t-on pas faites de ces êtres qui l'étaient déjà par leur contrainte et par leurs chaînes? [...] On a souvent parlé des bastilles abattues, et chaque maison en était une pour quelque épouse infortunée. Celles-là n'ont été ouvertes que du jour où le divorce a été établi [...]

Je le dis clairement, hautement: il n'y a de saint, de respectable, que l'union des êtres que le coeur associe [...] C'est à l'amour, non aux formalités ou aux solennités de nos mariages, que la nature accorde des enfants. Que nous faudra-t-il respecter davantage, ou ces formalités misérables, ces contrats, ces notaires, ces prêtres ministres de nos tyrannies domestiques, ou bien l'auguste consécration de la nature?[22]

Nature against institution, weakness oppressed by force, virtue defined by its encounter with misfortune, the constant recourse to notions of 'coeur' and 'sensibilité': the ancestry of this text is unmistakable. Similar evidence can be adduced from a passage in Mme de Condorcet's seventh letter to Cabanis. The work is largely devoted to demonstrating the fact that, given the natural sympathy of humankind, injustice and inhumanity must necessarily be attributed to the malign influence of bad institutions; the status of love in unreformed societies is presented as a case in point. She imagines a society in which the abolition of aristocratic prejudice means that marriages cease to be 'des conventions et des marchés de fortune, dont la conclusion rapide ne permet de reconnaître que long-temps après si les convenances personnelles s'y rencontrent, et où le prix de l'amour, commandé plutôt qu'obtenu, est adjugé en même temps que la dot, avant que l'on sache si l'on peut aimer', and concludes that

C'est la société qui, en mettant trop long-temps des entraves aux unions qu'un goût mutuel eût formées, [...] a donné naissance aux passions dangereuses et corrompues qui ne sont point l'amour, et qui l'ont rendu si rare. (pp. 421–2)

An often-quoted passage from Cabanis's 'Rapports du physique et du moral de l'homme' develops the theme further and introduces variations which are taken up in Tracy's *De l'Amour*. Certainly, Cabanis speaks in familiar terms of the obstacles placed in the way of love by aristocratic society: 'ces barrières maladroites que les parents, ou les institutions civiles prétendent lui opposer, et tous les autres obstacles qu'il rencontre dans les préjugés relatifs à la naissance, aux rangs, à la fortune'.[23] But his overall argument is that such obstacles are the direct cause of a particularly hyperbolic representation of love with which he takes issue. Love, he says, 'tel que le développe la nature, n'est pas ce torrent effréné qui renverse tout: ce n'est point ce fantôme théâtral qui se nourrit de ses propres éclats, se complaît dans une vaine représentation, et s'enivre lui-même des effets qu'il produit sur les spectateurs' (p. 313). Cabanis, then, is seeking to break free of what he takes to be a simplistic dichotomy: rejection of the aristocratic model should not drive us into uncritical acceptance of inflated sentimental definitions of love, 'car, sans barrières et obstacles, il peut y avoir beaucoup de bonheur dans l'amour, mais non du délire et de la fureur' (p. 313).

The critique of sentimental stereotypes is extended in Tracy's *De l'Amour*, the most celebrated Ideological text on love, and of course a crucial reference in the deconstruction of the sentimental topos which will be undertaken by Stendhal. Tracy's satire on sentimental representations of love is in fact closely related to the analysis proposed in *Quels sont les moyens de fonder la morale chez un peuple?*: the social practices of which sentimental love is a structural element are a perfect illustration of his view that 'prescrire, prohiber et punir sont des choses très faciles, mais que le grand art consiste à faire vouloir'. Thus, on the one hand, young men are kept in a state of supposedly virtuous isolation from women, but on the other they are fed a literary diet of total affective excess, with the result that 'aussitôt qu'une femme mariée leur fait la moindre grimace, ils sont persuadés que seule une passion des plus violentes peut la porter si loin'.[24]

Tracy's stated objective in *De l'Amour* is to consolidate marriage in modern society, through a programme of rational reform. The statement of the importance of the task is profoundly unsentimental in tone:

Le mariage est lié à tous nos intérêts; de là vient que, quand on en traite, il est nécessaire de faire entrer en ligne de compte la fortune, les plans d'établissement et d'avancement, la façon dont peuvent s'accorder la position sociale des personnes intéressées et l'époque où l'on vit. De là vient que c'est la chose la plus difficile du monde que d'obéir uniquement aux impulsions du coeur. (p. 15)

Tracy, in short, seems to be reintroducing the social considerations which the sentimental text marginalises: 'si dans leurs différends la nature est toujours du parti de l'Amour, Hymen a toujours été protégé par tous les législateurs et tous les moralistes' (p. 25).

Yet, when it comes to the programme of reform which would achieve these aims, Tracy pursues a line of reasoning entirely consistent with the sentimental project: increased social freedom for the unattached; help for those whose marriages were entered into lightly and mistakenly (i.e. divorce); and the exclusion from marriage projects of 'des considérations étrangères à l'amour'. In all societies where class distinctions and the gap between rich and poor are marked, where the patronage of the powerful is the route to success, where inheritance laws encourage the non-productive accumulation of wealth, and where paternal authority is excessive,

> vous verrez que beaucoup de mariages sont déterminés par ces motifs et sont par conséquent malheureux ou pour le moins assez tristes, et qu'ils sont souvent troublés par ces sentiments qu'inspire la nature, qui ne perd jamais ses droits, alors que le mariage par son institution primitive devrait les rendre plus fermes et plus assurés. (pp. 29–30)

Sentimental notions of the primacy of the heart have their place in Tracy's analysis, but it is only a place: rather than being isolated and celebrated, as in pure sentimentalism, the sentimental moment fits into a larger social project. The nature of that insertion relates, on the one hand, to the discussion of human motivation in *Quels sont les moyens de fonder la morale chez un peuple?* and, on the other, to the general intellectual model of liberalism. Placing social obstacles in the way of nature is folly not because, by virtue of some Manichean dichotomy, nature is always right and society always wrong, but because nature is a force which society must realistically accept as a given. Speaking warmly of the example offered by certain Swiss cantons – the *Lettre à d'Alembert* comes to mind – Tracy argues that giving free rein to the choice of young people, far from opening the way to anarchy, is an essential condition for the development of maturity. Once the choice of the heart has been made freely, couples will of their own volition consider the social and economic dimensions of marriage. It is here that a strong parallel with the theory of economic liberalism is apparent. Tracy writes:

> Dans mes spéculations, je prends pour guide la Nature, et il est si vrai que le bon ordre que j'ai décrit est si conforme à son voeu, qu'il s'établit lui-même quand quelque passion trop artificielle ne vient pas s'y opposer. (p. 32)

The workings of the heart and the workings of an economy manifest the same formal characteristics: in both cases, the legislator's task is to minimise barriers, to remove obstacles, to allow individual motivations and self-interests to operate, for, by virtue of the same law of nature, this freedom – of the heart, of economic agents – will produce order. A metaphor used by Tracy in his description of the free sentimental economy suggests some awareness of the parallels:

Les jeunes gens des deux sexes ont besoin de se connaître pour se choisir. Ils ont affaire dans le monde, comme les négociants en Bourse, et tout le monde doit comprendre que leurs affaires s'avancent et mûrissent à mesure qu'ils commencent à se retirer du tumulte. (p. 32)

In conclusion, it appears that *idéologie* represents a significant restriction of sentimentalism. Certainly, there are important formal parallels between the sentimental aesthetic and empiricist theories of sympathy taken over and developed in the Ideological milieu; furthermore, sentimental formulations concerning charity and the importance of individual passion in marital relations point to the existence of important continuities. Ultimately, however, the *Idéologues'* liberalism is determining: whatever place sentiment may have in the private sphere, in the public one the interaction of human beings is envisaged not in terms of interiority, meeting, communication, but as the clash of self-contained units coexisting through balance, and producing harmony almost despite themselves. The controversies discussed in the first part of this chapter concerning the role of self-interest and the nature of morality now take on a clearer significance: the free market's miraculous creation of order out of the chaos of individual action *legitimises* self-interest. Mandeville's formulation, in which private vices are seen to equate to public virtues, still holds, and this represents a direct challenge to sentimentalism's representation of altruism as coterminous with the social project. Sentimental narrative and the theory of economic liberalism may share a preoccupation with the removal of barriers, judged to prevent the natural circulation in one case of affection and in the other of wealth; but such a parallel is so formal as to appear devoid of any concrete social or ideological meaning, and seems to rely for readability on an extremely high degree of symbolic coding. It seems far more reasonable to conclude that, as in enlightened debates about poor relief, different modes of thought apply to different areas of activity: the sentimental model applies to a sphere beyond the reach of economic categories, to which belong the family, women, children and those whose misfortune has denied them the capacity to work and therefore the status of economic agents.

CHAPTER 6

Beyond sentimentalism? Madame de Staël

A number of factors suggest that an analysis of the work of Madame de Staël through the prism of sentimentalism would be useful and instructive. An enthusiastic reader of Rousseau, she is a daughter of the Enlightenment who goes through the experience of the Revolution and the Empire chastened but unchanged in her faith in the basic tenets of Enlightenment. She writes both imaginative and historical–social works, thus spanning at least part of the range which this study seeks to cover. She is a Protestant. Finally, and most importantly, she is a woman and a feminist: given the crucial importance of women in the stock dramatis personae of sentimentalism, and the potential feminism of some of the claims regarding love and marriage which sentimentalism has been seen to articulate, it seemed inadmissible not to devote a chapter to the most famous woman writer of the period.

The essay *De l'influence des passions sur le bonheur des individus et des nations*, begun in 1792 and published in 1796, provides a clue to the role which sentimentalism plays in the career of Madame de Staël. The essay is incomplete: the second part, which would have corresponded to the element 'et des nations' in the title, was never written, with the result that, formally, the essay concerns only the happiness of individuals. It is divided into three sections: 'Des passions', 'Des sentiments qui sont l'intermédiaire entre les passions et les ressources qu'on trouve en soi', and 'Des ressources qu'on trouve en soi'. This tripartite structure reflects the fundamental notion that the passions place the individual in a position of dependency with respect to others, and that a wise philosophy would counsel the

cultivation of 'les ressources qu'on trouve en soi', which elimi-
nate the danger of disappointment inherent in dependency
upon others. This argument is reflected at numerous points in
the text, where a youthful belief in the possibility of sentimental fulfilment gives way, in a temporal progression, to an
adult realisation of the futility of such dreams and of the
consequent desirability of self-reliance. The optimism of youth
is decribed in the following terms:

On veut d'abord consacrer sa vie à être aimé de ses amis, à captiver la
faveur publique. Il semble qu'on ne s'est jamais assez mis à la
disposition de ceux qu'on aime; qu'on ne leur ait jamais assez prouvé
qu'on ne pouvait exister sans eux; que l'occupation, les services de
tous les jours, ne satisfassent pas assez, au gré de la chaleur de l'âme,
le besoin qu'on a de se dévouer, de se livrer en entier aux autres.

The belief in the good faith of the other, in the transparency of
the subject's intentions and qualities, is total:

Comment la vérité, et la vérité du sentiment, ne persuaderait-elle
pas? Comment ne finirait-elle pas par être reconnue? [...] Vos
paroles, votre voix, vos accents, l'air qui vous environne, tout vous
semble empreint de ce que vous êtes réellement, et l'on ne croit pas à
la possibilité d'être long-temps mal jugé: c'est avec ce sentiment de
confiance qu'on vogue à pleines voiles dans la vie.[1]

The individual described here believes that the internal life of
the subject can be faithfully externalised; in the same way, in
the discussion of friendship, the highest level of intimacy is
achieved when 'les deux amis peuvent réussir à confondre leurs
existences, à transporter l'un dans l'autre ce qu'il y a d'ardent
dans la personnalité' (pp. 188–9).

  Jean Starobinski has argued that the dark side of Madame
de Staël's imagination, her preoccupation with suicide and
melancholy, is a function, precisely, of a logically anterior faith
in the total nature of sentimental communication. Speaking
particularly of the Staëlian concept of love, he writes:

L'être aimant s'anéantit tout entier au profit de l'être aimé. La
rhétorique amoureuse, qui fait de l'être aimé *ma vie*, est vécue ici au
sens littéral dans la mesure où la littéralité se laisse vivre. L'être ne
s'appartient plus, il n'est plus rien pour lui-même, il s'est tout entier
mis sous la garde et sous la dépendance de l'être aimé.[2]

This rhetoric of love is demonstrably related to the sentimental tradition, with its characteristic tendency to inflate the value of feeling by weighing it against the most valued commodities and always finding it more valuable. The chapter 'De l'amour' represents a lengthy and fulsome eulogy of love. Madame de Staël recalls an incident during a stay in England: out walking with a couple who have been happily married for twenty-five years, she and her hosts meet some gypsies, and she expresses pity for their material and moral deprivation. The husband replies with a rhetorical figure which is the precise reason for the inclusion of the anecdote, which has nothing to do with the poverty of gypsies:

Eh bien! [...] si, pour passer ma vie avec elle, il avait fallu me résigner à cet état, j'aurais mendié pendant trente ans, et nous aurions encore été bien heureux! – Ah! oui, s'écria sa femme, même ainsi nous aurions été les plus heureux des êtres! (pp. 132–6)

The comfortable bourgeois affirming that thirty years of begging is as nothing compared to their love is, of course, straight sentimentalism, and Madame de Staël quotes it without apparent embarrassment.

De l'influence des passions also offers contrasting perceptions of that fundamental sentimental category, misfortune, by young and old.

Ce mot terrible, le malheur, s'entend dans les premiers jours de la jeunesse, sans que la pensée le comprenne. Les tragédies, les ouvrages d'imagination, vous représentent l'adversité comme un tableau où le courage et la beauté se déploient; la mort, ou un dénouement heureux, terminent, en peu d'instants, l'anxiété qu'on éprouve. Au sortir de l'enfance, l'image de la douleur est inséparable d'une sorte d'attendrissement qui mêle du charme à toutes les impressions qu'on reçoit.

This literary perception of misfortune is replaced, in the subject who has reached the advanced age of twenty-five years (Madame de Staël was twenty-five in 1791), by a far darker perception: it becomes something 'long comme la vie',

sombre, desséchant l'émotion, [qui] ne laisse dans l'âme qu'une seule impression inquiète et brûlante. La souffrance est alors le centre de toutes les pensées, elle devient le principe unique de la vie; on ne se reconnaît que par la douleur. (pp. 214–6)

At first sight, then, *De l'influence des passions* would suggest that Madame de Staël associates the language and preoccupations of sentimentalism with youthful illusion, and that the movement towards maturity is perceived as a *dépassement* of the sentimental. And yet that is not really the case. The three 'ressources qu'on trouve en soi' which emerge in the third section of the work as a surer foundation for happiness than reliance on others are philosophy, study and 'la bienfaisance'; this last chapter, taking up one of the central philosophical preoccupations of the sentimental tradition of the eighteenth century, is of fundamental importance, since it lays the foundations for a theory of pity as a social virtue which, as I shall show later, runs as a constant throughout Madame de Staël's political, social and historical writings.

Madame de Staël follows Rousseau, and the major part of Enlightenment tradition, in defining *bienfaisance* as 'la vertu primitive', the only one to be 'gravée dans le coeur [...] L'homme bon est de tous les temps et de toutes les nations.' It exists in us 'comme le principe de la vie, sans être l'effet de notre propre volonté; elle semble un don du ciel comme toutes les facultés, elle agit sans se connaître' (pp. 233–4). She insists particularly on the non-reflexive, spontaneous nature of *bienfaisance*: if she has a criticism of Smith's 'excellent' *Theory of Moral Sentiments*, it is that his definition of sympathy is too restrictive, relying on the observing subject having experienced that which the sufferer is experiencing. Sympathy participates in the 'jouissances du sentiment', with the crucial difference that it does not expect a return from the person who is its object. It 'ne jouit que de ce qu'elle donne' and, 'n'ayant voulu que le plaisir même de son action, ne peut jamais s'être trompée dans ses calculs' (pp. 234–5).

To insist on the non-intellectual nature of pity is to see it as a reactive process, again in the sentimental tradition. The unmediated nature of the sentimental reaction to the sufferings of others suggests that physical sensibility is involved:

il semble que l'organisation physique elle-même soit destinée à en recevoir l'impression. Une voix qui se brise, un visage altéré, agissent sur l'âme directement comme les sensations; la pensée ne se met point entre deux, c'est un choc, une blessure.

And, again totally in line with the central tradition of sentimentalism, Madame de Staël goes on to point to the moral nature of this reaction:

Ce qu'il y a de plus sublime encore dans cette disposition de l'homme, c'est qu'elle est consacrée particulièrement à la faiblesse; et lorsque tout concourt aux avantages de la force, ce sentiment lui seul rétablit la balance, en faisant naître la générosité; ce sentiment ne s'émeut que pour un objet sans défense, qu'*à l'aspect* de l'abandon, qu'*au cri* de la douleur; lui seul défend les vaincus après la victoire.[3]

Finally, Madame de Staël goes on to insist, as she will on numerous occasions throughout her career, on the relationship of pity to the Revolution. She takes issue with the Robespierrist notion that 'la pitié est un sentiment puérile qui s'oppose à toute action nécessaire à l'intérêt général', and describes the Terror as 'un système continuel, et par conséquent à froid, de méconnaître toute pitié'. In her view, revolutionary situations, characterised by their suspension of the 'état social' and the introduction of passion into public reasoning, need the voice of pity more than any other circumstance (pp. 252–3).

In short, the importance of *bienfaisance* is such that, if one were to construct 'l'arbre de la morale, comme il en existe un des sciences, c'est à ce devoir, à ce sentiment dans son acception la plus étendue, que remonterait tout ce qui inspire de l'admiration et de l'estime' (p. 239).

De l'influence des passions does not, then, signify the abandonment of sentimental values as the illusion of youth. Rather, the text points to a shift away from sentimentalism in the private sphere, conceived as unreliable and a source of unhappiness, towards a cultivation of sentimentalism in the public sphere, where it can be the basis of civilised liberal values. This structure, which appears diametrically opposed to the division of private and public spheres in the thought of the *Idéologues* – whom Madame de Staël could not tolerate –

reproduces in a curious way an analysis of her career offered by Simone Balayé.[4] She argues that Madame de Staël maintains and prolongs Enlightenment values in the public sphere, but that her biography and her novels are marked by a significant break with Enlightenment. This rupture, according to Balayé, is particularly apparent in the pessimism and despair which mark the record of Madame de Staël's individual experience as a woman and as a woman writer. This is the dark side of Madame de Staël, in opposition to an Enlightenment belief in progress and perfectibility. Substituting 'sentimentalism' for 'Enlightenment' in Balayé's analysis, I propose in the following pages to examine on the one hand the 'public' work – the political, social and historical texts – and, on the other, the novels, against this basic hypothesis: that the former demonstrate a remarkable degree of continuity in their adherence to a set of values which will be described as sentimental, whereas the novels, while taking as their starting-point the dominant sentimental rhetoric, push this inheritance harder and further in the direction of innovation and renewal.

Madame de Staël is not alone in giving considerable importance to the notion of pity and to related narrative procedures in her treatment of the Revolution. The epigraph to her *Considérations sur la Révolution française* is taken from Rousseau: 'La liberté d'une nation ne vaut pas la vie d'un innocent'. This summarises her view of the argument that public safety justifies the Terror. But her arguments can be more political in character. Echoing the view of moderate opinion during the Revolution – Vergniaud, for instance, uses a similar argument when calling for the 'appel au peuple' in the trial of Louis at the end of December 1792 (see above, p. 154) – she argues that the error of the Revolution was to create the martyrs around which its enemies could then mobilise. 'Il importait [...] de ne jamais mettre les partisans des vieilles institutions dans une situation qui pût inspirer aucune espèce de pitié', she writes of the Assemblée Constituante's measures against the 'prêtres réfractaires'. 'Jamais on ne peut oublier ceux qui souffrent; la nature humaine à cet égard vaut mieux qu'on ne croit.'[5] In another passage, a very clearly sentimental *mise en scène* is used to isolate the point where an oppressed people becomes a mob. The context is the march on the Tuileries of 20 June 1792:

Si quelque sentiment vrai les avait animés, s'ils étaient venus récla-mer contre les injustices, contre la cherté des grains, contre l'accrois-sement des impôts, contre les enrôlements militaires, enfin contre tout ce que le pouvoir et la richesse peuvent faire souffrir à la misère, les haillons dont ils étaient revêtus, leurs mains noircies par le travail, la vieillesse prématurée des femmes, l'abrutissement des enfants, tout aurait excité la pitié. Mais leurs affreux jurements entremêlés de cris, leurs gestes menaçants, leurs instruments meurtriers, offraient un spectacle épouvantable, et qui pouvait altérer à jamais le respect que la race humaine doit inspirer. (p. 273)

Pity is the touchstone of the authenticity and justification of popular demands; and that pity is inspired in the observing subject, whose class position is unspoken but who is implicitly the arbiter of what is politically legitimate, by a series of features denoting powerlessness, oppression, suffering and poverty. Outside of those conditions, the nature of popular political action changes fundamentally: the victim becomes the terrorist, and the human becomes something verging on the non-human.

In *De l'influence des passions*, she writes that the century which has been marked by a rationalist challenge to religious belief has also seen 'les plus grands exemples de la puissance de la religion'. The evidence which she adduces for this statement has to do principally with the victims of the Revolution who, in the cruellest circumstances, maintained their dignity and their devotion to their loved ones:

nous avons vu des femmes nées timides, des jeunes gens à peine sortis de l'enfance, des époux qui, s'aimant, avaient dans cette vie ce qui peut seul la faire regretter, s'avancer vers l'éternité, sans croire être séparés par elle [...] et, moins lasse que nous des tourments de la vie, supporter mieux l'approche de la mort.

As for Louis, she writes:

C'est à l'instant où le malheur est sans espoir, que la puissance de la foi se développe tout entière dans la conduite de Louis [...] Il reçut passivement tous les arrêts du malheur, et se montra cependant sensible pour ce qu'il aimait, comme si les facultés de sa vie avaient doublé à l'instant de sa mort.[6]

In both cases, impending death serves, as in the sentimental tradition, to intensify the richness of the inner life which is about to be cut short; but Madame de Staël, typically, builds on this stereotype to project an image of the after-life, which is the real point of these two passages. As in the conclusion of *Delphine*, the religious experience of after-life appears as a projection of the experiential: it can be extrapolated from the power of the idea and the strength of feeling in the human soul.

Looking beyond the specific context of the Revolution, I would suggest that Madame de Staël's views on pity, and the use which she makes of sentimental figures, form a coherent whole, even if that coherence remains unformalised and implicit. Notions of pity, and figures of sentimentalisation, occur frequently in her discussions of political liberty, of the rule of law, and of the notion of public opinion. In the *Considérations*, a substantial chapter is devoted to England, conceived as a model of political liberty. Madame de Staël praises the success of public subscriptions for hospitals, educational and charitable institutions, but this is the least interesting part of her argument. She attributes particular importance to the institution of habeas corpus, arguing, I think, that the defence of the freedom of the individual is the root of a broader social freedom, because it treats as sacrosanct that fundamental sentimental category, *innocence*. (The author of *Caleb Williams* might have disagreed.) The jury system constitutes a guarantee of individual freedom, by its very egalitarianism: the members of the jury have 'une sympathie naturelle' with the accused 'puisqu'ils sont d'ordinaire choisis dans une classe semblable à la sienne; et, lorsque les jurés sont forcés de prononcer la sentence d'un criminel, il est du moins certain lui-même que la société a tout fait pour qu'il pût être absous, s'il le méritait; et cette conviction doit porter quelque calme dans son coeur'.[7] The English seem to possess a particular sentimental sympathy for the victim:

Si quelque chose peut séduire l'équité du peuple anglais, c'est le malheur. Un individu persécuté par une force quelconque pourrait inspirer un intérêt non mérité, et par conséquent passager; mais cette

noble erreur tient d'une part à la générosité du caractère anglais, et
de l'autre à ce sentiment de liberté qui fait éprouver à tous le besoin
de se défendre mutuellement contre l'oppression; car c'est sous ce
rapport surtout qu'en politique il faut traiter son prochain comme
soi-même. (p. 544)

The tears of the people are also expressive of English liberty in
relation to the way in which respect for the great is articulated
after their death. In Westminster Abbey, 'les penseurs et les
rois reposent sous la même voûte: là leurs querelles sont
apaisées [...] et les mèmes larmes les arrosent'. Nelson's
funeral was marked by a similar unanimity of public grief,
with the enormous crowd showing itself to be 'respectueuse
dans l'expression de sa douleur' (p. 543). Here, then, the contexts in which a sentimental reaction to misfortune takes place
in English society are seen as expressive of a fundamental
truth about the nature of equality and solidarity in English
society: the notion, perhaps, of a national identity which is
constructed from the network of sentimental relations linking
individuals and institutions.

The fine final pages of the *Considérations* confirm these associations. Liberty, whatever the enemies of the Revolution may
say about the ineluctable opposition between 1789 and religion, is of Christian origin: 'le christianisme a véritablement
apporté la liberté sur cette terre, la justice envers les opprimés,
le respect pour les malheureux, enfin l'égalité devant Dieu,
dont l'égalité devant la loi n'est qu'une image imparfaite.'
The political virtues of liberty and justice are defined, implicitly, according to a sentimental model: recognition of the
other's humanity, defence of the weak and innocent, self-
sacrifice.

Rien que la liberté ne peut remuer l'âme dans les rapports de l'ordre
social. Les réunions d'hommes ne seraient que des associations de
commerce ou d'agriculture, si la vie du patriotisme n'excitait pas les
individus à se sacrifier à leurs semblables. La chevalerie était une con-
frérie guerrière qui satisfaisait au besoin de dévouement qu'éprouvent
tous les coeurs généreux [...] Partout où vous rencontrez du respect
pour la nature humaine, de l'affection pour ses semblables, et cette
énergie d'indépendance qui sait résister à tout sur la terre, et ne se

prosterner que devant Dieu, là vous voyez l'homme image de son créateur, là vous sentez au fond de l'âme un attendrissement si intime qu'il ne peut vous tromper sur la vérité. (pp. 604–6)

The role of feeling is double here: at a primary level, it is that which provokes the forms of behaviour on which freedom is built; but the 'attendrissement' at work here is also the reaction of the historical or political observer, for whom, as in the spectacle of the crowd at the Tuileries on 20 June 1792, it is the ultimate touchstone of authenticity. For Madame de Staël, in the final analysis, the heart cannot deceive.

In *De la littérature*, Madame de Staël writes:

Lorsque la pensée peut contribuer efficacement au bonheur de l'homme, sa mission devient plus noble, son but s'agrandit. Ce n'est plus seulement une rêverie douloureuse parcourant tous les maux de l'univers, *sans les soulager*, c'est une arme puissante que la nature donne et dont la liberté doit assurer le triomphe.[8]

Implicitly, but very clearly, the righting of wrongs, the consolation of misfortune, is seen as the function of thought, and this notion may be generalised to encompass a good part of Madame de Staël's thinking about the social function of the writer and of literature. A crucial passage occurs in the chapter of *De la littérature* entitled 'De la littérature dans ses rapports avec le bonheur'. Literature and thought guarantee that 'le type de ce qui est bon et juste ne s'anéantira plus; l'homme que la nature destine à la vertu ne manquera plus de guide; enfin (et ce bien est infini) la douleur pourra toujours éprouver un attendrissement salutaire'. Literature is permanence; an idea, once abroad in the world, cannot be stopped; this is classic Enlightenment idealism. Madame de Staël then goes on to set up an opposition between the *isolation* of man alone and the sense of *community* which literature can afford. 'Les écrits conservateurs des idées, des affections vertueuses' can be an antidote to 'cette tristesse aride qui naît de l'isolement, cette main de glace qu'appesantit sur nous le malheur, lorsque nous croyons n'exciter aucune pitié'. The rest of the passage must be quoted at some length to show how powerful is the notion of the *communauté des âmes sensibles* inherited from the sentimental tradition:

Ces écrits font couler des larmes dans toutes les situations de la vie; ils élèvent l'âme à des méditations générales qui détournent la pensée des peines individuelles; ils créent pour nous une société, une communication avec les écrivains qui ne sont plus, avec ceux qui existent encore, avec les hommes qui admirent, comme nous, ce que nous lisons. Dans les déserts de l'exil, au fond des prisons, à la veille de périr, telle page d'un auteur sensible a élevé peut-être une âme abattue: moi qui la lis, moi qu'elle touche, je crois y retrouver encore la trace de quelques larmes; et par des émotions semblables, j'ai quelques rapports avec ceux dont je plains si profondément la destinée [...] Ce qui peut seul soulager la douleur, c'est la possibilité de pleurer sur sa destinée, de prendre à soi cette sorte d'intérêt qui fait de nous deux êtres pour ainsi dire séparés, dont l'un a pitié de l'autre [...] L'infortuné qui, par le concours de quelques calomnies propagées, est tout-à-coup généralement accusé, serait presque [...] dans la situation d'un vrai coupable, s'il ne trouvait quelques secours dans ces écrits qui l'aident à se reconnaître, qui lui font croire à ses pareils, et lui donnent l'assurance que, dans quelques lieux de la terre, il a existé des êtres qui s'attendriraient sur lui, et le plaindraient avec affection, s'il pouvait s'adresser à eux. (pp. 39–40)

This is a remarkable passage. It bears the marks of exile, as it also reflects the more general impact of the Terror: the whole notion of an imagined community to whom the condemned person appeals his or her innocence has as its classic reference point the prison writings of the Girondins. But the notion of the community of readers goes back also to Diderot's *Eloge de Richardson* (see above, p. 80): sensibility as the shared value drawing together a disparate community, and prefiguring the power and legitimacy which history has so far denied to the class of virtuous men and women. One should note the tense-shifts which are used to extend the republic of letters into an historical as well as a geographical space. However the richest notation is reserved for the end: the immediate continuation of the passage quoted reads as follows: 'Qu'elles sont précieuses ces lignes toujours vivantes qui servent encore d'ami, d'opinion publique et de patrie!' Here, Madame de Staël puts a very precise gloss on the notion of community, which she extends from the level of personal relations outwards through public opinion to the nation and perhaps, metaphorically, to a wider sense of *patrie*.

The chapter entitled 'Du dix-huitième siècle jusqu'en 1789' contrasts the function of literature in the century of Louis XIV with its function in the eighteenth century. The basic opposition is between *gloire* and *le bien public*; in continuity with the courtroom drama of Baculard's *Les Époux malheureux*, literature's role is to defend the oppressed:

L'écrivain, l'orateur se sent exalté par l'importance morale ou politique des intérêts qu'il traite; s'il plaide pour la victime devant l'assassin, pour la liberté devant les oppresseurs, si les infortunés qu'il défend écoutent en tremblant le son de sa voix, pâlissent lorsqu'il hésite, perdent tout espoir si l'expression triomphante échappe à son esprit convaincu; si les destinées de la patrie elle-même lui sont confiées, il doit essayer d'arracher les caractères égoïstes à leurs intérêts, à leurs terreurs, de faire naître dans ses auditeurs ce mouvement du sang, cette ivresse de la vertu qu'une certaine hauteur d'éloquence peut inspirer momentanément, même à des criminels. (p. 288)

Madame de Staël's view of eloquence is linked to the notion of community, for eloquence, too, is an eminently social, communicative form of activity:

Ce n'est pas, en effet, l'homme isolé, l'homme armé seulement de ses facultés individuelles, qui atteint de son propre essor à ces pensées d'éloquence dont l'irrésistible autorité dispose de tout notre être moral: c'est l'homme alors qu'il peut sauver l'innocence, c'est l'homme alors qu'il peut renverser le despotisme, c'est l'homme enfin lorsqu'il se consacre au bonheur de l'humanité: il se croit, il éprouve une inspiration surnaturelle. (pp. 288–9)

The inspiration of eloquence seems to lie somehow with those in whose favour it is pleading: the speaker is not solely responsible, for behind him lies a community, defined once again through the sentimental figure of the struggle of innocent humanity against the forces of obscurantism.

Chapter 2,8, 'De l'éloquence', considers eloquence in the light of the Revolution. Madame de Staël rejects the view that eloquence has been revealed by the revolutionary experience to be a potentially disastrous appeal to the feelings of the mob: 'Je crois [...] qu'on pourrait soutenir que tout ce qui est éloquent est vrai [...] L'éloquence ayant toujours besoin du mouvement de l'âme, ne s'adresse qu'aux sentiments des hommes, et les sentiments de la multitude sont toujours pour la vertu' (p. 416). The problem which she seeks to address is a different one: 'Comment arriver à l'âme endurcie contre les paroles par tant d'expressions mensongères'? (p. 406). This is the familiar Staëlian theme of the triumph of egotism, self-interest, *esprit de parti, persiflage*, in the wake of the Revolution, partly attributable, although perhaps not at the time of composition of *De la littérature*, to Napoleon. In such a cultural climate, the eloquence of sentimentalism is powerless:

> Voulez-vous du moins faire entendre aux caractères haineux quelques paroles de bienveillance? Vous serez également repoussé. Si vous parlez au nom de la puissance, ils vous écouteront avec respect, quel que soit votre langage; mais si vous réclamez pour le faible, si votre nature généreuse vous fait préférer la cause délaissée par la faveur et recueillie par l'humanité, vous n'exciterez que le ressentiment de la faction dominante. Vous vivez dans un temps où l'on est indigné contre le malheur, irrité contre l'opprimé, où la colère s'enflamme à l'aspect du vaincu, où l'on s'attendrit, où l'on s'exalte pour le pouvoir [...] Que fera l'éloquence au milieu de tels sentiments, l'éloquence à laquelle il faut, pour être touchante et sublime, un péril à braver, un malheureux à défendre? (pp. 410–11)

Her answer, as the previous analysis might suggest, is to appeal to 'la véritable nation', the silent majority whose feelings have not been corrupted by the storms of the previous decade.

The other important point to be made about eloquence in Madame de Staël's vision is that it partakes of the sentimental problematic of the outer and the inner. It holds out the possibility of true communication precisely because it offers a means of bridging the gap between the inner spaces, respectively, of the speaker and the listener, and thus uniting them in the community of enlightenment.

> Que pouvez-vous sur la volonté libre des hommes, si vous n'avez pas cette force, cette vérité de langage qui pénètre les âmes, et leur inspire ce qu'elle exprime? (p. 31)

Madame de Staël's commentary is couched in terms of an opposition between two forms of persuasion: that which obtains the voluntary agreement of the subject, as opposed to the use of force. Such an opposition is of course crucially topical in the France of 1800.

> En gagnant des batailles, on peut soumettre les ennemis de la liberté; mais pour faire adopter dans l'intérieur les principes de cette liberté même, il faut que l'esprit militaire s'efface; il faut que la pensée, réunie à des qualités guerrières, au courage, à l'ardeur, à la décision, fasse naître dans l'âme des hommes quelque chose de spontané, de volontaire, qui s'éteint en eux lorsqu'ils ont vu pendant long-temps le triomphe de la force. (p. 36)

The arms of sentiment are used to obtain what is habitually referred to as *rational* consent.

With the problem of the relationship between the inner and the outer, we are approaching the heart of Madame de Staël's thought: it is here that are negotiated questions such as the merits of Protestantism and Catholicism, the relationship of individual consciousness and authority, the role of introspection, the nature of immanence and transcendence. She shares with the sentimental tradition a conviction that human beings can find within themselves the moral resources to manage their lives: in this sense, she synthesises many of the themes current in eighteenth-century writing concerning the religion of humanity, the law of nature 'gravée dans tous les coeurs', in short, an immanent morality based on the notion that man is naturally a social creature and that life in society is therefore the fulfilment of a basic code to which each individual has access through his or her individual conscience. At the same time, she fundamentally transforms this tradition, not least by virtue of her very great talent. The transformation is both an intellectual and an aesthetic one. As a theorist, she clarifies some of the issues at stake: above all, she states, clearly, repeatedly and coherently, that introspection can furnish human beings with the key to their moral nature, that moral law is immanent, that we should trust our heart. But at the same time – and it is here that the transformation is as much aesthetic as intellectual – she extrapolates from this conviction into a dimension which is unclear in much of the previous sentimental tradition: she grasps the question of the transcendent and the religious, and formalises what was perhaps implicit in much sentimental writing, but was never addressed. A deity, a transcendent dimension, the notion of the immortality of the soul, exist for her, and exist as a dynamic of the soul, as an extension of those immanent dimensions which can be grasped experientially. If sentimentalism, like the *fête révolutionnaire*, can be understood as in some sense a substitute religious dimension, a grasping towards the replacement of the transcendent by something more immediately rooted in the experientially given, then Madame de Staël completes the process by allowing the transcendent dimension to proclaim itself. And she does this while remaining within the tradition which takes as its starting point the immanent. In that, she is a daughter of Enlightenment, and profoundly faithful to the Protestant tradition.

The belief in introspection is a powerful one in Madame de Staël. At the conclusion of *De la littérature*, she appears to apologise for having 'mêlé [...] les affections de mon âme aux idées générales que doit contenir ce livre'. But it is these affections which guide the process of thought, and help us to discover ideas.[9] Love is praised in *De l'influence des passions* as the source of more ideas than any great book,[10] while *De l'Allemagne* offers this description of the importance of the soul as the centre of human activity:

L'âme est un foyer qui rayonne dans tous les sens; c'est dans ce foyer que consiste l'existence; toutes les observations et tous les efforts des philosophes doivent se tourner vers ce *moi*, centre et mobile de nos sentiments et de nos idées.[11]

There is no anti-intellectualism in this conviction: for Madame de Staël, it is self-evident that 'la sensibilité, l'imagination et la raison servent l'une à l'autre'.[12] She is fiercely hostile to eighteenth-century sensationalism and materialism, which she considers morally bankrupt and assimilates to the much-despised 'persiflage', and praises the German philosophers who 'ont été les premiers, dans le dix-huitième siècle, qui aient mis l'esprit fort du côté de la foi, le génie du côté de la morale, et le caractère du côté du devoir'.[13]

The tendency towards introspection is identified as a general historical development in *De l'Allemagne*. Speaking of the epistolary novel, the specificity of which is to observe the human heart, she writes that 'cette disposition tient aux grands changements intellectuels qui ont eu lieu dans l'homme; il tend toujours plus en général à se replier sur lui-même, et cherche la religion, l'amour et la pensée dans le plus intime de son être' (vol. 2, p. 43). Later in the book, she speaks of another, closely related historical trend: Protestantism is the fruit of the irresistible tendency of human beings to want to examine rather than take on trust; 'mais quand l'homme sort de l'examen plus religieux qu'il n'y était rentré, c'est alors que la religion est invariablement fondée; c'est alors qu'il y a paix entre elle et les lumières, et qu'elles se servent mutuellement' (vol. 2, p. 224).

The relationship between the immanent and the transcendent which Madame de Staël establishes appears to me to be the culmination of these two tendencies. Part 4 of *De l'Allemagne*, 'La religion et l'enthousiasme', affirms at an early stage that the soul is the site of the notion of infinity, to which much religious significance is attached:

Le sentiment de l'infini est le véritable attribut de l'âme: tout ce qui est beau dans tous les genres excite en nous l'espoir et le désir d'un avenir éternel et d'une existence sublime; on ne peut entendre ni le vent dans la forêt, ni les accords délicieux des voix humaines; on ne peut éprouver l'enchantement de l'éloquence ou de la poésie; enfin surtout, on ne peut aimer avec innocence, avec pudeur, sans être pénétré de religion et d'immortalité. (vol. 2, p. 239)

Similarly, a few pages later, she writes that the 'sentiment religieux' is difficult to circumscribe in scientific language, partly because 'ce qui touche si intimement au mystère de l'existence ne peut être exprimé par les formes régulières de la parole', but partly also because of the subjective nature of the experience: 'l'un admire la divinité dans les traits d'un père, l'autre dans l'innocence d'un enfant' (vol. 2, pp. 240–1). Poetry and literature, nature and social affections: these, via the individual soul, are the vector of the transcendent dimension, which is thus always brought back to its immanent roots. That is why, in the ongoing debate within herself between Protestantism and Catholicism, Madame de Staël seems to me to return inevitably to the Protestant side. Even in her chapter on Catholicism in *De l'Allemagne*, her positions are fundamentally Protestant:

Comme tout était extérieur dans le culte païen, la pompe des images y est prodiguée; le sanctuaire du christianisme étant au fond du coeur, la poésie qu'il inspire doit toujours naître de l'attendrissement. Ce n'est pas la splendeur du ciel chrétien qu'on peut opposer à l'Olympe, mais la douleur et l'innocence, la vieillesse et la mort, qui prennent un caractère d'élévation et de repos, à l'abri des espérances religieuses.

She then proceeds to recount a (presumably Protestant) church service at Satigny, near Geneva, at which a father and son officiated jointly. The spectacle obviously combines religious feelings with the sentimental dimension of paternal–filial love, and leads to the following invocation:

Les hommes dont les affections sont désintéressées, et les pensées religieuses; les hommes qui vivent dans le sanctuaire de leur conscience, et savent y concentrer, comme dans un miroir ardent, tous les rayons de l'univers; ces hommes, dis-je, sont les prêtres du culte de l'âme, et rien ne doit jamais les désunir. (vol. 2, pp. 261–2)

Madame de Staël seems constantly drawn back to the immanent, sentimental dimension in her dealings with the transcendent.

If I have made no reference so far to Madame de Staël's feminism, this is not, I hope, out of a subconscious desire to subvert and marginalise it, but because it does not appear to me to be fully integrated into the rest of her thought. Before approaching the novels, which are the major site of her feminism, its place in her social and political thought should be traced.

In terms of explicitly formulated theoretical positions, Madame de Staël's view is not one which can be said to represent any great challenge to the established order. Chapter 3,19 of *De l'Allemagne* – 'De l'amour dans le mariage' – sets the tone:

On a raison d'exclure les femmes des affaires politiques et civiles, rien n'est plus opposée à leur vocation naturelle que tout ce qui leur donnerait des rapports de rivalité avec les hommes, et la gloire ne saurait être pour une femme qu'un deuil éclatant de bonheur. Mais si la destinée des femmes doit consister dans un acte continuel de dévouement à l'amour conjugal, la récompense de ce dévouement, c'est la scrupuleuse fidélité de celui qui en est l'objet. (vol. 2, p. 218)

The starting point, it seems, is that a sexual division of roles, and moreover a hierarchical one, is normal and given. The historical role of chivalry was, among other things, to protect the weaker sex, and since its demise 'la France a peut-être été, de tous les pays du monde, celui où les femmes étaient le moins heureuses par le coeur' (vol. 1, p. 71). The happiness of women, in other words, is to be built or destroyed within this framework: and unhappy marriage, in its various forms, is described in the fullest sentimental terms as the ultimate persecution of a defenceless victim. The contrast between the values of chivalry and those at work in a marriage 'où la femme aime et le mari respecte froidement [...] produit tous les malheurs du sentiment, les attachements illégitimes, la perfidie, l'abandon et le désespoir [...] Il y a dans un mariage malheureux une force de douleur qui dépasse toutes les autres peines de ce monde. L'âme entière de la femme repose sur l'attachement conjugal.' Despite the positions of Lebensei in *Delphine*, Madame de Staël's conclusion in *De l'Allemagne* is not, however, that the possibility of divorce would automatically resolve this injustice: 'il vaut encore mieux, pour maintenir quelque chose de sacré sur la terre, qu'il y ait dans le mariage une esclave que deux esprits forts' (vol. 2, pp. 219–20).

Chapter 1,3 of *De l'Allemagne* seems to represent the ultimate naturalisation of woman's acceptance of a subordinate role in society. Admittedly, the analysis here is set against the context of the ambient egotism which Madame de Staël sees as the hallmark of Napoleon's Empire; but, nevertheless, it does appear that *dévouement* is being raised here to the status of an eternal feminine virtue:

La nature et la société donnent aux femmes une grande habitude de souffrir, et l'on ne saurait nier, ce me semble, que de nos jours elles valent mieux que les hommes. Dans une époque où le mal universel est l'égoïsme, les hommes auxquels tous les intérêts positifs se rapportent, doivent avoir moins de générosité, moins de sensibilité que les femmes; elles ne tiennent à la vie que par les liens du coeur, et lorsqu'elles s'égarent, c'est encore par un sentiment qu'elles sont entraînées: leur personnalité est toujours à deux, tandis que celle de l'homme n'a que lui-même pour but. On leur rend hommage pour les affections qu'elles inspirent, mais celles qu'elles accordent sont presque toujours des sacrifices. La plus belle des vertus, le dévouement, est leur jouissance et leur destinée; nul bonheur ne peut exister pour elles que par le reflet de la gloire et des prospérités d'un autre, enfin, vivre hors de soi-même, soit par les idées, soit par les sentiments, soit surtout par les vertus, donne à l'âme un sentiment habituel d'élévation. (vol. 1, p. 65)

Perhaps we can detect here a hint of protest at a secondary role which elsewhere is apparently accepted as inevitable if not naturally given; but what denunciation of injustice there is, is oddly combined with a fulsome celebration of the sentimental virtues which this happy victimisation instils.

In parallel to this apparent acceptance of perceived inequality, Madame de Staël is unambiguous in her praise for the bourgeois family as a social model, both in the sense of a model for women to follow and in the broader sense of a general social prescription. England is seen as the exemplar in the field. In the provincial middle classes, 'on ne trouve que de bons ménages, des vertus privées, une vie intérieure entièrement consacrée à l'éducation d'une nombreuse famille qui, nourrie dans la conviction intime de la sainteté du mariage, ne se permettrait pas une pensée légère à cet égard'. Moreover, since there are no convents in England, young girls are brought up at home; 'et l'on peut voir par leur instruction et par leurs vertus, ce qui vaut mieux pour une femme, de ce genre d'éducation ou de celui qui se pratique en Italie'.[14] This comparison will of course be complicated by the criticism of the English bourgeois family model contained in *Corinne*.

Not only does such a society benefit women: domestic virtue is part of an overall social equation. A few pages later, Madame de Staël maintains that one of the effects of the Revolution in France has been to increase respect for marriage. In an analysis which is reminiscent of Rousseau's denunciations of the feminisation (or the effeminisation) of public life in the *Ancien Régime*, she asks:

Comment, sous un gouvernement arbitraire, les femmes se seraient-elles renfermées dans la vie domestique, et n'auraient-elles pas employé tous leurs moyens de séduction pour influer sur le pouvoir? [...] Le véritable caractère d'une femme, le véritable caractère d'un homme, c'est dans les pays libres qu'il faut le connaître et l'admirer. La vie domestique inspire aux femmes toutes les vertus [...] Une femme du peuple en Angleterre se sent un rapport avec la reine qui a soigné son mari, élevé ses enfants, comme la religion et la morale le commandent à toutes les épouses et à toutes les mères. Mais le genre de moeurs qu'entraîne le gouvernement arbitraire, transforme les femmes en une sorte de troisième sexe factice, triste production de l'ordre social dépravé.[15]

The opposition between an artificial social order and one based on nature is clear. Striking too is the sentimental theme of this natural order operating as a transcendence of social hierarchy, the commoner and the queen being united in motherhood. (The French fascination with the English royal family has older roots than one suspected.) This theme is echoed somewhere else by Madame de Staël when she condemns revolutionary attacks on Marie-Antoinette as an inadequate wife and mother as a base calumny, politicising that which should be beyond politics – in the realm, precisely, of nature.

All this from a woman whose life was so much more diverse than the model she espouses, and from the creator of Corinne, the exceptional woman, the woman of genius. Chapter 2,4 of *De la littérature* – 'Des femmes qui cultivent les lettres' – is the standard source for Madame de Staël's thought on this question. If she points out ironically that 'les hommes pardonnent plus facilement aux femmes de manquer aux devoirs qu'ils leur prescrivent, que de vouloir attirer l'attention par des talents distingués', her position remains that 'il vaut beaucoup mieux [...] que les femmes se consacrent uniquement aux vertus domestiques'. However, in accordance with Madame de Staël's enthusiasm for the English model, women should not be denied education; far from keeping women in the home, such an exclusion would have the effect of disqualifying women from being responsible for their daughters' education, and would encourage frivolity and thus prevent women from exercising a civilising influence on public opinion in the direction of humanity, generosity and sensibility.[16]

This, then, is the picture which emerges from Madame de Staël's social and political thought. In her picture of social woman, sentimental values and stereotypes are clustered around the notion of woman as spouse and mother. The injustice to which women are subjected, the misfortune against which she protests, is the disruption by society of woman's natural destiny, which is to experience the triple joys of love, marriage and maternity. 'L'amour dans le mariage' is the model which commands sentimental respect in Madame de Staël's social and political thought.

DELPHINE

Madelyn Gutwirth recognises the persistence in *Delphine* of sentimental conventions inherited from the fiction of the eighteenth century, but she appears to do little more than dismiss them as an empty shell, a superficial stylistic gloss having little real relation to the substance of the matters lying at the heart of Madame de Staël's fiction.[17] This underplaying of the sentimental aspects of the novel is related to the fact that she makes relatively little reference to Madame de Staël's social, political and historical work for, as I have tried to show, a reading of those works reveals the importance of sentimental language and figures in the constitution of Madame de Staël's abstract vision of the world, and therefore their symbolic importance in the Staëlian value-system. In the following pages, I propose an analysis of *Delphine* and *Corinne* which takes account of the sentimentalism which is inherent in them, and try to assess in what ways Madame de Staël's enterprise as a novelist transforms and transcends the sentimental tradition.

The birth of Delphine's love for Léonce is associated in a curious but very marked way with the heroine's sentimental credentials as a creature moved by *pity*. She first sees Léonce debilitated by the consequences of the attempt on his life: she herself comments that 'l'intérêt qu'inspire la souffrance trompe une âme sensible: il peut arriver de croire qu'on aime, lorsque seulement on plaint'.[18] Léonce, too, is affected by the evidence of Delphine's sympathy ('O pitié! douce pitié'); the external signs which he has witnessed must indicate an internal state: 'chacune des grâces de cette figure est le signe aimable d'une qualité de l'âme' (p. 174). There then occurs the episode at the Tuileries in which Delphine is the only person to sit with Mme de R, who enjoys a tarnished reputation in the aristocratic circles in which the novel takes place. Delphine's gesture, for such it is, is an explicit challenge to a social code conceived as going against nature: 'Oui, me disais-je alors, puisque encore une fois les convenances sociales sont en opposition avec la véritable volonté de l'âme, qu'encore une fois elles soient sacrifiées' (pp. 223–4). Léonce is impressed by this symbolic piece of behaviour, which manifests Delphine's inability to live by convention, and takes us straight to the heart of the novel's epigraph, 'Un homme doit savoir braver l'opinion, une femme s'y soumettre.' Delphine's commentary on the event makes clear its sentimental insertion: Mme de R is a deserving case because it is impossible to know what misfortunes are at the root of her bad reputation, misfortunes relating precisely to the fate of women in society.

'A-t-elle eu pour époux un protecteur, ou un homme indigne d'être aimé? ses parents ont-ils soigné son éducation? le premier objet de son choix a-t-il ménagé sa destinée? n'a-t-il pas flétri dans son coeur toute espérance d'aimer, tout sentiment de délicatesse? Ah! de combien de manières le sort des femmes dépend des hommes!' (p. 226)

Delphine's attitude to Thérèse d'Ervins forms a parallel to this episode at the Tuileries. The wrongs which Thérèse has suffered are real: she was the victim of an arranged marriage with a tyrannical husband, which her lover Serbellane evokes as a sin against nature: 'les indignes calculs d'une famille insensible les ont réunis, et Thérèse serait coupable de m'avoir choisi pour le compagnon de sa vie' (p. 323). Delphine comes to Thérèse's rescue, allowing her to use her home for a meeting with Serbellane, and this charitable gesture (and social *faux pas*) precipitates a chain of events the culmination of which is Léonce's marriage to Matilde. Discovering

Léonce's moves to marry Matilde, Delphine points to the link between her love and her pity:

Ne la comprend-il donc pas, cette pitié? [...] pouvais-je aimer comme j'aimais Léonce, et n'avoir pas un coeur accessible à cette compassion? L'amour et la bonté ne viennent-ils pas de la même source? (p. 248)

What is emerging, then, is an interrelated set of sub-plots and philosophical discourses surrounding the birth of Delphine's love, which inescapably mark it as sentimental: it is intimately linked, both psychologically within Delphine, and socially in the relationship between Delphine and Léonce, with Delphine's pity, her sensitivity to the sufferings of others – and in particular to the sufferings of female victims. But this constitution of Delphine as a sentimental heroine prepared to confront expected social behaviour in the name of humanity is simultaneously, and paradoxically, the prime cause of the failure and tragic nature of her love. Delphine's misfortune is that the object of this love is a man who cannot exist *without* social approval for his actions: in that sense, he is the direct opposite of the sentimental hero. Now, just as Delphine's love is being dashed, and she is formulating this as 'le bien suprême, l'amour dans le mariage' being snatched away from her (pp. 259–60), the Lebensei couple make their appearance in the novel, bringing with them a very explicit formulation of the problematic of the narrative in philosophical and social terms. Mme de Lebensei is a Catholic divorcee (divorce exists in the native Holland of her first husband) married to a Languedoc Protestant of Revolutionary sympathies. Her first husband had been a villain: avaricious, antiphilosophical, violent, he made his living from the slave trade 'en exerçant sur ses esclaves un despotisme tyrannique' (p. 287). Now, she has found happiness in marriage: in the garden of their home stands an altar to happiness bearing the inscriptions: 'A six ans de bonheur, Elise et Henri' and 'L'amour et le courage réunissent toujours les coeurs qui s'aiment'. Most importantly, their love signals the union of happiness and virtue in a solidarity which condemns the false categories of a corrupt civilisation: 'quel doux précepte de morale et de bonheur! Et la morale et le bonheur sont inséparables, quand les combinaisons factices de la société ne viennent pas mêler leur poison à la vie naturelle' (p. 291). Against this is set Mme de Lebensei's evocation of the misfortune of the unhappily married: 'S'il était une circonstance qui pût nous permettre une plainte contre notre Créateur, ce serait du sein d'un mariage mal assorti que cette plainte s'échapperait' (p. 288).

In counterpoint to Delphine's increasingly unhappy love for Léonce, we therefore have two triangular relationships – d'Ervins, Thérèse and Serbellane; Mme de Lebensei, her present and her former husband – where unhappiness in marriage is placed at the door of convention, and true love is held up as the union of duty and happiness, morality and instinct, under the benevolent eye of Nature. Moreover, two solutions to the triangular situation have already been adumbrated, and will be developed at a later point: Thérèse d'Ervins has opted for the convent solution, against the sentimental alternative of a flight to America where, in Serbellane's words 'nous emploierons [...] la fortune que je possède à des établissements utiles, à une bienfaisance éclairée' (p. 332), while the possibility of divorce has been introduced by the Lebensei subplot.

Meanwhile, Delphine's naturalness is being set in opposition to the necessary machinations of social existence. Mme d'Artemas advises Delphine that a woman cannot afford to follow her sensibility:

Une jeune femme sans père ou sans mari, quelque distinguée qu'elle soit, n'a point de force réelle ni de place marquée au milieu du monde. Il faut donc se tirer d'affaire habilement, gouverner les bons sentiments avec encore plus de soin que les mauvais, renoncer à cette exaltation romanesque qui ne convient qu'à la vie solitaire, et se préserver de ce naturel inconsidéré, la première des grâces de conversation, et la plus dangereuse des qualités en fait de conduite. (pp. 390–1)

This description of Delphine's sentimental virtues as *romanesques* occurs elsewhere in the novel;[19] and in the 'Quelques réflexions sur le but moral de Delphine' found in her papers after her death, Madame de Staël reflects bitterly on a corrupt society's rejection of moral ideals as a literary pipe-dream:

La plaisanterie [. . .] s'attaque maintenant à tous les sentiments forts
et vrais, qu'on est convenu de dénigrer sous le nom de mélancolie, de
philosophie, etc. que sais-je, l'une des formules reçues, l'une des
modes littéraires du moment [. . .] Dans notre pays et notre siècle, ce
n'est pas l'amour qui corrompt la morale, mais le mépris de tous les
principes causé par le mépris de tous les sentiments.[20]

The alignment of forces, I would suggest, remains entirely
consistent with the sentimental world picture.

This is the state of play prior to the extended crisis scene
which closes part 2 of the novel, and centres upon the death of
Mme de Vernon, the woman who had falsely manipulated
Delphine's generosity towards Thérèse d'Ervins in order to
settle her daughter Matilde's marriage to Léonce. Mme de
Vernon, in the knowledge that death is catching up with her,
opens her heart to Delphine in letter 2,41, explaining her
behaviour and asking for the heroine's forgiveness. She attributes the baseness of her behaviour to the social pressures
identified by Mme d'Artemas above:

Les femmes étant victimes de toutes les institutions de la société, elles
sont dévouées au malheur, si elles s'abandonnent le moins du monde
à leurs sentiments, si elles perdent de quelque manière l'empire
d'elles-mêmes. (p. 407)

She goes on to describe Delphine as the only person in the
world to possess the virtues of generosity and naturalness: 'c'est
en vous seule que j'espère pour verser des larmes sur ma tombe,
et conserver un souvenir de moi qui tienne encore à quelque
chose de sensible' (p. 415).

The extended death scene follows (pp. 426–36). I am not
maintaining that in itself it represents a significant shift in the
alignment of ideological forces set in play by the narrative,
although such a shift is undoubtedly in preparation, as I hope
to show later. The interest of the scene is rather that it stands
out as a supreme example of extended sentimental writing,
verging on the melodramatic or frenetic in its accumulation of
narrative reversals designed to enhance sentimental effect. The
scene is recounted by Mme de Lebensei, a suitably qualified
narrator of the sentimental. We see Delphine as the angel of

mercy, ministering to her dying friend despite the wrongs of which she has been the object. Then Matilde, informed that her mother is nearing the end, allows her confessor to come to the bedside, despite Mme de Vernon's previous refusal to see a priest. Delphine: 'Insensée, pensez-vous servir le souverainement bon, en causant à votre mère l'émotion la plus douloureuse?' Mme de Vernon then addresses her daughter in a tirade not entirely consistent with her state of health. Her mistake was to have entrusted the education of her daughter to a governess, thus preventing any affective relationship between herself and her daughter from being fostered. For the priest, she reserves a harangue of considerable violence, the philosophical tone of which is given when she says that

ce serait mal me présenter au juge de toute vérité, que de trahir ma pensée par des témoignages extérieurs, qui ne sont point d'accord avec mes opinions; j'aime mieux me confesser à Dieu dans mon coeur, qu'à vous, Monsieur, que je ne connais point, ou qu'à tout autre prêtre avec lequel je n'aurais point contracté des liens d'amitié ou de confiance [...] Nul homme ne peut m'apprendre si Dieu m'a pardonné, la voix de ma conscience m'en instruira mieux que vous. (p. 427)

The withdrawal of Matilde and the priest is immediately followed by another haemorrhage, causing Mme de Vernon to lose consciousness in the arms of Delphine. She is brought round, and Delphine is on her knees at the bedside, in the classic pose of the sentimental heroine ('le visage penché sur ses deux mains pour essayer de les réchauffer; ses beaux cheveux blonds, s'étant détachés, tombaient en désordre'), when Léonce enters, fresh from a seven-day and seven-night journey from Madrid through the freezing winter, and almost out of his mind at the news, communicated in a letter from Mme de Vernon, that Delphine had always loved him and that he had been deceived into marrying Matilde. He heaps accusations and imprecations on his dying mother-in-law, refusing the pleas of Delphine to have pity on a dying woman in the most emotionally florid phrases:

Pour qui, de la pitié? [...] pour qui? pour elle, ah! s'il est vrai qu'elle se meurt, faites que le ciel m'accorde de changer de sort avec elle, que

je sois sur ce lit de mort [. . .] et qu'elle porte à ma place les liens de fer
dont elle m'a chargé; qu'elle acquitte cette longue destinée de peines
à laquelle sa dissimulation profonde m'a condamné. (p. 431)

The recognisable sentimental tone here lies in the inflation of
emotion, the *surenchère* which takes the given reality (death)
and uses it metaphorically to state the far greater import of the
emotion felt by the subject.

It is Delphine, of course, who manages to rise above her own
unhappy love in the name of *dévouement*: faced with Léonce's
refusal to grant Mme de Vernon's request that the background
to their marriage be hidden from Matilde, Delphine intervenes, presenting herself as the redeemer of mother and
daughter:

Je te prends sous ma protection, s'il t'injurie, c'est moi qu'il offensera,
s'il ne prononce pas à tes pieds les paroles qui font du bien à l'âme,
c'est mon coeur qu'il aliénera: tu lui demandes de respecter le
bonheur de ta fille, hé bien! je réponds moi de ce bonheur, il me sera
sacré, je le jure à sa mère expirante. (p. 433)

The spectacle of Delphine's generosity makes Léonce in his
turn fall to his knees and ask for the dying woman's forgiveness,
after which he faints. Delphine now becomes the absolute
centre of the scene: fearing for the life of Léonce, her gaze is
fixed on him, while Mme de Vernon enters her final convul-
sions and dies in her arms.

The scene is a turning-point at least to the extent that it
represents Delphine at the intersection of the two forces which
are to tear her apart: her love and her generosity. In commit-
ting herself through the sentimental–melodramatic form of the
oath (which had known a brilliant career during the Revolution), she announces her decision that the happiness of others
(Matilde) must be placed before her own. This decision, of
course, will bring her into opposition with the values propounded by Lebensei. Aesthetically, what is important here is
the way in which the scene is brought to its culminating point
in a form of *tableau*, with Delphine physically represented at the
intersection of opposing forces. Léonce, too, will perceive the
scene in terms of a *tableau*, although what he sees is, character-

istically, somewhat different; in the following letter he writes that there is no future for them outside their love:

une seule image se détache de l'obscurité, de l'incertitude de mes souvenirs, c'est toi Delphine: je te vois aux pieds de ce lit de mort, cherchant à contenir ma fureur, me regardant avec douceur, avec amour; je veux encore ce regard; seul, il peut calmer l'agitation brûlante qui m'empêche de reprendre des forces. (p. 437)

The tension in the narrative from this point, then, is between renunciation and the fulfilment of love. Prompted by the fate of Thérèse d'Ervins, Delphine has already been tempted by the convent option, although her reflections on the question are prompted not by a religious motivation, but by a desire for 'cette vie solitaire, enchaînée, régulière, qui doit calmer enfin les mouvements désordonnées du coeur' (p. 355). Now, once again, she gives voice to this temptation, urging Léonce: 'Essayons d'une vie dévouée, d'une vie de sacrifices et de devoirs; elle a donné presque du bonheur à des âmes vertueuses.' Delphine initiates here the theme of self-fulfilment through self-sacrifice, renunciation and pain, which will become perhaps the dominant tone of the novel by its conclusion. But before that point is reached, the secular, immanent, sentimental solution is presented on two occasions: once in the episode of the de Belmont family, and then in Lebensei's plea in favour of divorce which provokes Delphine's clearest statement in favour of the ideology of sacrifice and pain.

The de Belmont episode is recounted by Léonce, and this is significant, in that it gives voice to the need which he feels perhaps more than Delphine to consummate their love in the face of all obstacles. Delphine and Léonce visit the family in their modest country retreat not far from Delphine's residence at Bellerive. The encounter demonstrates very powerfully the conjunction of sentimental figures with the drive to consummate love in the face of social opposition. De Belmont possesses a sentimental trump-card from the outset: he is blind. Furthermore, the reason for their retirement to the country far from their native Languedoc is the fact that Mme de Belmont's noble family were opposed to her marriage to a mere *roturier*, blind to boot. But it is precisely this apparent deprivation –

social and sensual – which constitutes the sentimental power of their example. His blindness means that all his impressions he receives from his beloved wife: it enhances the total nature of their love. As for the *déclassement*, it functions in exactly the same way as analysed elsewhere: defined as the triumph of natural love over the power of convention, it is the manifestation of human happiness, as de Belmont himself declares:

Je le dis [. . .] aux grands de la terre, aux plus beaux, aux plus jeunes; il n'est de bonheur pendant la vie que dans cette union du mariage, que dans cette affection des enfants, qui n'est parfaite que quand on chérit leur mère. (p. 516)

Léonce himself glosses the meeting in these classic terms:

Aveugles, ruinés, relégués dans un coin de la terre, ils sont heureux par l'amour dans le mariage; et moi qui pouvais goûter ce bien au sein de toutes les prospérités humaines, j'ai livré mon coeur à des regrets dévorants qui n'en sortiront qu'avec la vie. (pp. 518–9)

The de Belmonts, then, operate as a model of sentimental marriage in counterpoint to the trials of Delphine and Léonce. The model is an explicit reflection of Madame de Staël's theoretical positions on the question: the wife is in charge of the education of the daughter, the husband teaches the son, and husband and wife are united in their conviction that a wife must live a life of devotion to her husband, the latter possessing a natural superiority over his wife: 'malheur aux femmes obligées de conduire elles-mêmes leur vie, de couvrir les défauts et les petitesses de leur mari, ou de s'affranchir en portant seules le poids de l'existence' (p. 514).

One final feature of the episode is a clear adumbration of a theme which will come to the fore in *Corinne*. Father, mother and daughter perform a reapers' song from the south of France, which Delphine in particular finds irresistibly moving, to the extent that 'ses larmes la suffoquaient'. Part of this effect is achieved by the fact that the harpsichordist is blind: music played by a blind person strikes Léonce as the expression of a melancholy which is attached to 'une infirmité si malheureuse', but which the victim cannot normally express openly. But it seems that the major part of the effect is due to the fact that the performance is a family one, and that the subject-matter is germane to Delphine and Léonce's predicament. The girl sings to her mother:

> Accordez-moi donc ma mère,
> Pour mon époux, mon amant;
> Je l'aimerai tendrement,
> Comme vous aimez mon père.

The rest of the song confirms the agreement of the mother to this natural ambition. The sentimental feature here is, again, a formal one: it lies in the insertion of a quoted artefact, the function of which in the text is at once to encapsulate and to intensify the emotions of the represented characters. This is a *mise en scène* of sensibility.

Lebensei's letter to Delphine (4,16) is the major defence of immanent sentimental values in *Delphine*. This enlightened Protestant, sympathetic to the Revolution, informs Delphine that the Constituante is soon to institute divorce in France (this actually happened on 20 September 1792), and urges her and Léonce to avail of this in order to realise their love and found their happiness. He argues against the unnatural institution of arranged marriages, described as a tyrannical oppression and a form of chains, and attacks the Catholic church's defence of the indissolubility of marriage, linked in his eyes to its reliance on pain as 'le moyen le plus efficace pour le perfectionnement moral et religieux' of humanity (pp. 656–8). This is contrasted with the Protestant ethic at work in England, Holland, Switzerland and America: in this tradition, Christianity is closer to its charitable and humanitarian roots, and closer to Nature.

> Quoi! la Divinité, qui a voulu que tout fût facile et agréable pour le maintien de l'existence physique, aurait mis notre nature morale en opposition avec la vertu! [...] il faudrait réprimer sans cesse l'élan toujours renaissant de l'âme vers le bonheur; il faudrait réprimer ce sentiment doux en lui-même, quand il n'est pas injustement contrarié. (pp. 659–60)

There are circumstances in which it is necessary to sacrifice one's happiness to others, but that is with the aim of creating a greater sum of happiness. The consequence of divorce will be that 'les moeurs deviendront plus austères, le mariage sera plus respecté; et l'on sentira que tous ces biens sont dus à la possibilité de trouver le bonheur dans le devoir' (p. 662).

Delphine rejects this argument. While not in principle attached to the indissolubility of marriage, she cannot contemplate being the cause of the suffering of Matilde: the oath sworn to Mme de Vernon was not sworn lightly. She returns to the truth which was amply demonstrated in the opening phase of the novel: love and pity are inseparable emotions, which can never 'triompher l'un de l'autre';

le bonheur de l'amour dispose tellement le coeur à la sympathie qu'il est impossible de braver, pour l'obtenir, le spectacle ou le souvenir de la douleur [...] quand on a combattu la pitié, on a tué son bon génie, et tous les instincts du coeur ne parlent plus. (p. 666)

Perhaps Lebensei's 'système bienfaisant' has not left sufficient place for 'ces combinaisons de la destinée qui commandent de se vaincre soi-même; je suis dans une de ces situations déchirantes'.

Delphine's position then is to refuse to assimilate virtue and happiness; if their compatibility is a desirable social goal, they are not reconcilable in her case, and she must obey the voice of duty, even if the price of sacrifice is pain. Delphine's refusal of Lebensei's vision is closely related to their disagreement about the role of pain in human destinies. Lebensei's rejection of the Catholic cult of pain is countered by Delphine when she compares the selfishness and suspicion of most men with the dominant emotions of those who have suffered:

nous ne sommes pas ainsi, nous qui avons souffert: oui, dans toutes les relations de la vie, dans tous les pays du monde, c'est avec les opprimés qu'il faut vivre; la moitié des sentiments et des idées manquent à ceux qui sont heureux et puissants. (p. 682)

Frank Bowman has shown that the association 'mélancolie – douleur – prière – conscience de Dieu' was already established in Madame de Staël's work at the time of *Delphine*. He argues, no doubt rightly, that Delphine's view of pain and Lebensei's rejection of it should not be seen as radically opposed, since Lebensei's is a rejection of the *cult* of pain which denies humanity, whereas Delphine affirms simply the sense of pain, which enables the subject to act in this world, and is in that sense 'libératrice'.[21] Moreover, the continuities between the passage quoted above and the association between suffering and virtue which is central to the whole sentimental project are obvious. And yet, something new is happening in Madame de Staël's presentation of suffering. Fragment III in part 5 of the novel is crucial here: renewing the reflection begun in *De l'influence des passions*, the author has Delphine reflect on the insufficiency of literary representations of suffering when compared to the reality which she now knows:

Le malheur n'est plus à mes yeux la touchante parure de l'amour et de la beauté, c'est une sensation brûlante, aride; c'est le destructeur de la nature, séchant tous les germes d'espérance qui se développent dans notre sein [...] Dans les ouvrages dramatiques, vous ne voyez l'être malheureux que sous un seul aspect, sous un noble point de vue, toujours intéressant, toujours fier, toujours sensible; et moi, j'éprouve que dans la fatigue d'une longue douleur, il est des moments où l'âme se lasse de l'exaltation, et va chercher encore du poison dans quelques détails inaperçus, dont il semblait qu'un grand revers devrait au moins affranchir. (pp. 740–1)

It is to passages such as this that Simone Balayé's view of the significance of Madame de Staël as a novelist applies: she confronts the problematic relationship between happiness and virtue, which the sentimental tradition had sought to reconcile when it assigned moral objectives to the novel 'au milieu des cris, des larmes, de la frénésie'.[22] A readiness and an ability to analyse the nature of suffering and its consequences upon the human being as a social animal would in this view be one of the marks of the transition from sentimentalism to Romanticism.

Despite this new post-sentimental understanding of suffering, which is an important feature of the novel, *Delphine* seems to me to continue to validate the sentimental vision in ways which are important to its meaning. In my view, and Balayé would I think agree,[23] Lebensei remains the ideological focus of the novel. It is his brand of Protestant optimism, uniting the transcendent and the immanent in a secular philosophy of progress and perfectibility, which remains the dominant public value of *Delphine*. This is expressed in his letter to Léonce urging him and Delphine to consider void the monastic vows which she has made: 'Dieu qui parle à l'homme par la voix de la nature, lui interdit d'avance des engagements contraires à tous les sentiments comme à toutes les vertus sociales' (p. 900). But it also finds expression in a less publicly ideological area but one which is dramatically crucial in *Delphine*, particularly in view of the novel's closing scene: the attitude to death.

The question is of course raised on various occasions before the closing scene. The death of Mme de Vernon introduces an opposition between competing attitudes to death: on the one hand a Catholic attitude based upon the authority of the priest, the dogma of sin and salvation, and the concretisation of the process of dying around an externalised ceremony; on the other hand an enlightened attitude which privileges the individual's conscience and relationships with those who were close during life. In part 5 of the novel, Delphine attends a Protestant first communion, and reflects on the fact that, rather than using the means of 'superstition', it expresses a religion based upon the immanent:

Notre âme n'a pas besoin de superstition pour recevoir une impression religieuse et profonde; le ciel et la vertu, l'amour et la mort, le bonheur et la souffrance en disent assez à l'homme, et nul n'épuisera jamais tout ce que ces idées sans terme peuvent inspirer. (pp. 800–1)

Some letters later, Lebensei witnesses the death of Matilde and, in his description of it to Delphine, he too rejects superstition and external ceremony in favour of an attitude centred upon the life of the dying person, his/her affections and relationships:

Celui qui meurt regretté de ce qu'il aime doit écarter de lui cette pompe funèbre; l'affection l'accompagne jusqu'à son dernier adieu, il dépose sa mémoire dans les coeurs qui lui survivent, et les larmes de ses amis sollicitent pour lui la bienveillance du ciel. (p. 874)

The function of memory here is reminiscent of the function of literature as the founding of a community of sensitive souls, evoked in *De la littérature*: communication between consciousnesses is the mark of true human activity (see above, p. 204).

It is in the light of all this that the conclusion of *Delphine* is significant. The death of Delphine and Léonce is refracted through the theme of survival. Survival, as Balayé points out, of the Lebenseis and of their son;[24] but the survival, above all, of the lovers' memory, articulated in a manner entirely consistent with Lebensei's analysis, and using formal means inherited from the sentimental tradition: the surviving friend lost in reverie at their graveside. Serbellane buries the couple on a river bank, a place surrounded by poplars, and then departs for Switzerland, to see to the needs of Isore, the daughter of Thérèse d'Ervins whom Delphine had promised to bring up. (Survival also of the victims of superstition, and a reminder of the solidarity of sentiment.) Then Serbellane returns to their graveside, and is tempted, in his despondency, to join them in death, when it seems to him that he hears the voice of the lovers telling him 'Supporte la peine, attends la nature et fais du bien aux hommes.' His final act is the sentimental gesture *par excellence*, the marking on a tree of an inscription, through which the feelings of an individual at a given moment attain the status of a permanent record: 'On ne me répond pas, mais peut-être on m'entend.'

In short, the discourse of humanist optimism emerges from *Delphine* tempered by an acute awareness of suffering; but that discourse, which is centrally articulated by Lebensei through the inherited figures of sentimentalism, remains the message of the novel, as its hostile reception in 1802–3 confirms. As we close the novel, the image of the couple united in love remains a dominant metaphor for a social order based on such values.

Madelyn Gutwirth argues that a tension exists in *Delphine* between what she too calls the *immanent* model of satisfaction through family and motherhood, and the novel's serious contribution to an emergent feminism. In her view, it is a women's dimension which is required for an understanding of the place of pain in Madame de Staël's narrative. The irruption of suffering is an expression, mediated through the conventions of fiction, of the suffering of a woman who wishes to be more than the society in which she lives allows her to be. It is the Revolution, by destroying previous models of insertion of women into the polity without proposing a new model, which renders the problematic of a woman's place in society acute for Madame de Staël; in response, *Delphine* represents a challenge to the immanent, sentimental model based on domesticity and the ideal of self-sacrifice and devotion: 'If this is your image of real femininity, I will show how splendid it can be, but how truly little it is wanted by your society if it is taken seriously as an ideal.'[25] For Gutwirth, Madame de Staël's evocation of suffering – precisely that aspect of her work which goes beyond sentimentalism – is the core of her feminism:

In the image of the compromised, trapped, encircled Delphine whom no one will approach in society, we discern how Mme de Staël has distilled the sense of her unacceptability to others. This work conse-crates her post-Revolutionary understanding that she may not present herself or any woman resembling herself as a heroine.[26]

In what sense can feminism be said to represent a limit to the sentimental vision? Despite sentimentalism's evident alignment with a 'progressive' model of marital and family relations – marriages based on consent rather than parental choice, a new attentiveness to the humanity of children – is it the case that this remains a model defined by men, and that the emancipa-tion of women which it entails goes only as far as men are prepared to allow? Certainly, the privileged status of women as objects of sentimentalisation is suspect: 'tears are only eloquent when they flow down fair cheeks' writes Mary Wollstone-craft,[27] suggesting that powerlessness is the condition of senti-mentalisation. In this view, the limit of sentimentalism would be the point where the sentimentalised subject manifests the desire for power, stakes a claim to being a social actor in the full sense of the term. And yet, to suggest that there exists a predetermined ideological meaning to a particular form of discourse is wrong, as I tried to argue in chapter 3. Dominique Godineau quotes a wonderful passage from a speech by a young woman, Joséphine Fontanier, at a meeting of her section in Year 2. She is arguing against a model of womanhood, associated with the *Ancien Régime*, in which beauty and ornamentation are the dominant values:

Ah! citoyens, oseriez-vous prétendre au nom de républicains, si vous pensiez encore que la beauté est la première qualité d'une femme [...]? Non, non, citoyens, laissons aux cours des despotes et aux villes corrompues qui renferment leurs esclaves abrutis cette fausse manière d'apprécier la moitié du genre humain [...] Plus d'idées frivoles pour nous; indifférentes désormais sur la couleur d'un ruban, sur la finesse d'une gaze, sur la forme ou le prix de nos boucles d'oreille; *nos vertus seront toute notre parure et nos enfants nos bijoux.*[28]

A claim is being made here about the political and symbolic liberation of women, and their relationship to a revolutionised society; the metaphorical substitution of natural for social attributes – 'nos vertus seront toute notre parure' – is typically sentimental, and the reference to children shows that, even in a statement about the public role of women, the domestic sphere has not lost its symbolic importance. The feminism of Joséphine Fontanier's position coexists with the sentimentalism of her language, as historical contradictions must coexist.

Nevertheless, Geneviève Fraisse has argued convincingly that, for feminism in the period of the French Revolution, this dividing line between the private and the public, the domestic and the political and historical, constitutes a crucial boundary.[29] Given that Madame de Staël's second novel, *Corinne*, is centrally preoccupied with woman as public figure, I propose now to look at that novel, and to ask to what extent the work's feminism involves changes in the use and status of sentimental figures and language.

CORINNE

Simone Balayé writes that the core of *Corinne* is 'le conflit de la femme de génie et de la société', and goes on to argue that this insistence on the intellectual rather than the moral, political and religious definition of the individual in conflict with society sets *Corinne* apart from *Delphine*, whereas too many critics have seen them as 'le calque l'un de l'autre'.[30] Both novels are stories of unhappy love, both are about the tragic inability of a woman to find happiness in society. But where *Delphine* operates fundamentally within the established Enlightenment frame of individual love in conflict with social convention, *Corinne* employs what is at first glance a similar narrative structure to pose in a far more rigorous fashion questions about the place of women in society. The novel juxtaposes two visions of women's destiny, and these are to be understood in terms of an opposition between two sets of associated terms: on the one hand, domesticity, family, immanence, submission to man, social construction and control, all these being associated geographically with Britain; on the other hand, independent genius, woman as celebrity and public figure, art as transcendence, sexual freedom, natural abandon, all of these associated with Italy. Madelyn Gutwirth offers a very fine analysis of *Corinne* which demonstrates the importance of this series of oppositions.[31]

The notion of sentimentalism offers a less complete account of *Corinne* than of its predecessor, and this is precisely because of the new ground which the novel tries to break. It does, however, have its share of sentimental scenes, and plenty of tears are shed by hero and heroine. Perhaps the most excessively sentimental (and melodramatic) scene is the parting in Venice (Book xvi, chapter 3). In Book xv,3 Oswald's love for Corinne expresses itself in his willingness to risk catching a contagious disease from the loved one, in a clear reference to the *inoculation* scene in *La Nouvelle Héloïse*. The episode at Ancona (1,4), in which Oswald demonstrates his humanity by rescuing the inmates of a burning lunatic asylum, is a sentimental *topos* which is picked up later (xv,5) when Oswald and Corinne return to the town, witness the gratitude of the population, and Corinne explicitly points to the feelings of respect and submission which these masculine exploits inspire in her. At a more structural level, *Corinne*, like *Delphine*, relies upon an opposition between social convention and a form of authenticity at once sentimental and moral: in Book xii, 'Histoire de Lord Nelvil', Maltigues represents a cynical social view of morality based entirely on respecting convention and appearance – a morality, moreover, clearly associated with Paris in a novel which shifts between England and Italy. Oswald it is who opposes the sentimental view of a moral code which at times demands self-sacrifice, a notion entirely foreign to the world of Maltigues.

In the final analysis, however, Oswald shows that he cannot break loose from his social roots and the assumptions with which he was brought up. I want to argue that, in the characterisation of Oswald, typically sentimental forms of behaviour and ways of seeing are constantly tugging him back towards his origins, towards fidelity to his dead father's expectations, to the social model represented by England. Oswald cries often and easily, and Corinne finds this attractive (xiii,5). Frequently, in the novel, his tears are provoked by the tension between the memory of his father and his love for Corinne. It is, of course, the revelation of his father's preference for Lucile over Corinne as his future wife which will prove determining. The first chapter of Book viii develops this theme at length, and can be read as a systematic and extended exercise in sentimental writing. After a sleepless night spent torn between these two conflicting forces, Oswald turns to his father's image:

O toi! dit-il en s'adressant au portrait de son père; toi, le meilleur ami que j'aurai jamais sur la terre, je ne peux plus entendre ta voix; mais apprends-moi par ce regard muet, si puissant encore sur mon âme, apprends-moi ce que je dois faire pour te donner dans le ciel quelque contentement de ton fils.[32]

The portrait is the token of the father, his mark or trace, the sign of his simultaneous absence and presence. Oswald begins by asking his father's indulgence: his happiness demands that he make his life with Corinne. Then the argument shifts to a moralised plane when he speaks of having 'l'honneur de protéger, de sauver une telle femme'. But immediately, another shift takes place: 'La sauver? reprit-il tout à coup; et de quoi? d'une vie qui lui plaît, d'une vie d'hommages, de succès, d'indépendance?' We are thus at the heart of the wider debate, which continues with the appearance of Edgermond, who knows and admires Corinne, but believes that 'une telle femme n'est pas faite pour vivre dans le pays de Galle [...]: il n'y a que les Anglaises pour l'Angleterre [...] je pense comme Thomas Walpole: *que fait-on de cela à la maison?* et *la maison* est tout chez nous' (vol. 1, pp. 193–4). Edgermond then brings in the

sentimental arguments: he knew Oswald's mother 'que votre
respectable père a tant regrettée: c'était une personne tout à
fait semblable à ma jeune cousine; et c'est comme cela que je
voudrais avoir une femme'. Of course, it is the reference to his
parents which strikes to the heart: 'Insensé que je suis! s'écria-t-
il quand il fut seul, je veux savoir quelle est l'épouse que mon
père me destinait; et ne le sais-je pas, puisque je puis me
retracer l'image de ma mère, qu'il a tant aimée' (vol. 1,
p. 194). Again, the memory of the lost one makes its appearance, this time functioning as a model for the present, and
suggesting the reassuring permanence of social reproduction at
the heart of the family model, opposed to the unknown mystery
of Corinne and of Italy. The emotion is too much: in a recur-
rence of his illness, a blood-vessel bursts in his chest, and he
wishes that he could die now, having seen Corinne for one last
time.

Corinne now appears, in the role of the bedside carer rather
than the woman of genius, driven by 'le mouvement irrésistible
qui fait voler au secours de ce qu'on aime' (vol. 1, p. 196).
That evening, Oswald asks her to read to him from his father's
thoughts on death, which he always consults as a source of
solace in his illness. The text is in fact largely a sentimental
death-bed scene, in which a dying but virtuous man imagined
by Oswald's father consoles his 'épouse fidèle', wipes away her
tears, recalls their happiness together and then, turning to his
children, recommends to them the path of courage and virtue:

Approchez-vous de moi! ... que je vous aperçoive encore, que la
bénédiction d'un serviteur de Dieu soit sur vous ... Il meurt ... O
anges du ciel! recevez son âme, et laissez-nous sur la terre le souvenir
de ses actions, le souvenir de ses pensées, le souvenir de ses espérances.
(vol. 1, pp. 199–200)

A complex series of mirror-images is at work here, in a typically
sentimental process of intertextual reference within the text.
Oswald's dead father has composed a moralising death-bed
scene which is now being read to Oswald in a trembling voice
by Corinne as he lies in his own sick-bed. That the text is in fact
borrowed from Necker's *Cours de morale religieuse* only further
complicates the process of *enchâssement*. The emotions provoked

by the death scene mean that the reading has to be abandoned. Now, Oswald tries to build a bridge between his father and Corinne:

Oui, lui dit Oswald en lui tendant la main, oui, chère amie de mon coeur, tes larmes sont confondues avec les miennes. Tu le pleures avec moi, cet ange tutélaire dont je sens encore le dernier embrassement, dont je vois encore le noble regard; peut-être est-ce toi qu'il a choisie pour me consoler. (vol. 1, p. 200)

The attempt to reconcile the two poles of his dilemma actually brings Oswald close to what will later decide the lovers' fate: his father's expressed wish that he marry Lucile, not Corinne. At this stage, however, Corinne conceals this information, and her attempts to remain cryptic give an odd lack of closure to the sentimental epiphany: in this and other such scenes, one feels that, in a strange undermining of the movement towards sentimental contact and fulfilment which is implicit in the form and the language, the characters somehow do not meet at all. In particular, Corinne appears almost as an observer rather than a character fully embedded in the representational coding of the scene.

Oswald's return to Britain confirms the role of sentimental framing on the side of a traditional social model. While Corinne waits in black despondency, Oswald rediscovers the charm of an ordered society, of domestic predictability as against what is revealingly described as 'le désir infini d'un bonheur romanesque' (vol. 2, p. 168). His intention in visiting Lady Edgermond is to persuade her to recognise Corinne as the daughter of her husband's first marriage, but he comes under the spell of Lucile, who appears as the epitome of domesticated and virtuous womanhood: innocent, devoted to the wellbeing of her severe mother, her eyes modestly downcast like the English ladies on the ship in the Bay of Naples, in short a perfect representative of the virtues of the British model of womanhood which Corinne found most unacceptable during her unhappy stay in the Edgermond household. Systematically, in Book XVI, chapters 5 and 6, Oswald's reaction to Lucile is described as one of *attendrissement*; and it is made very clear that it is precisely these qualities in Lucile which prompt his reaction. It is when she shows concern for her mother, when she recites the evening prayer before the assembled household, that he finds her innocence and devotion touching. Lucile's is a conscious effort to keep back emotion, to prevent its externalisation; in a passage reminiscent of Roederer, the delicacy of her skin, which 'trahissait à son insu les émotions que sa profonde réserve cachait de toute autre manière', is contrasted with a more direct expression of the internal life characteristic of the South. Later, Corinne will watch as Lucile weeps in a London theatre, and Oswald, also present but in a different part of the auditorium, reacts with *attendrissement* to the spectacle of Lucile's tears (vol. 2, pp. 200–1).

In short, it is as though certain features of the sentimental aesthetic were specifically attached to Oswald's point of view, and were used by Madame de Staël as a device which not only characterises Oswald, but also makes clear his relation to one of the fundamental ideological questions which the novel addresses.

Simone Balayé has pointed out the importance of aesthetic debates in *Corinne*. Oswald's view of art is a utilitarian one, while Corinne points the way towards an aesthetic of 'l'art pour l'art'. According to Balayé, music and architecture occupy pride of place in Madame de Staël's aesthetic hierarchy, because they are 'les deux formes les plus abstraites, les seules qui laissent à la pensée toute sa liberté'.[33] Corinne argues that, of all the arts, music is the one which 'agit le plus directement sur l'âme. Les autres la dirigent vers telle ou telle idée; celui-là seul s'adresse à la source intime de l'existence' (vol. 1, p. 234). Similarly, speaking of the fountains in St Peter's Square, she argues that such a monument 'n'a point [...] de sens déterminé; et l'on est saisi, en le contemplant, par cette rêverie sans calcul et sans but qui mène si loin la pensée' (vol. 1, p. 94). Conversely, when Corinne returns to Italy after renouncing Oswald, her attempts at writing are a failure:

Se sentant alors incapable de détourner sa pensée de sa propre situation, elle peignait ce qu'elle souffrait; mais ce n'était plus ces idées générales, ces sentiments universels qui répondent au coeur de tous les hommes; c'était le cri de la douleur; [...] c'était le malheur, mais ce n'était plus le talent. (vol. 2, p. 237)

The opposition, then, is between an abstract, transcendent view of art, associated with Antiquity and with the South, and a model, associated with modernity and with the North, in which the function of the artefact is to express individual emotion, often of a melancholy nature.

In Book VIII,3, Oswald argues in favour of the pictorial representation of literary scenes, 'afin que tous les plaisirs de l'imagination et de l'âme fussent réunis'. This crossing of boundaries between genres is, I have argued, a feature of the sentimental aesthetic. Corinne takes issue with Oswald: 'Vous [...] n'aimez pas les arts en eux-mêmes, mais seulement à cause de leurs rapports avec le sentiment ou l'esprit. Vous n'êtes ému que par ce qui retrace les peines du coeur'. The following chapter has Corinne show Oswald round her collection of paintings in her house at Tivoli (VIII,4). They have come to the end of the collection: the last painting, by J. G. Wallis, represents a scene from Ossian. The son of Caibar sleeps on his father's grave, awaiting the bard who will sing in honour of the departed. The scene is a winter landscape. 'A l'aspect du tableau, le tombeau de son père et les montagnes d'Ecosse se retracèrent à sa pensée, et ses yeux se remplirent de larmes.' Corinne then takes up her harp, and sings a Scottish lament in which a warrior bids farewell to his country and his mistress (Corinne will teach Oswald's daughter this lament at the end of the novel). 'Oswald ne résista point à l'émotion qui l'oppressait, et l'un et l'autre s'abandonnèrent sans contrainte à leurs larmes.' Oswald then verbalises the nature of this emotion: 'Cette patrie, qui est la mienne, ne dit-elle rien à ton coeur?' Will she not come and live with him there, in a reconciliation of the two forces which are tearing him apart? (vol. 1, pp. 222-3).

Oswald's relationship to the cultural artefact is funda-mentally a sentimental one: art is important in as much as it mirrors and heightens the lived experience of an individual or a community. Like the emblem, like the reported narrative or spectacle, the work of art offers a kind of expressive *dédoublement* of experience: Oswald is at once subject and spectator, for the work of art allows him to theatricalise his own situation, and to amplify his own reaction to it. In that sense, the scene from Ossian and his father's thoughts on death fulfil a similar role. And Corinne, despite her aesthetic views, appears quite self-conscious in her use of the work of art as a detonator of the emotional explosion.

The closing phase of the novel in a way brings together the two tendencies which I have noted: the association of senti-mental ways of seeing with the domestic model, and a senti-mental attitude to the work of art. Oswald, who has drifted into a cold marriage with Lucile, returns to Italy with his wife and his daughter Juliette. The journey appears to represent an attempt – recounted essentially from Oswald's point of view – to assuage his feelings of guilt towards Corinne, and perhaps to reappropriate something of the lost Corinne, to integrate into the social model which he has chosen some of the values which are associated with the now dying heroine. This attempted reconciliation is marked by the sentimentalisation of what had been an increasingly cold marital relationship and, secondly, by the typically sentimental use of the child figure, in the form of Juliette, to build a bridge between Oswald and Corinne. After the crossing of the Alps which has terrified Lucile, Oswald is made aware of the sentimental power of the mother-child couple in a *tableau* description of Lucile holding the child on her knees as she dries her in front of the fire (vol. 2, p. 270); in the following chapter, the literary *tableau* is mirrored and reinforced when the couple admire the *Madonna della Scala* by Correggio. Oswald discovers a likeness between Lucile–Juliette and the Madonna and child represented in the painting, and it is the concordance between work of art and lived experience which prompts him to express his tenderness towards Lucile in the phrase 'Ce tableau, dans peu de temps, n'existera plus; mais moi j'aurai toujours sous les yeux son modèle' (vol. 2, p. 275). Art, characteristically, functions as a mirror, and a catalyst, to the life of the emotions. The following chapter, moreover, continues the interplay between art and narrative:

the couple go to see Domenichino's *The Sibyl* in Bologna, and Oswald explicitly points the contrast between the two models of womanhood:

La Sibylle ne rend plus d'oracles; son génie, son talent, tout est fini: mais l'angélique figure du Corrège n'a rien perdu de ses charmes, et l'homme malheureux qui fit tant de mal à l'une ne trahira jamais l'autre. (vol. 2, p. 278)

The sentimental framing of the mother and child couple confirms Oswald as the father-husband.

In the closing pages of the novel, where Corinne for a long time refuses to see Oswald, what communication there is between the former lovers is transacted largely through the figure of the daughter Juliette, once again framed sentimentally. The dying poet teaches the child some of her arts; in xx,4, Juliette describes to her parents her meetings with Corinne in the naïve language of the child. This involves a purely external description of their meetings, since the child is unaware of the affective significance which attaches to word and gesture:

'Elle a beaucoup pleuré en me voyant, dit Juliette; je ne sais pourquoi. Elle m'embrassait et pleurait; et cela lui faisait mal, car elle a l'air bien malade' [...] Lord Nelvil ne répondit plus, et s'éloigna pour cacher son attendrissement. (vol. 2, p. 292)

The technique is a sentimental one; it is akin to the use of silence or of gesture as a notation of the deepest emotional tumult, in that an absence is used to suggest a presence so overwhelming that it goes beyond the expressive power of language. The whole scene proceeds in a similarly sentimental vein. Juliette, glimpsed during a music lesson, resembles Corinne in every detail, and the power of the impression is dependent upon the fact that it is articulated pictorially: 'On croyait voir la miniature d'un beau tableau, avec la grâce de l'enfance en plus, qui mêle à tout un charme innocent.' The effect on Oswald is powerful, and it is only strengthened when Juliette plays for him the very air which Corinne had played for him at Tivoli in front of the Wallis painting. Once again, emotion is intensified by its re-presentation in emblematic form within the text. 'Ah! mon Dieu! s'écria lord Nelvil; et il embrassa sa fille en versant beaucoup de larmes' (vol. 2, pp. 292–3).

But what of Corinne? She, too, is liberal in her shedding of tears, and participates, however ambiguously, in the sentimental epiphanies which I have described. But the *isolation* of Corinne in the final scene of the novel does appear to be symptomatic of a tendency in the novel as a whole. In a final symbolic transaction involving one of the several portraits which figure in the novel,[34] she asks the priest to remove from her breast the image of Oswald, and replace it with one of Christ. Corinne's suffering, like Delphine's, is increasingly experienced not in the dialogical forms characteristic of sentimentalism, but in the form of the fragment, which is essentially soliloquy, or in a solitary relationship with God which places her firmly in a transcendent dimension. On at least two previous occasions, Corinne is shown weeping alone in a religious setting (vol. 2, pp. 135 and 227). This is surely related to another feature of the closing sections of the novel: that powerful sentimental category, *le malheur*, is increasingly interpreted not according to the standard sentimental coding (injustice, *tyrannie, persécution*) but as an expression of *fatality*. Misfortune has no immanent meaning, it has no identifiable originator or cause, and it is not to be struggled against. Book xvii, in particular, suggests this new interpretation of misfortune: written from Corinne's point of view, the prose admirably suggests the way in which her links with society have been cut, and misfortune is experienced in a kind of metaphysical isolation. As she hands over to the blind beggar the letter which breaks her ties with Oswald,

ses regards, sa main tremblante, sa voix solennelle et troublée, tout annonçait un de ces terribles moments où la destinée s'empare de nous, où l'être malheureux n'agit plus que comme l'esclave de la fatalité qui le poursuit. (vol. 2, p. 220)

There are echoes of *Caleb Williams* here.

This analysis should not, however, obscure the fact that, to the very end, the narrative structure of misfortune continues to be associated with one fundamental political meaning. It clearly is the case that the novel does not have a figure like

Lebensei, who in *Delphine* represents the link between sentimental narratives and public ideological meanings. On the
other hand, in parallel with the discourse about fatality, the
feminist meaning of misfortune is very clearly formulated: by
Castel-Forte, in the reproaches he addresses to Oswald when
the latter returns to Florence (vol. 2, pp. 283–4); by Corinne,
in the Fragments (vol. 2, pp. 238–43); and by Corinne, in the
final chapter, when the transcendent dimension appears to be
in total control.

Les hommes ne savent pas le mal qu'ils font, et la société leur
persuade que c'est un jeu de remplir une âme de bonheur, et d'y faire
ensuite succéder le désespoir. (vol. 2, p. 301)

Corinne is a victim, and as such she is the bearer of a feminist
critique of patriarchal society. But at the same time, by her use
of sentimental techniques in the characterisation of Oswald,
Madame de Staël suggests that, if men are indeed responsible
for the sufferings of women, it is because they assent to a
pre-existing model which possesses its own grammar and its
own powers of reproduction. In that sense, the place of sentimentalism in *Corinne* is a new one; rather than being an unseen
and omnipresent structuring force within the narrative, it is
rendered opaque, revealed as a historical construct which can
be analysed. That is a measure of the power of Corinne/
Madame de Staël's vision of woman as an independent subject.

Conclusions

I have argued that sentimental narratives occupy a central place in the project of the French Enlightenment. Making such an argument requires a readiness to open up links – between categories, between genres and text types, between periods – which have sometimes been artificially separated. Between categories: reason and sentiment can no longer be posited as contradictory polarities in eighteenth-century cultural formations; rationality can be accessed experientially and affectively, just as the constitution of reason as a historical category uses textual procedures entirely consonant with sentimental narratives. Between genres and text types: one of my basic presuppositions throughout is that the formal, as opposed to the thematic analysis of texts is the best route to their historical significance. The links which I have shown between literary texts (both canonical and marginal) and other forms of discourse – political, social, economic and historical – rely on a principle of comparability which is essentially formal. Between periods: in my narrative, the French Revolution is neither a point of departure nor a point of arrival, but rather the central historical experience around which transformations in ideological and discursive formations are articulated.[1] Enlightenment does not stop in 1789, or 1793, or 1800, any more than these dates represent the beginning of Romanticism, and I believe that, here also, the notion of sentimentalism offers a perspective, a principle of comparability, which brings out the continuities between supposedly separate periods and movements and thus allows us to isolate those elements where change and realignment do indeed take place.

Sentimentalism's central contribution to Enlightenment and consequently to the modernity in which we are still living can be viewed from different angles. The relationship between sentimentalism and *secularisation* is obvious and direct. The sentimental text shares with the *fête révolutionnaire*, and melo-drama, a particular predilection for seeing the experience of the individual as informed by and contributing to universal categories. The two levels are in a dialectical relationship. Individualism and universalism represent a crucial axis in the philosophy of the Revolution, and one which appears to substi-tute an immanent definition of morality for a transcendent one. Substitution does, however, imply that the new form takes over some of the functions of the old, and the movement from individual to universal can be seen as closely related to the principle of transcendence, in the sense that it inscribes the significance of the immediately perceptible in another, not immediately perceptible, dimension. The celebratory tone of sentimental texts confirms that, partially at least, they fulfil a role previously devolved to a religious morality. Peter Brooks speaks of the *sentimentalisation* of ethics.[2]

Taking *individualism* as the angle of vision, something slightly different emerges. One crucial function of the sentimental aesthetic is the externalisation of the inner life of the indi-vidual: the signs by which that inner reality may be read and interpreted are an important site of meaning and exchange. I have shown how this aesthetic feature relates to the preoccu-pations of eighteenth-century psychology, epistemology and ethics. In this sense, the sentimental text participates in the movement described by Louis Dumont: 'l'artificialisme moderne' is the 'application systématique aux choses de ce monde d'une valeur extrinsèque, imposée [...] A mon sens, cette disposition est sous-jacente aussi bien à ce que Weber a appelé la rationalité des modernes.'[3] This 'valeur extrinsèque' is precisely the interiority of the individual, externalised and brought into the public domain by the sentimental text.

The twin notions of *public opinion* and *community* are the third angle from which sentimentalism's place within Enlighten-ment can be viewed. This is in a sense the opposite pole to the inner and the individual; here, the sentimental text figures a social relationship. From humble beginnings in the pre-linguistic signs of the Other's suffering, a textual structure of perception and reaction, echoing the philosophical categories of imagination and sensibility, refracts individual experience outwards into the social realm: here is a social morality based on nature, not authority. Revolutionary rhetoric uses the tools of sentimentalism to mobilise an audience on the side of the writer or speaker and, particularly in the later phase of the Revolution, imagines the conflict between the Revolution and its enemies, and its own appeal to the opinion of the people, in terms which closely resemble those of the sentimental text. Madame de Staël, for her part, develops the notion of a community of sensitive souls in a very original direction: it is present in her work in the form of the republic of letters, an imagined network of enlightened opinion stretching through time and space, the ultimate court of humanity to which the suffering individual may appeal. But, in a typically Staëlian development, this process of universal expansion outwards is also a turning inwards, in the sense that the pronouncements of this external audience are indistinguishable from the inner voice of conscience.

If secularisation, individualism and public opinion represent three ways of viewing the general, structural relationship between sentimentalism and Enlightenment, the interest of such a model is that it allows us to approach specific social or political themes, or specific types of discourse. The purpose of such analysis is to reveal the articulation between the over-arching structure, and the actual social and political substance of ideological conflict and struggle in a particular area. To the extent to which it is possible to separate the construction of a model and its application to particular cases, this type of analysis is the particular focus of the second half of the book, from chapter 3 or 4 onwards. What conclusions can we draw from this analysis?

Chapter 3 looks at the representation of individual passion and of poverty, in relation to the sentimental questioning of hierarchy. Both representations share two fundamental features: the model of social relations held up by the text corresponds only partially to the real social behaviour or the identifiable social project of the rising bourgeoisie, or indeed of any class, in other words texts are to be read as discursive practices and not as a mimesis; and, secondly, there is a clear social disparity between those who occupy the central role of victim in the sentimental text, and the person or class occupying the site of enunciation. In that sense, it is apparent that the ideological functioning of sentimentalism is an ambiguous one: at once an appeal for the overcoming of hierarchy, and an indirect apology for hierarchy, an ambiguity shared with the French Revolution itself. This, however, is much clearer where hierarchy, wealth, social position, are explicitly the object of representation. Love narratives are much harder to read, and in particular the watershed between the validation of passion and the ideology of renunciation is resistant to ideological interpretation. This difficulty has to do with the degree to which discourse about passion is symbolised as a form of discourse about the city,[4] and it is complicated by the fact that this is a male discourse at the centre of which stands the figure of woman. This, of course, constitutes a further reason for focussing in a later chapter on the work of Germaine de Staël.

Set against the enormously complex hermeneutics of social hierarchy, the rhetoric of Revolution seems to offer a welcome simplicity. The Revolution is a wonderful laboratory for the study of texts, because it represents a moment when discourse expands to fill the social and historical space: for a brief moment, the relation between text and history is total and transparent. In the debates of 1793 and 1794, and in the *fête*, it is almost as though the historical actors were acting out a text, as though history had become for them a question of saying the right thing, of acting in conformity with a script or a grammar which of necessity must produce the right moral outcome, the ultimate happy ending. But this transparency is illusory: whatever the determining influence of the Revolution in terms of cultural and ideological formations in the early nineteenth century (and this influence is enormous), discourse corresponds only partially with social practice, and the complexities

and contradictions involved in the relationship between sentimentalisation and social hierarchy are certainly a more accurate picture of the place of sentiment in the mentalities of the
period than the textual patterns emanating from Parisian
debate, however fascinating the latter may be.[5]

In the case of the *Idéologues*, despite the fact that their work is
relatively homogeneous in ideological terms, the application of
the conceptual template of sentimentalism to a particular
corpus of texts produces ambiguous results; but this ambiguity
is in fact revealing of certain transformations which are under
way. It is difficult, for instance, to determine the ideological
orientation of sentimental categories in the debates on the
nature of morality between the *Idéologues* and the Kantian
school: on the one hand, the formal parallel between the
sentimental text and the empiricist genealogy of moral feeling
remains; but, at the same time, a realignment appears, in the
sense that other features of sentimental discourse, in particular
its Manichean urge to counterpose right and wrong, victim
and persecutor in the most stark and radical way, are now
associated with Kantian influences and with a rehabilitation of
'traditional' definitions of morality. This rehabilitation is
based on a view which associates the perceived excesses of the
Revolution with a materialist morality. In a sense this association is wrong, given the entirely voluntarist and transcendent
resonances of the discourse of a Robespierre or a Saint-Just; the
equation which is being promoted is in fact part of the emerging myth of a rationalist (or materialist) Revolution, itself part
of the reason–sentiment dichotomy which is largely a creation
of the post-Revolutionary period. But, of course, the fact that
the association is 'wrong' in the eyes of the dispassionate
historical observer is irrelevant: those who were alive at the
time were concerned not with the formal analysis of texts, but
with making sense of the reality of lived experience by means of
the intellectual and cognitive tools available to them. New
meanings accrue to forms as historical circumstances change:
and for the historian of texts and ideologies to refuse to see this,
and to cling to the notion that particular forms must *of necessity*
carry with them the ideological meanings which marked their

birth, is to evacuate the whole dimension of cultural change and conflict.

The problematic meaning of narratives of love is taken up again in the treatment of Madame de Staël. If narratives of love written by men appear ambiguous and overdetermined, then the relatively explicit feminist dimension of Madame de Staël's fiction, the identity of gender between the enunciating and the represented subject, and the clarity with which the suffering of the subject is articulated in an autobiographical mode do clarify many issues. *Corinne* in particular also suggests a questioning of some of the ideological assumptions of the sentimental aesthetic. In the non-fictional writings, the sentimental base of Madame de Staël's theory of public opinion, which is essentially an agenda for political liberalism, stands out with great clarity and coherence. Here, then, the sentimental heritage is at its most unambiguous in the enunciation of public values; for the *Idéologues*, on the other hand, sentiment is, in the last analysis, confined to the private sphere, and is marginalised at a public level in favour of a laissez-faire economic model, just as enlightened attitudes towards poor relief are predicated on the assumption that only those who are unfit to work deserve the status of sentimental objects, economic activity in this sense becoming invisible to the sentimental gaze. Is this to be read as a parting of the ways between a Kantian, introspective, potentially Romantic view (represented by Madame de Staël) and a more publicly oriented, hard-nosed Republican attitude, concerned with institutional engineering and legislative reform rather than moral pedagogy? Yet both Madame de Staël and the *Idéologues* can justifiably claim to represent an Enlightenment tradition, and to be carrying on the heritage of the Revolution. Is the distinction then more to do with the roots of two different traditions of liberalism, one economic and the other political and cultural?

As always, what was anticipated as a point of arrival turns out to be just another point of departure. As this work approaches (temporary) completion, several new perspectives appear on the horizon, with the Revolution, once again, standing in a pivotal position. My interests and sympathies have

taken me in the direction of writers and thinkers whose fundamental allegiances are with Enlightenment and Revolution,
and yet, in Gorjy and even in Vernes, we have glimpsed
another type of sentimental vision: here, the Terror represents
a watershed, and the sentimental celebration of misfortune
undergoes a transformation, becoming aligned with a message
of protest at the abuses, the excesses – and, in some cases, the
essence – of the Revolution. There is much work to be done on
this realignment. Just one direction is suggested by the use of
the notion of *pity* by Delille and Michaud: developing and
making explicit the conservative potential of Rousseau's model
of Clarens, these writers offer the reassuring and nostalgic
picture of an organic society in which pity neutralises and
renders acceptable a rigid hierarchy. The Revolution, in exe-
cuting the king, finally cut the knots binding society together:

> Tant que d'un Dieu suprême on adore les lois,
> La Pitié dans les coeurs fait entendre sa voix;
> Mais, quand un peuple impie outrage sa puissance,
> Alors elle se tait.[6]

At the same time, as in the later Vernes but I think with
different ideological implications, the figure of the chain of
being and the conceptual framework of theodicy re-emerge,
with pity representing part of that mysterious alchemy which
produces Good out of Evil, happiness out of perceived suffering, Order out of the perceived inequality of social existence.
'Ordre admirable, dans lequel la faiblesse a son empire, qui fait
céder la force elle-même; où l'infortune a son pouvoir, qui
balance quelquefois l'éclat de la prospérité.'[7]

A related, but much more complex question concerns the
impact of the Revolution in the transition from Enlightenment
to Romanticism. Roland Mortier has suggested that the Revolution occupies a determining position in the intellectual
evolutions which produced, not Romanticism as a whole, but
'*un certain* romantisme, celui de Joubert, de Fontanes, de Chateaubriand, de Ballanche, du jeune Lamennais...' For such
writers, he says, the Revolution represents 'une véritable
expérience intérieure, une tragédie existentielle, la révélation

au grand jour d'incompatibilités et de contradictions à peine ressenties auparavant'.[8] The particular area where I see a need for more work is in the ideological reading of narratives, specifically narratives of love. The Enlightenment sentimental tradition cautions a definition of love which carries the individual out towards the Other: the dynamic of the narrative is towards the fulfilment of individual desire, and the unnatural opposition of corrupt social institutions only heightens the natural rights of the heart. Now, although it is clear that the tragic treatment of love, even within the sentimental tradition, does not wait for 1795 to manifest itself, the post-revolutionary period is particularly marked by an imagination in which the connotations of love become tragic. In Mme Cottin, Mme de Genlis's *La Duchesse de la Vallière*, in *René* and *Atala* love remains an *élan* in the direction of the Other, but the linearity of desire, the belief that such narratives can have happy endings, is broken. What replaces it is a model in which desire, under the pressure of unsurmountable obstacles, functions in a circular, self-reflexive mode, standing as a metaphor for the difficulty or impossibility of an immanent existence in this world, a sign pointing towards transcendent dimensions. To what extent is this related to what Jochen Schulte-Sasse calls the autonomisation of the aesthetic, and does the Revolution play a determining role in this process?[9] To what extent is the gender dimension determining in this type of narrative? And what are the relations between that gender dimension and the constitution of the Romantic aesthetic?[10]

Other potential lines of research are less immediately connected with the Revolution, but rather look forward to the evolution of the sentimental heritage in the nineteenth century. The thematic and formal similarities between sentimentalism and melodrama are clear, and have been mentioned more than once in the preceding pages; what, then, might the kinds of analysis I have undertaken here reveal if applied to melodramatic narratives of the first half of the nineteenth century, beginning with Eugène Sue? What is the place of sentimentalism in the lyricism of those two giants, Hugo and Michelet? Finally, there is certainly a rich seam of socio-political texts stretching forward to the Third Republic, in which, in various competing and contradictory ways, the procedures and categories of sentimental writing are brought to bear on questions of political reform, class relations, social welfare and education. *Le Visiteur du pauvre* (1820) by Degérando, the former *Idéologue* and later a mainstay of the Société de morale chrétienne, represents a specific evolution in the sentimental treatment of poverty, and illustrates Foucault's remark in *Surveiller et punir* that, whereas in the feudal world, it is the rich and powerful who enjoy the privilege of full individuation, in the 'univers disciplinaire' it is the object of control who is most fully characterised as an individual: here, the beneficent observer and legislator goes amongst the poor armed with his *endéiamètre*, a highly structured tabular framework for noting the external signs which are the key to the inner state of the observed subject.[11] Half a century later, clear evidence of the continued presence of sentimentalism in public discourse is provided by that pedagogical classic of the Third Republic, *Le Tour de la France par deux enfants*, which I have analysed elsewhere.[12] Similarly, the discourse of solidarism in late nineteenth-century Radical circles is conscious of the historical precedent of Revolutionary debates on poor relief and social justice; from my perspective, what would need examination here would be the way in which altered historical circumstances, including the availability of positivist and scientific models for the understanding of society and social reform, lead to transformations of inherited discursive forms.[13]

Notes

INTRODUCTION: THE POLITICS OF TEARS

1 On Britain and Russia respectively, see two recent books: John Mullan, *Sentiment and Sociability. The Language of Feeling in the Eighteenth Century*, Oxford, 1988; Gitta Hammarberg, *From the Idyll to the Novel. Karamzin's Sentimental Prose*, Cambridge, 1991.

2 'Rapport de Roland Mortier', in *Le Préromantisme: hypothèque ou hypothèse?*, ed. Paul Viallaneix, Paris, 1975, pp. 97–113, at pp. 112–13.

3 In *Studies on Voltaire and the Eighteenth Century*, 24 (1963), pp. 1207–21; reprinted in *Clarté et ombres du siècle des Lumières*, Geneva, 1969, pp. 114–24.

4 Frank Baasner, *Der Begriff 'sensibilité' im 18. Jahrhundert. Aufstieg und Niedergang eines Ideals*, Heidelberg, 1988.

5 J. S. Spink, 'Sentiment, sensible, sensibilité: les mots, les idées d'après les "moralistes" français et britanniques au début du 18e siècle', *Zagadnienia Rodzajow Literackich*, 20, 1 (1977), pp. 33–46; 'From 'Hippolyte est sensible' to 'Le fatal présent du ciel': the position of "bienfaisance"', in *The Classical Tradition in French Literature*, *Essays presented to R. C. Knight*, ed. H. T. Barnwell, A. H. Diverres, G. F. Evans, F. W. A. George and V. Mylne, London, 1977, pp. 191–202; 'Rousseau et la morale du sentiment (lexicologie, idéologie)', in *Rousseau after 200 Years*, Proceedings of the Cambridge Bicentennial Colloquium, ed. R. A. Leigh, Cambridge, 1982, pp. 239–50; 'Diderot et la réhabilitation de la pitié', in *Denis Diderot 1713–1784. Colloque international 4–11 juillet 1984*, ed. A.-M. Chouillet, Paris, 1985, pp. 51–60.

6 Jean Sgard and Michel Gilot, 'La vie intérieure et les mots', in *Le Préromantisme*, ed. Viallaneix, pp. 509–28. R. S. Ridgway's rarely cited *Voltaire and Sensibility* (Montreal and London, 1973) is an extremely useful study of the place of sensibility in Voltaire's vision, which argues, in different terms from my own, that no

249

significant opposition exists between sensibility and rationalism in this, supposedly the most rationalist of the 'philosophes'.

7 Baasner, *Der Begriff 'sensibilité'*, pp. 17–27. Other works belonging to this movement include: Gustave Lanson, *Nivelle de la Chaussée et la comédie larmoyante*, Paris, 1887, esp. pp. 225–58, 276ff; Daniel Mornet, *Le romantisme en France au XVIIIe siècle*, Paris, 1912; Paul Van Tieghem, *Le Préromantisme*, 3 vols., Paris, 1924–47; Pierre Trahard, *Les Maîtres de la sensibilité française au XVIIIe siècle*, 4 vols., Paris, 1931–3. Trahard's *La sensibilité révolutionnaire*, Paris, 1936, does address the point of contact between discourse and society, and remains useful.

8 In *Revue d'histoire littéraire de la France*, 36 (1929), pp. 603–10. I owe this valuable reference to Baasner, *Der Begriff 'sensibilité'*, p. 20.

9 A. Monglond, *Le Préromantisme français*, 2 vols., Grenoble, 1930, vol. 2, pp. 394–422, at p. 417.

10 *Revue d'histoire littéraire de la France*, p. 607.

11 Daniel Mornet, *Les Origines intellectuelles de la Révolution française* (Paris, 1933), 2nd ed., Paris, 1934, pp. 95ff, 258–65, 474.

12 Paul Van Tieghem, 'Quelques aspects de la sensibilité préromantique dans le roman européen au XVIIIe siècle', *Edda*, 27 (1929), pp. 146–75; here, p. 164. Van Tieghem's 'Les droits de l'amour et l'union libre dans le roman français et allemand (1760–1790)', *Neophilologus*, 12 (1927), pp. 96–103, analyses the political dimensions of sentimental love.

13 Michael Fried, *Absorption and Theatricality. Painting and Beholder in the Age of Diderot*, Berkeley, Los Angeles and London, 1980; Jay Caplan, *Framed Narratives: Diderot's Genealogy of the Beholder*, Theory and History of Literature, 19, Minneapolis, 1985.

THREE SENTIMENTAL WRITERS

1 Robert L. Dawson, *Baculard d'Arnaud, Life and Prose Fiction*, Studies on Voltaire and the Eighteenth Century, 141–2, Banbury, 1976, pp. 13–28. For details on Grimm, see p. 18.

2 Henri Coulet, *Le Roman jusqu'à la Révolution*, 2 vols., Paris, 1967–8, vol. 1, p. 439.

3 Jean-Louis Lecercle, 'Baculard, ou l'embonpoint du sentiment', in *Approches des Lumières, Mélanges offerts à Jean Fabre*, Paris, 1974, pp. 295–308, at 296–7.

4 J.-J. Rousseau, *Oeuvres complètes*, ed. B. Gagnebin and M. Raymond, La Pléiade, 4 vols., Paris, 1959–69, vol. 2, pp. 1450–1.

5 Lecercle, 'Baculard', pp. 306–7.

6 *Les Epoux malheureux* in *Oeuvres complètes*, 11 vols., Paris, 1803, vols. 10–11, at vol. 10, p. 270.

7 Lecercle, 'Baculard', p. 297.

8 *Les Epoux malheureux*, vol. 10, pp. 189–90.

9 Caplan, *Framed Narratives*.

10 *Les Epreuves du sentiment*, 4 vols., Neuchâtel, 1773, vol. 1, p. 6.

11 *Les Délassements de l'homme sensible*, 2nd series, 6 vols., Paris, 1787, vol. 3, p. 299.

12 *Les Délassements de l'homme sensible*, 1st series, 6 vols., Paris, 1783–6, vol. 3, pp. 236–7.

13 'Or la négativité du mal aura toujours selon Rousseau la forme de la supplémentarité. Le mal est extérieur à une nature, à ce qui est par nature innocent et bon. Il survient à la nature. Mais il le fait toujours sous l'espèce de la suppléance qui devrait ne point se manquer à soi'. J. Derrida, *De la grammatologie*, Paris, 1967, pp. 208–9.

14 *Délassements*, 1st series, vol. 5, p. 331.

15 Ibid., 2nd series, vol. 6, pp. 80–7.

16 Ibid., 1st series, vol. 1, p. 81.

17 Ibid. 2nd series, vol. 1, p. 211.

18 Ibid., 2nd series, vol. 3, pp. 116–18.

19 Ibid., 1st series, vol. 5, pp. 289ff.

20 *La vraie grandeur, ou Hommage à la bienfaisance de son altesse sérénissime Monseigneur le duc d'Orléans*, Paris, 1789, p. 44.

21 *Délassements*, 1st series, vol. 5, pp. 81–2.

22 Ibid., 1st series, vol. 1, p. 61 (my italics).

23 *Le Nouveau voyage sentimental*, London and Paris, 1784, p. 12.

24 On poverty and attitudes to it in eighteenth-century France, see Olwen Hufton, *The Poor of Eighteenth-Century France*, Oxford, 1974; Alan Forrest, *The French Revolution and the Poor*, Oxford, 1981.

25 *Mémoire sur les dépôts de mendicité*, Paris, 1789, p. 6.

26 On this evolution, see *Europe*, no. 659, March 1984; the issue is devoted to the *roman gothique*.

27 *Victorine*, 2 vols., Paris, 1789, vol. 2, p. 134.

28 *Blançay*, 3rd ed., 2 vols., Paris, 1792, vol. 2, p. 124.

29 *Tablettes sentimentales du bon Pamphile pendant les mois d'Août, Septembre, Octobre et Novembre, en 1789*, Paris, 1791, p. 202.

30 *Victorine*, vol. 2, pp. 155–6.

31 For further discussion of the issues involved here, with reference to Fried's *Absorption and Theatricality*, see below, pp. 83–5.

32 *Ann'Quin Bredouille*, 6 vols., Paris, 1791–2, vol. 5, pp. 112–53. The six volumes of the work appear as volumes 12–17 of the *Oeuvres de Gorjy*, 17 vols., Paris, 1789–92.

33 *Tablettes sentimentales*, pp. 161–9.

34 *Ann'Quin Bredouille*, vol. 6, pp. 124–5.

35 J.-B.-G. Galiffe, *Notices généalogiques sur les familles genevoises*, 3 vols., Geneva, 1857–92; Albert de Montet, *Dictionnaire biographique des Genevois et des Vaudois*, 2 vols., Lausanne, 1878, vol. 2, pp. 607–8.

36 Archives d'Etat de Genève
Correspondence de Jacob Vernes: archives de famille, 1st series, *sv. Vernes*; correspondence of J.-B. Say: MS hist. 242.
Bibliothèque publique et universitaire de Genève
Correspondence of Jacob Vernes: MS fr. 298–300; correspondence of J.-B. Say: MS suppl. 1036 folios 165–8; correspondence of L.-F. Wartmann: MS fr. 670.

37 J.-B.-G. Galiffe, *D'un siècle à l'autre. Correspondances inédites entre gens connus et inconnus du XVIIIe et XIXe siècles*, 2 vols., Geneva, 1877–8, vol. 1, pp. 316–17. See also Peter Marc, *Genève et la Révolution*, 2 vols., Geneva, 1921–50.

38 François Vernes, *Le Voyageur sentimental, ou ma promenade à Yverdon*, Neuchâtel, 1786; the episode occupies pp. 185–200.

39 For a fuller discussion of these issues, see chapter 2.

40 J.-M. Goulemot, 'Un roman de la Révolution. *Le Voyageur sentimental en France sous Robespierre* de François Vernes', *Europe*, 659 (March 1984), pp. 80–8.

41 *Le Voyageur sentimental en France sous Robespierre*, 2 vols., Geneva and Paris, Year 7, vol. 1, pp. v–vi.

42 Vol. 1, p. 260. This must be Robespierre's famous report to the Convention of 18 floréal Year 2, discussed below, pp. 160–1.

43 François Vernes, *Mathilde au Mont-Carmel*, 2 vols., Paris, 1822.

44 For the correspondence, see L. C. Sykes, *Madame Cottin*, Oxford, 1949, pp. 369–87.

45 Marie-Joséphine-Sophie Cottin, *Oeuvres*, 12 vols., Paris, 1820; *Mathilde* comprises vols. 8–11.

46 *Oeuvres*, vol. 11, p. 73. See Madame Cottin's comments on *Atala* in Sykes, *Madame Cottin*, p. 338.

47 'Le moyen âge à Coppet', in *Actes et documents du 2me colloque de Coppet* (10–13 July 1974), Geneva, Paris, 1977, pp. 375–99.

48 *Le Printemps d'un proscrit, suivi de plusieurs lettres à M. Delille sur la pitié*, Paris, 1803, p. 182.

49 *Histoire des Croisades*, Paris, 1849, Book 28, chapter 8.

50 *Mathilde au Mont-Carmel*, vol. 1, pp. i–ix.

51 *L'Homme politique et social*, Paris, 1831, p. 3.

52 *L'Homme religieux et moral*, Paris, 1829, pp. 82–3.

53 *L'homme politique et social*, pp. 3–4.

54 Ibid., pp. 66–7.

55 Ibid., pp. 54–5.
56 *L'Homme religieux et moral*, pp. 96–7.
57 Ibid., p. 123n.

TOWARDS A MODEL OF THE SENTIMENTAL TEXT

1 Peter Brooks, *The Melodramatic Imagination*, New Haven and London, 1976; Fried, *Absorption and Theatricality*; Peter Szondi, '*Tableau* and *coup de théâtre*: on the social psychology of Diderot's bourgeois tragedy', *New Literary History*, 11 (1980), pp. 323–43; Caplan, *Framed Narratives*.
2 Vladimir Propp, *Morphology of the Folktale* (1927), English translation, 2nd ed., Austin, TX, 1968, p. 21.
3 On the place of the print within narrative, see Claude Labrosse, *Lire au dix-huitième siècle. La Nouvelle Héloïse et ses lecteurs*, Paris and Lyon, 1985, pp. 209–40.
4 Denis Diderot, *Oeuvres esthétiques*, ed. P. Vernière, Paris, 1968, p. 90.
5 Diderot, *Oeuvres esthétiques*, p. 794.
6 For a fuller development of this idea in relation to Mme de Condorcet, see below, pp. 179–82.
7 Caplan, *Framed Narratives*.
8 Diderot, *Lettre sur les sourds et muets*, in *Oeuvres complètes*, ed. H. Dieckmann, J. Proust and J. Varloot, Paris, 1975– , vol. 4 (1978), p. 161.
9 Diderot, *Oeuvres esthétiques*, p. 154.
10 Ibid., p. 99.
11 Ibid., pp. 30–1.
12 Ibid., p. 33.
13 Quoted by Szondi, '*Tableau* and *coup de théâtre*', p. 339
14 Vernes, *Le Voyageur sentimental*, p. 184.
15 Diderot, *Oeuvres esthétiques*, p. 99.
16 Caplan, *Framed Narratives*, pp. 18–19.
17 Brooks, *Melodramatic Imagination*, pp. 55–80.
18 Diderot, *Oeuvres esthétiques*, pp. 101–2.
19 Peter Szondi, '*Tableau* and *coup de théâtre*', p. 326.
20 Caplan, *Framed Narratives*, p. 38.
21 Brooks, *Melodramatic Imagination*, pp. 70–8.
22 Fried, *Absorption and Theatricality*, pp. 103–4; on the theme of absorption, see also pp. 7–70.
23 Etienne Bonnot de Condillac, *Essai sur l'origine des connaissances humaines* (1746), preceded by Jacques Derrida, 'L'Archéologie du frivole', Paris, 1973, pp. 193–5.

24 Brooks, *Melodramatic Imagination*, pp. 1–23.
25 The passage from one mode to the other is discussed above in relation to Vernes's *Voyageur sentimental en France sous Robespierre*: see pp. 57–8. Baculard is a writer standing at the frontier between the two genres, even if such a statement seems to contradict the notion that the French Revolution is the historical key to the emergence of melodrama.
26 This is, I think, Caplan's view; see also Jochen Schulte-Sasse's afterword to Caplan, 'Art and the sacrificial structure of modernity: a sociohistorical supplement', Caplan, *Framed Narratives*, pp. 97–115. In particular, Schulte-Sasse emphasises the process of aestheticisation whereby the critical element in sentimentalism is progressively disarmed and channelled into harmless, compensatory forms of consumption.
27 On individualism and universalism, see J.-P. Sartre, *Situations 2*, Paris, 1948, pp. 17–19. The Protestant overtones of the relation between the individual and the universal are striking. Peter Brooks points out (p. 37) that, in melodrama, characterisation is replaced by the repeated use of moral epithets which establish character as a kind of moral cipher or integer: 'femme admirable', 'femme vertueuse', 'respectable vieillard', etc. The same is endlessly true of sentimentalism: the individual is an exponent of the general.
28 See Theodor Adorno and Max Horkheimer, *Dialectic of Enlightenment* (1944), London, 1979. Peter Brooks writes very perceptively on the parallelism between dumb-show and abstract discourse, *Melodramatic Imagination*, pp. 58ff.
29 G. Bruno, *Le Tour de la France par deux enfants* (1877), Paris, recent reprint, no date. See below, p. 248, note 11.
30 Suzanne Gearhart, *The Open Boundary of History and Fiction: A Critical Approach to the French Enlightenment*, Princeton, NJ, 1984, pp. 45–6.
31 Ibid., p. 54.
32 Lessing to Nicolai, 29 November 1756, in *Lessings Briefwechsel mit Mendelssohn und Nicolai über das Trauerspiel*, ed. R. Petsch, (1910), reprinted Darmstadt, 1967, p. 69; quoted by Szondi, '*Tableau* and *coup de théâtre*', pp. 336ff.
33 Jean Le Rond d'Alembert, *Oeuvres philosophiques, historiques et littéraires*, 10 vols., Paris, 1805, vol. 1, pp. 263–4.
34 A.-R.-J. Turgot, *Oeuvres*, ed. E. Daire and H. Dussard, 2 vols., Paris, 1844, vol. 2., pp. 586–97 and 597–611.
35 Nicolas de Condorcet, *Esquisse d'un tableau historique des progrès de l'esprit humain*, Paris, 1970, p. 145.
36 Bronislaw Baczko, *Lumières de l'Utopie*, Paris, 1978.

LOVE AND MONEY: SOCIAL HIERARCHY IN THE
SENTIMENTAL TEXT

1 E. Sieyès, *Qu'est-ce que le Tiers Etat?*, ed. Roberto Zapperi, Geneva, 1970, p. 119.

2 Vernes, *Le Voyageur sentimental*, p. 16. See also the analysis of Baculard's *Fanny*, chapter 1, pp. 16–18.

3 Béatrice Didier, Michel Gilot, Marie-Françoise Luna, Michel Maillard, Jean Oudart and Jean Sgard, 'Le mot *amour*', in *Aimer en France 1760–1860, Actes du colloque de Clermond-Ferrand (1977)*, ed. Paul Viallaneix and Jean Ehrard, Clermont-Ferrand, 1980, pp. 117–29, esp. p. 117, emphasises how the history of love as social praxis and individual feeling is also the history of a representation, and vice versa.

4 Various contributors to *Aimer en France 1760–1860* point to the parallelism between love and freedom/democracy in the history of ideas and mentalities: see in particular Elisabeth Guibert, 'Barrières à l'amour, barrières à la circulation des richesses dans la société française d'Ancien Régime', pp. 453–9; and concluding debate, especially pp. 626–7, where Kaplow remarks that 'L'idée de l'amour, de la liberté de l'amour me paraît inséparable de celle de la liberté tout court', and Maurice Agulhon comments that, in the *Chartreuse de Parme*, love is imported to Milan together with 'les idées françaises'.

5 Lawrence Stone, *The Family, Sex and Marriage in England 1500–1800*, London, 1977, p. 226.

6 Quoted by Christopher Frayling, 'The composition of *La Nouvelle Héloïse*', in *Reappraisals of Rousseau, Studies in honour of R. A. Leigh*, ed. S. Harvey, M. Hobson, D. Kelley and S. S. B. Taylor, Manchester, 1980, p. 181.

7 J.-J. Rousseau, *Oeuvres complètes*, vol. 2, p. 89. All references to Rousseau, with the exception of the *Essai sur l'origine des langues* and the *Lettre à d'Alembert sur les spectacles* (see below, notes 10 and 11), will be to the Pléiade *Oeuvres complètes* (see chapter 1, n.4), and will be given in abbreviated form, e.g. *O.C.*, 2, p. 89.

8 Jacques Derrida, *De la grammatologie*, Paris, 1967, p. 61.

9 Joel Schwartz, *The Sexual Politics of Jean-Jacques Rousseau*, Chicago and London, 1984, pp. 27–32.

10 J.-J. Rousseau, *Essai sur l'origine des langues* (chapters 1–11, 20), ed. Eric Zernik, Paris, 1983, p. 74.

11 J.-J. Rousseau, *Lettre à d'Alembert sur les spectacles*, ed. M. Fuchs, Lille and Geneva, 1948, pp. 175–6, 174.

12 Ibid., p. 159.

13 Ibid., p. 73.

14 F.-J. Dusausoir, *La Fête de Jean-Jacques Rousseau*, Paris, Year 3, p. 13.

15 Louis J. Courtois, ed., 'Rousseau jugé par Etienne Dumont', in *Annales de la société Jean-Jacques Rousseau*, 22 (1933), pp. 154–203, at pp. 169–70.

16 Some instances of this discourse can be found in the following: Anon., *Prosopopée de J.-J. Rousseau*, Paris, 1791, pp. 3–8; Anon., *Fête champêtre célébrée à Montmorency, en l'honneur de J.-J. Rousseau*, Paris, 1791, pp. 5, 10–16; F.-L. d'Escherny, *Eloge de J.-J. Rousseau*, 1790, in *J.-J. Rousseau peint par lui-même*, 4 vols., Paris, 1819, vol. 1, pp. 3–72, esp. pp. 3–7.

17 Jean Biou, 'Le Rousseauisme, idéologie de substitution', in *Roman et lumières au XVIIIe siècle*, Centre d'études et de recherches marxistes, Paris, 1970, pp. 115–28.

18 Labrosse, *Lire au dix-huitième siècle*.

19 Germaine de Staël, *Lettres sur les ouvrages et le caractère de Jean-Jacques Rousseau*, 2nd ed., 1798, reprint, Geneva, 1979, pp. 20–1.

20 Lionel Gossmann, 'The Worlds of *La Nouvelle Héloïse*', *Studies on Voltaire and the Eighteenth Century*, 41 (1966), pp. 235–76, at p. 242.

21 Ibid., p. 272.

22 Jochen Schulte-Sasse, 'Art and the sacrificial structure of modernity: a sociohistorical supplement', afterword to Jay Caplan, *Framed Narratives*, pp. 100–1. See above, pp. 88–9.

23 K. Marx, *The Holy Family* in K. Marx and F. Engels, *Collected Works*, 45 vols., London, 1975–91, vol. 4, pp. 5–209, at p. 195.

24 E. Zola, *Germinal*, Paris, Livre de Poche, n.d., pp. 90–4.

25 In particular Olwen Hufton, *The Poor of Eighteenth-Century France*, Oxford, 1974; Alan Forrest, *The French Revolution and the Poor*, Oxford, 1981.

26 *Quatrième rapport du Comité de mendicité*, Imprimerie nationale, Paris, 1791, pp. 4–5.

27 *Plan de travail du Comité de mendicité*, Imprimerie nationale, Paris, 1790, pp. 4–5.

28 Abbé Nicholas Baudeau, *Idées d'un citoyen sur les besoins, les droits et les devoirs des vrais pauvres*, 2 vols., Amsterdam and Paris, 1765, vol. 1, pp. 70–2.

29 *Quatrième rapport du Comité de mendicité*, pp. 88–9.

30 Baudeau, *Idées d'un citoyen*, vol. 2, p. 135. For the possible Dutch origins of Baudeau's proposal, see Simon Schama, *The Embarrassment of Riches*, 2nd ed., London, 1988, pp. 22–4.

31 Joseph Dupré, *Moyens d'exciter l'industrie nationale et de détruire la mendicité*, Paris, 1790, pp. 9–10.

32 B. Barère, *Rapport sur les moyens d'extirper la mendicité, et sur les secours*

que doit accorder la République aux citoyens indigents, 22 floréal Year 2; in P.-J.-B. Buchez and P.-C. Roux, *Histoire parlementaire de la Révolution française*, 40 vols., Paris, 1834–8, vol. 33, pp. 24–62. See also Forrest, *The French Revolution and the Poor*, pp. 82–3.

33 Louis-Sébastien Mercier, *L'Indigent*, Paris, 1772, pp. 6, 67.

34 Jean Starobinski, Introduction to *Discours sur l'inégalité* in Rousseau, *Oeuvres complètes*, vol. 3, 1964, reprinted in *Jean-Jacques Rousseau. La transparence et l'obstacle*, Paris, 2nd ed., 1971, pp. 330–55; here, pp. 334–5.

35 Bronislaw Baczko, 'Rousseau and Social Marginality', *Daedalus* (Summer 1978), pp. 27–40, at p. 39.

36 Jean Starobinski, 'Don fastueux et don pervers. Commentaire historique d'une Rêverie de Rousseau', *Annales ESC*, 41,1 (Jan–Feb 1986), pp. 7–26.

37 Ibid., p. 18.

38 Robert Mauzi, *L'idée du bonheur au XVIIIe siècle*, Paris, 1960, p. 168.

39 This was one of the main themes of the bicentennial conference, Paris, 6–12 July 1989: see *L'Image de la Révolution française*, ed. Michel Vovelle, 3 vols., Paris, Oxford, New York, Peking, Frankfurt, Sydney and Tokyo, 1989.

SENTIMENTALISM IN THE RHETORIC OF THE REVOLUTION

1 The use of the language of sensibility by the Revolution, or more exactly by the Montagne, has often been used as a stick with which to beat either the Revolution, or sensibility, or both. From Mme de Genlis to André Monglond, passing through Taine, Robespierre's references to virtue were part of a syllogism which proved his hypocrisy (André Monglond, *Le Préromantisme français*, 2 vols., Grenoble, 1930, vol. 2, pp. 405–22). Pierre Trahard's *La sensibilité révolutionnaire* (1936) rejected this analysis: implicitly defining *sensibilité* as sensitivity to the suffering of the other, he documents the Revolutionaries' use of the language of sentiment, suggesting its relation to the denunciation of social injustice, and then goes on to look at the changes undergone by this mode of thought in a group of men who had to confront the reality of the Terror, as its victims but particularly as its perpetrators. Here, his aim is to defend the sincerity of the men of 1793–4, if not the correctness of their political choices. Looking a little further back, A. Aulard's *L'éloquence parlementaire pendant la Révolution française* (Paris, 3 vols., 1882, 1885–6) is not particularly helpful in the analysis of the *discourse* of the Revolutionaries. There is, however,

recent work in this area: *La Mort de Marat* (ed. Jean-Claude Bonnet, Paris, 1986) looks at the discursive construction of that event; and *La Carmagnole des Muses. L'homme de lettres et l'artiste devant la Révolution* (ed. Jean-Claude Bonnet, Paris, 1988) also contains work on Revolutionary discourse. The political lexicology team of ENS Saint-Cloud-CNRS has produced a *Dictionnaire des usages socio-politiques* (1770–1815), ed. F. Dougnac, A. Geffroy and J. Guilhaumou, Paris, 1985– ; see also Jacques Guilhaumou, *La Langue politique et la Révolution française*, Paris, 1989.

2 Henri-Baptiste Grégoire, *Motion en faveur des juifs*, Paris, 1789, pp. 11–12.

3 Henri-Baptiste Grégoire, *Lettre aux philanthropes sur les malheurs, les droits et les réclamations des gens de couleur de Saint Domingue, et des autres îles françaises de l'Amérique*, Paris, 1790, pp. 9–10.

4 G.-H. de Mirabeau, *Mémoires biographiques, littéraires et politiques de Mirabeau écrits par lui-même, par son père, son oncle et son fils adoptif*, ed. Lucas Montigny, 8 vols., Paris, 1834–5, vol. 7, p. 147; quoted by Françoise Thésée, 'Autour de la société des amis des noirs: Clarkson, Mirabeau et l'abolition de la traite (août 1789 – mars 1790)', *Présence africaine*, 125 (1983), pp. 3–82, at p. 43.

5 Letter dated 16 November 1789; quoted by Thésée, p. 28.

6 J.-P. Brissot de Warville, *Mémoire sur les noirs de l'Amérique septentrionale lu à l'Assemblée de la Société des Amis des Noirs, le 9 février 1789*, Paris, 1789, p. 29.

7 Olivier Blanc, *Une femme de libertés. Olympe de Gouges*, 2nd ed., Paris, 1989, pp. 73–4.

8 *Journal politique et national*, 2 (1790), pp. 322–3; quoted by Blanc, p. 70.

9 Thésée, 'Autour de la société des amis des noirs', p. 46.

10 Blanc, *Une femme de libertés*, p. 87.

11 Ibid., p. 107.

12 Dominique Godineau, *Citoyennes tricoteuses. Les femmes du peuple à Paris pendant la Révolution française*, Aix-en-Provence, 1988, pp. 280–2.

13 J.-M. Lequinio, *Les Préjugés détruits*, 2nd ed., Paris, 1793, pp. 3–4.

14 Gérard Walter, *Marat*, Paris, 1933, pp. 435–6.

15 Ibid., pp. 396–7. There is more than an echo, also, of the 'hôtel des bonnes gens' in Vernes's *Voyageur sentimental en France sous Robespierre*, vol. 1, p. 211.

16 *L'ami du peuple*, 5 January 1790; in J.-P. Marat, *Oeuvres*, ed. A. Vermorel, Paris, 1869, pp. 82–4.

17 J.-P. Marat, *Les Chaînes de l'esclavage* (1774), Paris, Year 1, title page.

18 Marat, *Oeuvres*, p. 102.
19 Marat, *Les Chaînes de l'esclavage*, p. 189.
20 *L'Ami du peuple*, 18–19 September 1789, in *Oeuvres*, p. 58
21 Ibid., pp. 111–14.
22 Walter, *Marat*, p. 438.
23 *L'Ancien Moniteur* (May 1789–November 1799), 32 vols., reprint, Paris, 1847, vol. 14, p. 855.
24 Trahard, *La sensibilité révolutionnaire*, pp. 86–8.
25 See below, pp. 199–200.
26 P.-V. Vergniaud, *Oeuvres de Vergniaud, Guadet, Gensonné*, ed. A. Vermorel, Paris, 1866, p. 183.
27 *L'Ancien Moniteur*, vol. 18, p. 492.
28 *Archives parlementaires* (1st series, 1787–1799), ed. J. Mavidal and E. Laurent, then Institut d'histoire de la Révolution française, Paris, 1867– , vol. 82, pp. 34–5.
29 Ibid., p. 36.
30 Ibid., pp. 364–6.
31 See, for instance, Jules Claretie's account of Desmoulins's words as he went to the scaffold: 'On te trompe, peuple, ce sont tes serviteurs qu'on immole! C'est moi qui, en 89, t'appelais aux armes! c'est moi qui ai poussé le premier le cri de la liberté! Mon crime, mon seul crime est d'avoir versé des larmes!': *Camille Desmoulins, Lucile Desmoulins, étude sur les dantonistes*, Paris, 1875, p. 358. But Saint-Just uses a similar rhetoric in his planned defence of Robespierre: 'Quel droit exclusif avez-vous sur l'opinion, vous qui trouvez un crime dans l'art de toucher les âmes? Trouvez-vous mauvais que l'on soit sensible?': *Oeuvres complètes*, ed. Ch. Vellay, 2 vols., Paris, 1908, vol. 2, p. 488, quoted by Trahard, *La sensibilité révolutionnaire*, p. 45.
32 Camille Desmoulins, *Le Vieux Cordelier*, ed. Henri Calvet, Paris, 1936, pp. 123, 187.
33 J. Pétion de Villeneuve, *Mémoires inédits de Pétion, et mémoires de Buzot et de Barbaroux*, ed. C.-A. Dauban, Paris, 1866, pp. xlix–li.
34 Alphonse Aulard, *L'éloquence parlementaire pendant la Révolution française: Les orateurs de la Législative et de la Convention*, 2 vols., Paris, 1885–6, vol. 1, p. 216.
35 L.-A. de Saint-Just, *Rapport [...] relatif aux personnes incarcérées du 8 ventôse an 2*, Paris, Imprimerie nationale, no date, pp. 5, 10, 12–13, 14–15.
36 *L'Ancien Moniteur*, vol. 19, p. 611.
37 Albert Soboul, *Les sans-culottes parisiens de l'an II. Mouvement populaire et gouvernement révolutionnaire*, Paris, 1958, pp. 710–15.
38 Alphonse Aulard, *La société des Jacobins. Recueil de documents*, 6 vols., Paris, 1889–97, vol. 5, p. 529.

39 Ibid., vol. 4, p. 699 (26 March 1792).
40 M. Robespierre, *Discours et Rapports à la Convention*, ed. Marc Bouloiseau, Paris, 1965, pp. 250, 258, 262–3.
41 Ibid., p. 285. See also Georges Gusdorf, *Les Sciences humaines et la pensée occidentale*, vol. 8: *La Conscience révolutionnaire. Les Idéologues*, Paris, 1978, p. 164, for *fêtes* proposed by Sieyès.
42 L.-A. de Saint-Just, *L'Esprit de la Révolution, suivi de Fragments sur les Institutions républicaines*, Paris, 1963, pp. 168–9, 160–1.
43 In Buchez and Roux, ed., *Histoire parlementaire de la Révolution française*, vol. 33, pp. 151–62; here, pp. 151–2.
44 Quoted by Mona Ozouf, *La fête révolutionnaire*, Paris, 1976, p. 258.
45 Jean Starobinski, 'Principes et volonté', *1789, Les emblèmes de la raison*, Paris, 1979, pp. 39–48.

SENTIMENTALISM AND *IDÉOLOGIE*

1 *Décade philosophique, littéraire et politique*, Paris, Year 2–Year 12; messidor–fructidor Year 3, pp. 548–9. For the whole anecdote, see pp. 355–61, 410–21, 471–8, 541–9.
2 *Décade philosophique*, germinal–prairial Year 3, p. 156.
3 Ibid., p. 165.
4 Ibid., pp. 235–9; for the whole anecdote, pp. 156–65, 229–39.
5 Marc Régaldo, *Un milieu intellectuel. La Décade philosophique 1794–1807*, Paris and Lille, 1976, pp. 1211–12.
6 A. Destutt de Tracy, *Quels sont les moyens de fonder la morale chez un peuple?*, Paris, Year 6, pp. 17–19.
7 Tracy's response might be that the liberal economy does not rely on moral spontaneity in the sense that it takes as its starting point the legitimate *self-interest* of each individual. But in terms of form, the dichotomy in the text is a real one.
8 J.-B. Say, *Olbie, ou Essai sur les moyens de réformer les moeurs d'une nation*, Paris, Year 8, p. 15.
9 J.-H. Bernardin de Saint-Pierre, *Oeuvres complètes*, ed. L. Aimé-Martin, 12 vols., Paris 1830–1, vol. 7; Bernardin's report occupies pp. 329–42; Aimé-Martin's introduction, pp. 315–28. François Picavet, in *Les Idéologues*, Paris, 1891, pp. 214–16, believes that Cabanis's tirade is an invention of Aimé-Martin.
10 François Picavet, *La Philosophie de Kant en France de 1773 à 1814*, Paris, 1888, throughout, but esp. p. 3.
11 Archives of the Institut de France, *Registre indicatif des mémoires lus par les membres de la Classe des Sciences morales et politiques*, manuscript.
12 Fonds Duca, Bibliothèque de l'Arsenal. Quoted by Hermann Hofer, 'Mercier admirateur de l'Allemagne et ses reflets dans le

préclassicisme et classicisme allemands', in *Louis-Sébastien Mercier précurseur et sa fortune*, ed. Hermann Hofer, Munich, 1977, pp. 73–116, at p. 106.

13 In *Mémoires de l'Institut national des Sciences et Arts*, Classe des Sciences morales et politiques, 5 vols., Paris, Year 4–Year 12, vol. 4 (vendémiaire Year 11), pp. 544–606.

14 *Magasin encyclopédique*, 8th year, vol. 2 (Year 1–1802), pp. 79–81. A translation of Mercier's text appeared in the *Monthly Magazine*, vol. 14, No. 4 (1 November 1802), pp. 333–5. Further echoes of Mercier's *Institut* speeches on the subject of innate ideas may be found in *Décade philosophique*, germinal–prairial Year 8, pp. 238–41, 306–9, and *Mémoires de l'Institut*, Classe des Sciences morales et politiques, vol. 4, vendémiaire Year 11, pp. 27–8.

15 The second is to be found in P.-L. Roederer, *Oeuvres*, ed. A.-M. Roederer, 8 vols., Paris, 1853–9, vol. 8, pp. 129–305.

16 Sophie de Condorcet, 'Huit lettres sur la sympathie', in Adam Smith, *Théorie des sentiments moraux*, trans. Sophie de Condorcet, 2 vols., 2nd ed., Paris, 1830, vol. 2, pp. 320–2.

17 Roederer, *Oeuvres*, vol. 8, p. 195. No date is given for the composition of this 'Observation', but since he speaks in it of not yet having had an opportunity to read the work of Mme de Condorcet analysed above, we may suppose that it is after 1798, and perhaps relatively contemporaneous with the publication of her translation of Smith.

18 P.-J.-G. Cabanis, 'Rapports du physique et du moral de l'homme', in *Oeuvres philosophiques*, ed. C. Lehec and J. Cazeneuve (Corpus général des philosophes français, vol. 44, 1), Paris, 1956, part 1, p. 578.

19 Kenneth Margerison, *P-L Roederer: Political Thought and Practice during the French Revolution*, Philadelphia, 1983, pp. 92–3. On thought-control in *idéologie*, see Michel Foucault, *Surveiller et punir. Naissance de la prison*, Paris, 1975, p. 105.

20 Cabanis, *Oeuvres philosophiques*, part 2, p. 6.

21 The law of 20 September 1792, the last day of the Legislative Assembly, introduced divorce and secularised the *état-civil*. The definitive version of the *Code civil*, promulgated on 21 March 1804, reduced the accepted motives for divorce and reinstated paternal authority, although within time limits and with a ban on disinheritance as a means of pressure on the offspring. The civil code also represented a significant reduction in women's rights within the family, even compared with the pre-revolutionary situation. See F. Furet and M. Ozouf, *Dictionnaire critique de la Révolution française*, Paris, 1988, pp. 511–17.

22 Roederer, *Oeuvres*, vol. 8, p. 176.

23 Cabanis, *Oeuvres philosophiques*, part 1, p. 313.
24 A. Destutt de Tracy, *De l'Amour*, ed. Gilbert Chinard, Paris, 1926, p. 38.

BEYOND SENTIMENTALISM? MADAME DE STAËL

1 *Essai sur les fictions*, followed by *De l'influence des passions sur le bonheur des individus et des nations*, introduction by Michel Tournier, Paris, 1979, pp. 76–8.
2 Jean Starobinski, 'Suicide et mélancolie chez Mme de Staël' in *Madame de Staël et l'Europe*, Actes du colloque du Coppet (18–24 juillet 1966), Paris, 1970, pp. 242–52 at p. 246.
3 *De l'influence des passions*, p. 251. My italics underline the standard sentimental vocabulary linking spectacle to perceiving subject.
4 Simone Balayé, 'A propos du "Préromantisme": continuité ou rupture chez Mme de Staël', in *Le Préromantisme*, ed. Viallaneix, pp. 153–68.
5 *Considérations sur la Révolution française*, introduction and notes by Jacques Godechot, Paris, 1983, p. 220.
6 *De l'influence des passions*, pp. 205–7.
7 *Considérations sur la Révolution française*, p. 531.
8 *De la littérature considérée dans ses rapports avec les institutions sociales*, ed. Paul Van Tieghem, Geneva and Paris, 1959, pp. 330–1. My italics.
9 *De la littérature*, p. 430.
10 *De l'influence des passions*, p. 134.
11 *De l'Allemagne*, preface by Simone Balayé, 2 vols., Paris, 1968, vol. 2., p. 96.
12 Ibid., vol. 2, p. 95.
13 Ibid., vol. 2, p. 227.
14 *Considérations sur la Révolution française*, p. 552.
15 Ibid., pp. 591–2.
16 *De la littérature*, pp. 332–6.
17 Madelyn Gutwirth, *Madame de Staël, Novelist. The Emergence of the Artist as Woman*, Urbana, Chicago and London, 1978, esp. pp. 103–6, 141–4.
18 *Delphine*, ed. Simone Balayé and Lucia Omacini ('Textes littéraires français', no. 346), Geneva, 1987, p. 172.
19 Similar uses of the term can be found on pp. 394 and 409.
20 *Delphine*, pp. 1005–7.
21 Frank P. Bowman, 'Mme de Staël et l'apologétique romantique', in *Madame de Staël et l'Europe*, pp. 157–71, esp. pp. 164–7.

22 Simone Balayé, *Madame de Staël. Lumières et liberté*, Paris, 1979, p. 153.
23 Ibid., pp. 122–36, and '*Delphine*, Roman des Lumières: pour une lecture politique', in *Le Siècle de Voltaire. Hommage à René Pomeau*, ed. Christiane Mervaud and Sylvain Menant, 2 vols., Oxford, 1987, vol. 1, pp. 37–46.
24 Simone Balayé, '*Delphine*, Roman des Lumières', p. 45.
25 Gutwirth, *Madame de Staël, Novelist*, p. 130.
26 Ibid., p. 150.
27 Mary Wollstonecraft, *Vindication of the Rights of Woman* (1792), in *The Works of Mary Wollstonecraft*, ed. J. Todd and M. Butler, 7 vols., London, 1989, vol. 5, pp. 60–266, at p. 153.
28 Quoted by Dominique Godineau, *Citoyennes tricoteuses*, p. 278. My italics.
29 Geneviève Fraisse, *Muse de la raison. La démocratie exclusive et la différence des sexes*, Aix-en-Provence, 1989. Two important works in this area which appeared when the present book was in press are: Lynn Hunt, *The Family Romance of the French Revolution*, Berkeley and Los Angeles, 1992; Madelyn Gutwirth, *The Twilight of the Goddesses. Women and Representation in the French Revolutionary Era*, New Brunswick, NJ, 1992.
30 Balayé, *Madame de Staël. Lumières et liberté*, p. 137.
31 Gutwirth, *Madame de Staël, Novelist*, pp. 209–33.
32 *Corinne ou l'Italie*, ed. Claudine Hermann, 2 vols., Paris, 1979, vol. 1, p. 191.
33 'Fonction romanesque de la musique et des sons dans *Corinne*', *Romantisme*, 3 (1972), pp. 17–32, esp. p. 22; 'Du sens romanesque de quelques oeuvres d'art dans *Corinne* de Madame de Staël', *Mélanges offerts à André Monchoux*, Toulouse, 1979, pp. 345–64, esp. p. 345.
34 Simone Balayé, 'Du sens romanesque', pp. 346–52.

CONCLUSIONS

1 David J. Denby, 'Transformations du discours sentimental autour de la Révolution française', in *La Littérature et ses avatars. Discrédits, déformations at réhabilitations dans l'histoire de la littérature*, ed. Yvonne Bellenger, Paris, 1991, pp. 255–65.
2 Brooks, *Melodramatic Imagination*, pp. 44, 54–5.
3 Louis Dumont, *Essais sur l'individualisme moderne*, Paris, 1983, pp. 76–7.
4 Niklas Luhmann, *Love as Passion. The Codification of Intimacy*, trans. Jeremy Gaines and Doris L. Jones, Cambridge, 1986.

5 François Furet, *Penser la Révolution française*, Paris, 1978.

6 J. Delille, *Oeuvres complètes*, ed. Amar Du Rivier, 14 vols., Paris, 1824, vol. 1, p. 81.

7 Joseph-François Michaud, *Le Printemps d'un proscrit, suivi de plusieurs lettres à M. Delille sur la Pitié*, Paris, 1803, pp. 148–51. Delille translated Pope's *Essay on Man* in 1765; Antoine Rivarol translated Soame Jenyns's *Essay on the Necessity of Evil*: *Essai sur la nécessité du mal*, Paris, 1791.

8 Roland Mortier, 'Le Traité *Du Sentiment* de P.-S. Ballanche: un programme littéraire antiphilosophique et post-révolutionnaire', in *Approches des Lumières, Mélanges offerts à J. Fabre*, Paris, 1974, pp. 319–31.

9 See above, pp. 113–14, and chapter 2, note 26.

10 Jennifer Birkett's 'Madame de Genlis: The New Men and the Old Eve', *French Studies*, 42, 2 (April 1988), pp. 150–64, tackles this difficult area.

11 J.-M. Degérando, *Le Visiteur du pauvre*, Paris, 1820. Michel Foucault, *Surveiller et punir*, Paris, 1975, pp. 194–5.

12 In 'Transformations du discours sentimental', pp. 261–3.

13 There is an enormous literature here: the classic secondary source is Henri Hatzfeld, *Du Paupérisme à la sécurité sociale, essai sur les origines de la sécurité sociale, 1850–1940*, Paris, 1971. Daniel Mornet's comments on the contemporary relevance of Enlightenment sensibility (Introduction, note 10) are themselves an indication of precisely this historical self-awareness on the part of solidarism.

Bibliography

PRIMARY SOURCES

Alembert, Jean Le Rond d', *Oeuvres philosophiques, historiques et littéraires*, 10 vols., Paris, 1805, vol. 1

L'Ancien Moniteur (May 1789–November 1799), 32 vols., reprint, Paris, 1847

Archives parlementaires, first series, 1787–1799, ed. J. Mavidal and E. Laurent, then Institut d'histoire de la Révolution française, Paris, 1867–

Baculard d'Arnaud, François Thomas Marie de, *Euphémie, ou le triomphe de la religion*, Paris, 1768

Les Epreuves du sentiment, 4 vols., Neuchâtel, 1773

Les Délassements de l'homme sensible, 1st series, 6 vols., Paris, 1783–6; 2nd series, 6 vols., Paris, 1787

La vraie grandeur, ou Hommage à la bienfaisance de son altesse sérénissime Monseigneur le duc d'Orléans, Paris, 1789

Les époux malheureux, in *Oeuvres complètes*, 11 vols., Paris, 1803, vols. 10 & 11

Barère de Vieuzac, B., *Rapport sur les moyens d'extirper la mendicité, et sur les secours que doit la République aux citoyens indigents*, 22 floréal Year 2, in *Histoire parlementaire de la Révolution française*, ed. P.-J.-B. Buchez and P.-C. Roux, vol. 33, pp. 24–62

Baudeau, abbé Nicolas, *Idées d'un citoyen sur les besoins, les droits et les devoirs des vrais pauvres*, 2 vols., Amsterdam and Paris, 1765

Bernardin de Saint-Pierre, J.-H., *De la nature de la morale*, in *Oeuvres complètes*, ed. L. Aimé-Martin, 12 vols., Paris, 1830–1, vol. 7

Brissot de Warville, J.-P., *Mémoire sur les noirs de l'Amérique septentrionale lu à l'Assemblée de la Société des Amis des Noirs, le 9 février 1789*, Paris, 1789

Bruno, G., *Le Tour de la France par deux enfants* (1877), Paris, recent reprint, no date

Cabanis, Pierre-Jean-Georges, 'Rapports du physique et du moral de l'homme', in *Oeuvres philosophiques*, ed. C. Lehec and J. Cazeneuve (Corpus général des philosophes français, vol. 44.1), Paris, 1956, part 1

'Quelques principes et quelques vues sur les secours publics', in *Oeuvres philosphiques*, ed. C. Lehec and J. Cazeneuve (Corpus général des philosophes français, vol. 44.1), Paris, 1956, part 2

Comité de mendicité de l'Assemblée Nationale, *Plan de travail, 1er–7ème Rapports*, Paris, 1790–1

Condillac, Etienne Bonnot de, *Essai sur l'origine des connaissances humaines* (1746), preceded by Jacques Derrida, 'L'Archéologie du frivole', Paris, 1973

Condorcet, Antoine-Nicolas Caritat de, *Esquisse d'un tableau historique des progrès de l'esprit humain*, Paris, 1970

Condorcet, Sophie de, 'Huit lettres sur la sympathie', in Adam Smith, *Théorie des sentiments moraux*, trans. Sophie de Condorcet (1st ed., 1798), 2nd ed., 2 vols., Paris, 1830

Cottin, Marie-Joséphine-Sophie, *Mathilde*, in *Oeuvres*, 12 vols., Paris, 1820, vols. 8–11

La Décade philosophique, littéraire et politique, Paris, Year 2–Year 12

Degérando, J.-M., *Des signes et de l'art de penser, considérés dans leurs rapports mutuels*, Paris, Year 8

Le Visiteur du pauvre, Paris, 1820

Delille, J., *Oeuvres complètes*, ed. Amar Du Rivier, 14 vols., Paris, 1824, vol. 1

Desmoulins, Camille, *Le vieux cordelier*, ed. Henri Calvet, Paris 1936

Destutt de Tracy, Antoine, *Quels sont les moyens de fonder la morale chez un peuple?*, Paris, Year 6

'De la métaphysique de Kant, ou observations sur un ouvrage intitulé "Essai d'une exposition succinte de la critique de la Raison pure" par J. Kinker', in *Mémoires de l'Institut National des Sciences et Arts. Classe des Sciences morales et politiques*, 5 vols., Paris, Year 4–Year 12, vol. 4 (vendémiaire Year 11), pp. 544–606

De l'amour, introduction by Gilbert Chinard, Paris, 1926

Diderot, Denis, *Oeuvres esthétiques*, ed. P. Vernière, Paris, 1968

Oeuvres complètes, ed. H. Dieckmann, J. Proust and J. Varloot, Paris, 1975–

Dusausoir, François-Jean, *La Fête de Jean-Jacques Rousseau*, Paris, Year 3

Dupré, Joseph, *Moyens d'exciter l'industrie nationale et de détruire la mendicité*, Paris, 1790

Escherny, François-Louis d', 'Eloge de Jean-Jacques Rousseau', in *Jean-Jacques Rousseau peint par lui-même*, 4 vols., Paris, 1819, vol. 1, pp. 3–72

Fête champêtre célébrée à Montmorency, en l'honneur de Jean-Jacques Rousseau, Paris, 1791

Godwin, William, *Things as They Are, or the Adventures of Caleb Williams*, ed. Maurice Hindle, Harmondsworth, 1988

Gorjy, Jean-Claude, *Le nouveau voyage sentimental*, London and Paris, 1784

    Mémoire sur les dépôts de mendicité, Paris, 1789

    Victorine, 2 vols., Paris, 1789

    Blançay, 3rd ed., 2 vols., Paris, 1792

    Tablettes sentimentales du bon Pamphile pendant les mois d'Août, Septembre, Octobre et Novembre, en 1789, Paris, 1791

    Ann'Quin Bredouille, 6 vols., Paris, 1791–2, published as vols. 12–17 of *Oeuvres de Gorjy*, 17 vols., Paris, 1789–92

Grégoire, Henri-Baptiste, *Motion en faveur des juifs*, Paris, 1789

    Lettre aux philanthropes sur les malheurs, les droits et les réclamations des gens de couleur de Saint Domingue, et des autres îles françaises de l'Amérique, Paris, 1790

Lequinio, Jean-Marie, *Les Préjugés détruits*, 2nd ed., Paris, 1793

Lessing, Gotthold Ephraim, *Briefwechsel mit Mendelssohn und Nicolai über das Trauerspiel*, ed. R. Petsch (1910), reprinted Darmstadt, 1967

Magasin Encyclopédique, 7th year, vol. 5 (Year 9), 8th year, vol. 2 (Year 10)

Marat, Jean-Paul, *Oeuvres*, ed. A. Vermorel, Paris, 1869

    Les chaînes de l'esclavage (1st ed., 1774), Paris, Year 1

Mémoires de l'Institut national des Sciences et Arts, Classe des Sciences morales et politiques, 5 vols., Paris, Year 4–Year 12

Mercier, Louis-Sébastien, *L'Indigent*, Paris, 1772

    'De l'acte du moi, ou le fumeur', in *Magasin encyclopédique*, 8th year, vol. 2 (Year 10 – 1802), pp. 79–81

Michaud, Joseph-François, *Le Printemps d'un proscrit, suivi de plusieurs lettres à M. Delille sur la pitié*, Paris, 1803

    Histoire des Croisades (1st ed., 1811–22), Paris, 1849

    'Tableau historique des Croisades', in Cottin, *Oeuvres*, vol. 8

Mirabeau, G.-H., *Mémoires biographiques, littéraires et politiques de Mirabeau écrites par lui-même, par son père, son oncle et son fils adoptif*, ed. Lucas Montigny, 8 vols., Paris, 1834–5

Monthly magazine or British Register, vol. 14, no. 4 (1 November 1802)

Pétion de Villeneuve, J., *Mémoires inédites de Pétion, et mémoires de Buzot et de Barbaroux*, ed. C.-A. Dauban, Paris, 1866

Prosopopée de Jean-Jacques Rousseau, Paris, 1791

Registre indicatif des mémoires lus par les membres de la classe des Sciences morales et politiques, MS, Archives, Institut de France, no date

Robespierre, Maximilien, *Discours et rapports à la Convention*, ed. Marc Bouloiseau, Paris, 1965

Roederer, P.-L., *Cours d'organisation sociale*, in *Oeuvres*, ed. A.-M. Roederer, 8 vols., Paris, 1853–9, vol. 8, pp. 129–305

Rousseau, Jean-Jacques, *Oeuvres complètes*, ed. B. Gagnebin and M. Raymond, La Pléiade, 4 vols., Paris, 1959–69

  Essai sur l'origine des langues, ed. Eric Zernik, Paris, 1983

  Lettre à M. d'Alembert sur les spectacles, ed. M. Fuchs, Lille and Geneva, 1948

Saint-Just, Louis-Antoine de, *Oeuvres complètes*, ed. Ch. Vellay, 2 vols., Paris, 1908

  L'Esprit de la Révolution, followed by *Fragments sur les institutions républicaines*, Paris, 1963

  Rapport au nom des comités de salut public et de sûreté générale et Décret de la Convention nationale relatif aux personnes incarcérées du 8 ventose an 2, Paris, Imprimerie nationale, no date

Saint-Lambert, J.-F., Marquis de, *Principe des moeurs chez toutes les nations, ou Catéchisme universel*, Paris, Year 6

Say, Jean-Baptiste, Correspondence, Archives d'Etat de Genève, MS hist. 242

  Correspondence, Bibliothèque publique et universitaire de Genève, MS suppl. 1036, folios 165–8

  Traité d'économie politique, 5th ed., 3 vols., Paris, 1826

  Olbie, ou Essai sur les moyens de réformer les moeurs d'une nation, Paris, Year 8

Sieyès, Emmanuel, *Qu'est-ce que le Tiers Etat?*, ed. Roberto Zapperi, Geneva, 1970

Smith, Adam, *Théorie des sentiments moraux*, trans. Sophie de Condorcet, followed by *Huit lettres sur la sympathie* (1st ed., 1798), 2nd ed., 2 vols., Paris, 1830

Staël, Germaine de, *Considérations sur la Révolution française*, introduction and notes J. Godechot, Paris, 1983

  Corinne ou l'Italie, ed. Claudine Hermann, 2 vols., Paris, 1979

  De l'Allemagne, ed. S. Balayé, 2 vols., Paris, 1968

  De la littérature considérée dans ses rapports avec les institutions sociales, ed. Paul Van Tieghem, Geneva and Paris, 1959

  Delphine, ed. S. Balayé and L. Omacini ('Textes littéraires français', no. 346), Geneva, 1987

  Dix années d'exil, Brie-Comte-Robert, 1956

  Essai sur les fictions, followed by *De l'influence des passions sur le bonheur des individus et des nations*, introduction Michel Tournier, Paris, 1979

  Lettres sur les ouvrages et le caractère de Jean-Jacques Rousseau, 2nd ed., 1798, reprint, Geneva, 1979

Turgot, Anne-Robert-Jacques, *Oeuvres*, ed. E. Daire and H. Dussard, 2 vols., Paris, 1844

Vergniaud, Pierre-Victurnien, *Oeuvres de Vergniaud, Guadet, Gensonné*, ed. A. Vermorel, Paris, 1866

Vernes, François, *Le voyageur sentimental, ou ma promenade à Yverdon*, Neuchâtel, 1786

   Le voyageur sentimental en France sous Robespierre, 2 vols., Geneva and Paris, Year 7

   Mathilde au Mont-Carmel, 2 vols., Paris, 1822

   L'homme religieux et moral, Paris, 1829

   L'homme politique et social, Paris, 1831

   Seymour, ou quelques notes du bonheur, Paris, 1834

Vernes, Jacob, Correspondence, Archives d'Etat de Genève, archives de famille, 1st series, *sv. Vernes*

   Correspondence, Bibliothèque publique et universitaire de Genève, MS fr. 298–300

Watteville du Grabe, A. de, ed., *Législation charitable*, 2 vols., Paris, 1843–4

Wartmann, L. F., Correspondence, Bibliothèque publique et universitaire de Genève, MS fr. 670

Wollstonecraft, Mary, *Vindication of the Rights of Woman*, in *The Works of Mary Wollstonecraft*, ed. J. Todd and M. Butler, 7 vols., London, 1989, vol. 5, pp. 60–266

Zola, Emile, *Germinal*, Paris, Livre de Poche, no date

SECONDARY SOURCES

Adorno, Theodor, and Max Horkheimer, *Dialectic of Enlightenment* (1st ed., 1944), London, 1979

Aulard, Alphonse, *L'éloquence parlementaire pendant la Révolution française: les orateurs de l'Assemblée constituante*, Paris, 1882; *Les Orateurs de la Législative et de la Convention*, 2 vols., Paris, 1885–6

   La Société des Jacobins. Recueil de documents, 6 vols., Paris, 1889–97

Baasner, Frank, *Der Begriff 'sensibilité' im 18. Jahrhundert. Aufstieg und Niedergang eines Ideals*, Heidelberg, 1988

Baczko, Bronislaw, *Lumières de l'Utopie*, Paris, 1978

   'Rousseau and Social Marginality', *Daedalus* (Summer 1978), pp. 27–40

Balayé, Simone, 'Fonction romanesque de la musique et des sons dans *Corinne*', *Romantisme*, 3 (1972), pp. 17–32

   'A propos du "Préromantisme": continuité ou rupture chez Madame de Staël', in *Le Préromantisme: hypothèque ou hypothèse?*, ed. P. Viallaneix, Paris, 1975, pp. 153–68

   Madame de Staël. Lumières et liberté, Paris, 1979

'Du sens romanesque de quelques oeuvres d'art dans *Corinne* de Madame de Staël', in *Mélanges offerts à André Monchoux*, Toulouse, 1979, pp. 345–64

'Destins de femmes dans *Delphine*', *Cahiers staëliens*, 35 (1984), pp. 41–59

'*Delphine*, Roman des Lumières: pour une lecture politique', in *Le siècle de Voltaire. Hommage à René Pomeau*, ed. Christiane Mervaud and Sylvain Menant, Oxford, 1987, vol. 1, pp. 37–46

'Pour une lecture politique de *Corinne*', *Il gruppo di Coppet e l'Italia*, ed. M. Matucci, Pisa, 1988, pp. 7–16

Bénichou, Paul, *Le Sacre de l'écrivain 1750–1830. Essai sur l'avènement d'un pouvoir spirituel laïc dans la France moderne*, Paris, 1985

Biou, Jean, 'Le Rousseauisme, idéologie de subsitution', in *Roman et Lumières au XVIIIe siècle*, Centre d'études et de recherches marxistes, Paris, 1970, pp. 115–28

Birkett, Jennifer, 'Madame de Genlis: the New Men and the Old Eve', *French Studies*, 42.2 (April 1988), pp. 150–64

Blanc, Olivier, *Une femme de libertés. Olympe de Gouges*, 2nd ed., Paris, 1989

Bonnet, Jean-Claude, ed., *La Mort de Marat*, Paris, 1986

La Carmagnole des Muses. L'homme de lettres et l'artiste dans la Révolution, Paris, 1988

Bowman, Frank P., 'Madame de Staël et l'apologétique romantique', in *Madame de Staël et l'Europe*, pp. 157–71

Brooks, Peter, *The Melodramatic Imagination*, New Haven & London, 1976

Bryson, Norman, *Word and Image: French Painting of the Ancien Régime*, Cambridge, 1981

Buchez, P.-J.-B., and P.-C. Roux, eds., *Histoire parlementaire de la Révolution française*, 40 vols., Paris, 1834–8

Cailliet, Emile, *La Tradition littéraire des Idéologues*, Philadelphia, 1943

Caplan, Jay, *Framed Narratives: Diderot's Genealogy of the Beholder*, Theory and History of Literature, 19, Minneapolis, 1985

Chouillet-Roche, Anne-Marie, 'Le clavecin oculaire du Père Castel', *Dix-huitième siècle*, 8 (1976), pp. 141–66

Claretie, Jules, *Camille Desmoulins, Lucile Desmoulins, étude sur les dantonistes*, Paris, 1875

Coulet, Henri, *Le Roman jusqu'à la Révolution*, 2 vols., Paris, 1967–8

Courtois, Louis J., ed., 'Rousseau jugé par Etienne Dumont', *Annales de la société Jean-Jacques Rousseau*, 22 (1933), pp. 154–203

Dawson, Robert L., *Baculard d'Arnaud, Life and Prose Fiction*, Studies on Voltaire and the Eighteenth Century, 141–2, Banbury, 1976

Denby, David J., 'Le thème des croisades et l'héritage des Lumières au début du 19e siècle', *Dix-huitième siècle*, 19 (1987), pp. 411–21

'Images négatives de la Révolution française dans la littérature sentimentale des années 1790: le cas de Jean-Claude Gorjy', in *L'image de la Révolution française*, ed. Michel Vovelle, 3 vols., Paris, Oxford, New York, Peking, Frankfurt, Sydney and Tokyo, 1989, vol. 3, pp. 1905–13

'Transformations du discours sentimental autour de la Révolution française', in *La littérature et ses avatars. Discrédits, déformations et réhabilitations dans l'histoire de la littérature*, ed. Yvonne Bellenger, Paris, 1991, pp. 255–65

Derrida, Jacques, *De la grammatologie*, Paris, 1967

Didier, Béatrice, M. Gilot, M.-F. Luna, M. Maillard, J. Oudart and J. Sgard, 'Le mot amour', in *Aimer en France*, ed. P. Viallaneix, pp. 117–29

Dougnac, F., A. Geffroy and J. Guilhaumou, eds., *Dictionnaire des usages socio-politiques (1770–1815)*, Paris, 1985–

Dumont, Louis, *Essais sur l'individualisme moderne*, Paris, 1983

Europe, 659 (March 1984); special issue on 'le roman gothique'

Fabre, Jean, *Lumières et romantisme*, Paris, 1963

Forrest, Alan, *The French Revolution and the Poor*, Oxford, 1981

Foucault, Michel, *Surveiller et punir. Naissance de la prison*, Paris, 1975

Fraisse, Geneviève, *Muse de la raison. La démocratie exclusive et la différence des sexes*, Aix-en-Provence, 1989

Frayling, Christopher, 'The composition of *La Nouvelle Héloïse*', in *Reappraisals of Rousseau*, ed. S. Harvey *et al.*, pp. 181–214

Fried, Michael, *Absorption and Theatricality. Painting and Beholder in the Age of Diderot*, Berkeley, Los Angeles and London, 1980

Furet, François, *Penser la Révolution française*, Paris, 1978

Furet, François, and Mona Ozouf, *Dictionnaire critique de la Révolution française*, Paris, 1988

Galiffe, J.-B.-G., *D'un siècle à l'autre, Correspondances inédites entre gens connus et inconnus du XVIIIe et XIXe siècles*, 2 vols., Geneva, 1877–78

Notices généalogiques sur les familles genevoises, 3 vols., Geneva, 1857–92

Gaspard, Claire, 'Vertu: le sens robespierriste du terme', in *Dictionnaire des usages socio-politiques (1770–1815)*, ed. F. Dougnac *et al.*, Paris, vol. 2, 1987, pp. 197–210

Gaulmier, Jean, *L'idéologue Volney 1757–1820*, Beirut, 1951

Gearhart, Suzanne, *The Open Boundary of History and Fiction: a Critical Approach to the French Enlightenment*, Princeton, NJ, 1984

Gilot, Michel and Jean Sgard, eds., *Le Vocabulaire du sentiment dans l'oeuvre de Jean-Jacques Rousseau*, Geneva, Paris, 1980

Godineau, Dominique, *Citoyennes tricoteuses. Les femmes du peuple à Paris pendant la Révolution française*, Aix-en-Provence, 1988

Gossmann, Lionel, 'The worlds of *La Nouvelle Héloïse*', *Studies on Voltaire and the Eighteenth Century*, 41 (1966), pp. 235–76

Goujard, Philippe, 'Une notion-concept en construction: l'héroïsme révolutionnaire', in *Dictionnaire des usages socio-politiques (1770–1815)*, ed. F. Dougnac *et al.*, Paris, vol. 2, 1987, pp. 9–43

Goulemot, J.-M., 'Un roman de la Révolution: *Le Voyageur sentimental en France sous Robespierre* de François Vernes', *Europe*, 659 (March 1984), pp. 80–8

Guibert, Elisabeth, 'Barrières à l'amour, barrières à la circulation de la richesse dans la société française d'Ancien Régime', in *Aimer en France*, ed. Viallaneix, pp. 453–9

Guilhaumou, Jacques, *La Langue politique et la Révolution française*, Paris, 1989

Guillaume, James, ed., *Procès-verbaux du Comité d'instruction publique de la Convention nationale*, 5 vols., Paris, 1891–1907

Gusdorf, Georges, *Les Sciences humaines et la pensée occidentale*, vol. 8: *La Conscience révolutionnaire. Les Idéologues*, Paris, 1978

Gutwirth, Madelyn, *Madame de Staël, Novelist. The Emergence of the Artist as Woman*, Urbana, Chicago and London, 1978

    The Twilight of the Goddesses. Women and Representation in the French Revolutionary Era, New Brunswick, NJ, 1992

Hammarberg, Gitta, *From the Idyll to the Novel. Karamzin's Sentimental Prose*, Cambridge, 1991

Harvey, S., M. Hobson, D. Kelley and S. S. B. Taylor, eds., *Reappraisals of Rousseau. Studies in Honour of R. A. Leigh*, Manchester, 1980

Hatzfeld, Henri, *Du Paupérisme à la sécurité sociale, essai sur les origines de la sécurité sociale, 1850–1940*, Paris, 1971

Hofer, Hermann, 'Mercier admirateur de l'Allemagne et ses reflets dans le préclassicisme et le classicisme allemands', in *Louis-Sébastien Mercier précurseur et sa fortune*, ed. Hermann Hofer, Munich, 1977, pp. 73–116

Hufton, O., *The Poor of Eighteenth-Century France*, Oxford, 1974

Hunt, Lynn, *The Family Romance of the French Revolution*, Berkeley and Los Angeles, 1992

Kennedy, Emmet, *A 'Philosophe' in the Age of Revolution. Destutt de Tracy and the origins of 'Ideology'*, Philadelphia, 1978

King, Norman, 'Le moyen âge à Coppet', *Actes et documents du deuxième colloque de Coppet* (10–13 July 1974), Geneva, Paris, 1977, pp. 375–99

Labrosse, Claude, *Lire au dix-huitième siècle. La Nouvelle Héloïse et ses lecteurs*, Paris and Lyon, 1985

Lanson, G., *Nivelle de la Chaussée et la comédie larmoyante*, Paris, 1887

Launay, Michel, '*La Nouvelle Héloïse*, son contenu et son public', in *Jean-Jacques Rousseau et son temps*, ed. Michel Launay, Paris, 1969, pp. 179–84

Lecercle, Jean-Louis, 'Baculard, ou l'embonpoint du sentiment', in *Approches des Lumières. Mélanges offerts à Jean Fabre*, Paris, 1974, pp. 295–308

Leigh, R. A., ed., *Rousseau after 200 years. Proceedings of the Cambridge Bicentennial Colloquium*, Cambridge, 1982

Levi-Strauss, Claude, 'La structure et la forme. Réflexions sur un ouvrage de Vladimir Propp', in *Anthropologie structurale Deux*, Paris, 1973, pp. 139–73

Luhmann, Niklas, *Love as Passion. The Codification of Intimacy*, translated by Jeremy Gaines and Doris L. Jones, Cambridge, 1986

Luppé, Robert de, *Les idées littéraires de Madame de Staël et l'héritage des Lumières (1795–1800)*, Paris, 1969

Mandrou, Robert, 'Le baroque européen: mentalité pathétique et révolution sociale', *Annales ESC* (1960), pp. 898–914

Marc, Peter, *Genève et la Révolution*, 2 vols., Geneva, 1921–50

Margerison, Kenneth, *P. L. Roederer: Political Thought and Practice during the French Revolution*, Philadelphia, 1983

Marx, Karl, 'The Holy Family', in K. Marx and F. Engels, *Collected Works*, 45 vols., London, 1975–91, vol. 4, pp. 5–209

Mauzi, Robert, *L'idée du bonheur au XVIIIe siècle*, Paris, 1960

Monglond, André, *Le Préromantisme français*, 2 vols., Grenoble, 1930

Montet, Albert de, *Dictionnaire biographique des Genevois et des Vaudois*, 2 vols., Lausanne, 1878

Mornet, Daniel, *Le sentiment de la nature en France de Rousseau à Bernardin de Saint-Pierre*, Paris, 1907

Le Romantisme en France au dix-huitième siècle, Paris, 1912

Review of Monglond, André, *La vie intérieure du préromantisme français de l'Abbé Prévost à Joubert*, (Grenoble, 1929), in *Revue d'histoire littéraire de la France*, 36 (1929), pp. 603–10

Les origines intellectuelles de la Révolution française, 2nd ed., Paris, 1934

Mortier, Roland, 'Unité ou scission du siècle des Lumières?', in *Clarté et ombres du siècle des Lumières*, Geneva, 1969, pp. 114–24

'Madame de Staël et l'héritage des Lumières', in *Madame de Staël et l'Europe*, pp. 129–39

'Le Traité *Du sentiment* de P.-S. Ballanche: un programme littéraire antiphilosophique et post-révolutionnaire', in *Approches des Lumières. Mélanges offerts à Jean Fabre*, Paris, 1974, pp. 319–31

Mullan, John, *Sentiment and Sociability. The Language of Feeling in the Eighteenth Century*, Oxford, 1988

O'Neal, John C., 'Condillac's contribution to eighteenth-century French aesthetics', *Studies on Voltaire and the Eighteenth Century*, 264 (1989), pp. 1064–66

'The sensationist aesthetics of the French Enlightenment', *L'esprit créateur*, 28.4 (1988), pp. 95–106

Ozouf, Mona, *La Fête révolutionnaire*, Paris, 1976

Picavet, François, *La philosophie de Kant en France de 1773 à 1814*, Paris, 1888

Les Idéologues: Essai sur l'histoire des idées et des théories scientifiques, philosophiques, religieuses, etc. en France depuis 1789, Paris, 1891

Propp, Vladimir, *Morphology of the Folktale* (1927), English translation, 2nd ed., Austin, TX, 1968

Régaldo, Marc, *Un milieu intellectuel. La Décade philosophique, 1794–1807*, Paris and Lille, 1976

Ridgway, R. S., *Voltaire and Sensibility*, Montreal and London, 1973

Sartre, Jean-Paul, *Situations 2*, Paris, 1948

Schama, Simon, *The Embarrassment of Riches*, 2nd ed., London, 1988

Schulte-Sasse, Jochen, 'Art and the sacrificial structure of modernity: a sociohistorical supplement', in Caplan, *Framed Narratives*, pp. 97–115

Schwartz, Joel, *The Sexual Politics of Jean-Jacques Rousseau*, Chicago and London, 1984

Sgard, Jean and Michel Gilot, 'La vie intérieure et les mots', in *Le Préromantisme: hypothèque ou hypothèse?*, ed. Viallaneix, pp. 509–28

Shklar, Judith N., 'Jean-Jacques Rousseau and equality', *Daedalus* (Summer 1978), pp. 13–25

Soboul, Albert, *Les sans-culottes parisiens de l'an II. Mouvement populaire et gouvernement révolutionnaire*, Paris, 1958

Spink, J. S., 'Sentiment, sensible, sensibilité: les mots, les idées d'après les "moralistes" français et britanniques au début du 18e siècle', *Zagadnienia Rodzajow Literarckich*, 20.1 (1977), pp. 33–46

'From *Hyppolyte est sensible* to *Le fatal présent du ciel*: the position of "bienfaisance"', in *The Classical Tradition in French Literature, Essays presented to R. C. Knight*, ed. H. T. Barnwell, A. H. Diverres, G. F. Evans, F. W. A. George and V. Mylne, London, 1977, pp. 191–202

'Rousseau et la morale du sentiment (lexicologie, idéologie)', in *Rousseau after 200 years*, Proceedings of the Cambridge Bicentennial Colloquium, ed. R. A. Leigh, Cambridge, 1982, pp. 239–50

'Diderot et la réhabilitation de la pitié', in *Denis Diderot 1713–1784. Colloque International, 4–11 juillet 1984*, ed. A.-M. Chouillet, Paris, 1985, pp. 51–60

Madame de Staël et l'Europe. Actes du Colloque de Coppet (juillet 1966), Paris, 1970
Starobinski, Jean, 'Suicide et mélancolie chez Madame de Staël', in *Madame de Staël et l'Europe*, pp. 242–52
Jean-Jacques Rousseau. La transparence et l'obstacle, 2nd ed., 1971
1789, Les emblèmes de la raison, Paris, 1979
'Don fastueux et don pervers. Commentaire historique d'une Rêverie de Rousseau', *Annales ESC*, 41.1 (January–February 1986), pp. 7–26
Staum, Martin S., *Cabanis. Enlightenment and Medical Philosophy in the French Revolution*, Princeton, 1980
Stone, Lawrence, *The Family, Sex and Marriage in England 1500–1800*, London, 1977
Sykes, L. C., *Madame Cottin*, Oxford, 1949
Szondi, Peter, '*Tableau* and *coup de théatre*: on the social psychology of Diderot's bourgeois tragedy', *New Literary History*, 11 (1980), pp. 323–43
Thésée, Françoise, 'Autour de la Société des amis des noirs: Clarkson, Mirabeau et l'abolition de la traite (août 1789–mars 1790)', *Présence Africaine*, 125 (1983), pp. 3–82
Tillich Paul, 'Critique and Justification of Utopia', in *Utopias and Utopian Thought*, ed. Frank E. Manuel, Boston, 1966, pp. 296–309
Trahard, Pierre, *Les maîtres de la sensibilité française au XVIIIe siècle*, 4 vols., Paris, 1931–3
La sensibilité révolutionnaire, Paris, 1936
Van Tieghem, Paul, *Le Préromantisme*, 3 vols., Paris, 1924–47
'La sensibilité et la passion dans le roman européen au dix-huitième siècle', *Revue de littérature comparée*, 6 (1926), pp. 924–35
'Les droits de l'amour et l'union libre dans le roman français et allemand (1760–1790)', *Neophilologus*, 12 (1927), pp. 96–103
'Quelques aspects de la sensibilité préromantique dans le roman européen au XVIIIe siècle', *Edda*, 27 (1929), pp. 146–75
'Le Roman sentimental en Europe de Richardson à Rousseau: 1740–1761', *Revue de littérature comparée*, 20 (1940), pp. 129–51
Venturi, Franco, *Utopia and Reform in the Enlightenment*, Cambridge, 1971
Viallaneix, Paul, ed., *Le Préromantisme: hypothèque ou hypothèse?*, Paris, 1975
Viallaneix, Paul and Jean Ehrard, eds., *Aimer en France 1760–1860. Actes du colloque de Clermont-Ferrand (1977)*, Clermont-Ferrand, 1980
Vovelle, Michel, ed., *L'Image de la Révolution française*, 3 vols., Paris, Oxford, New York, Peking, Frankfurt, Sydney and Tokyo, 1989

Walter, Gérard, *Marat*, Paris, 1933

Das Weinende Saeculum. Colloquium der Arbeitsstelle 18. Jahrhundert, Gesamthochschule Wuppertal Universität Münster, 7–9 Oktober 1981, Heidelberg, 1983

Index

CAMBRIDGE STUDIES IN FRENCH

General Editor: Malcolm Bowie (*All Souls College, Oxford*)
Editorial Board: R. Howard Bloch (*University of California, Berkeley*),
Ross Chambers (*University of Michigan*), Antoine Compagnon
(*Columbia University*), Peter France (*University of Edinburgh*),
Toril Moi (*Duke University*), Naomi Schor (*Duke University*)

Also in the series (* denotes titles now out of print)